PHOTOIMPACT
SOLUTIONS

Jason Dunn with Kate Binder and James Rodel

PhotoImpact Solutions

Library of Congress Catalog Number 00-106696

ISBN 1-929685-12-2

5   4   3   2   1

Educational facilities, companies, and organizations interested in multiple copies or licensing of this book should contact the publisher for quantity discount information. Training manuals, CD-ROMs, and portions of this book are also available individually or can be tailored for specific needs.

Muska & Lipman Publishing
2645 Erie Avenue, Suite 41
Cincinnati, Ohio 45208
www.muskalipman.com
publisher@muskalipman.com

This book is composed in Melior, Columbia, Helvetica, and Courier typefaces using QuarkXpress 4.1.1, Adobe PhotoShop 5.0.2, and Adobe Illustrator 8.0.
Created in Cincinnati, Ohio, in the United States of America.

Credits

Publisher
Andy Shafran

Managing Editor
Hope Stephan

Development and Copy Editing
WordTech Communications
  Lori Jareo

Technical Editors
James "Iacobus" Rodel
Ulead
  Colwin Chan
  Victor Wong

Proofreader
Molly Flynn

Cover Designer
John Windhorst

Production Manager
Cathie Tibbetts

Production Team
DOV Graphics
  Stephanie Archbold
  Michelle Frey
  Tammy Norton

Indexer
Kevin Broccoli

Printer
C.J. Krehbiel

About the Authors

Jason Dunn

jasond@kensai.com (www.kensai.com)

Chapters 1, 2, 3, 7, 8, 9, 10, and 13
Jason Dunn has been using PhotoImpact for Web design and creative expression since version 3.0, and after abandoning Adobe PhotoShop 4.0 for Ulead products, he's never looked back. He has been providing content for Ulead's WebUtilities site (www.webutilities.com) on everything from fonts to JavaScript rollovers for nearly two years, has beta-tested numerous Ulead products and is involved daily in the Usenet newsgroup devoted to Ulead products.

As the owner of Kensai Design & Communications (www.kensai.com), he lends his skills to a myriad of projects in the writing, graphical, and Web design genres. He co-authored *Short Order Microsoft PhotoDraw 2000* (Hayden Books, ISBN 0789720485), and has tech edited several other computing titles.

Outside of the graphics realm, he's a contributing editor for Microsoft's *PocketPC.com* and, as a four-year veteran of the Microsoft Most-Valuable Professional program in the Windows CE arena, he spends several hours each day answering questions and assisting users in the public support newsgroups. He has been an active player in the evolving Windows Powered Devices market, and his dozens of *PocketPC.com* articles have also been translated into German and French.

His background is in communications, having earned a degree in public relations. When he's not sitting in front of one of his three computers, he's ripping one apart to upgrade one component or another. And if he's not doing that, he's playing bass guitar and singing, reading a good fantasy or sci-fi book, going for a walk through the Calgary, Alberta, Canada, suburb in which he lives or waiting for the next Matrix movie to be released.

Kate Binder

photois@prospecthillpub.com (www.prospecthillpub.com)

Chapters 4, 5, 6, and 12
Kate Binder is a production artist and freelance writer living in southern New Hampshire. The author of *Teach Yourself QuarkXPress 4 in 14 Days* and *Easy Adobe Photoshop*, she also writes articles on desktop production tools and techniques for *Publish* magazine. Her current favorite subjects for artwork creations in PhotoImpact are her four retired racing greyhounds. For more information, see www.adopt-a-greyhound.org/.

James Rodel

iacobus@rodelworks.com (http://www.rodelworks.com)

Chapter 11
James Rodel—Iacobus— is an independent Web designer and a co-partner with his mother, Dorothy, in RodelWorks, a home-based business based in Brockton, Massachusetts, that provides various Internet services to small and medium-sized businesses. RodelWorks was established in 1998. Iacobus also maintains a tutorial site at RodelWorks for PhotoImpact users.

Dedication

Jason: I dedicate this book to Ashley: my support, my comfort, my best friend, my one love. Your unending encouragement, compassion, and help allowed me to focus completely on making this the book I wanted it to be. Thank you for letting me make this my first priority.

And to the many great people in the comp.graphics.apps.ulead newsgroup: here it is, the book I've been promising for years. I hope it's everything you hoped it would be!

Kate: As always, my efforts here are dedicated to my partner and best friend: my husband, Don Fluckinger.

Iacobus: Chapter 11 is dedicated to my sister, Ann Marie. See you when I get there, sis!

Acknowledgments

A book like this is never done by a single person—it takes a whole team of people working together to pull it off. My special thanks go to the two contributors, James "Iacobus" Rodel and Kate Binder, who helped flesh out the content for this book and made the seemingly impossible time constraints actually work. We did it!

Thanks to everyone at Muska & Lipman for letting me write the book I wanted to write, for trusting my suggestions, and for putting up with my never-ending stream of questions and comments about every facet of the project. To Andy Shafran, your eagerness to get me involved was only matched by my eagerness to get started, so that was a great combination! To Hope Stephan, thank you for your gentle encouragements and kind words. And, of course, for keeping me on schedule. Lori Jareo, your excellent editing skills kept the book sharp. Thank you.

To my friends at Ulead, Colwin Chan and Victor Wong: Thank you for your prompt replies to my questions, for involving me in the beta in the first place, for being part of the company that made this incredible software, and for reading my many suggestions for version 7.0. I hope this is the first of many books that help people explore the wonderful products that Ulead creates.

To the indispensable graphics guru, Tony R. Celeste, thank you for always answering my questions, and for your insane work hours—you always seemed to be awake when I needed you!

My love and gratitude to my friends and family: Aaron, Cariann, Mom and Dad, thank you for your encouragement and understanding. To my friend Todd, I appreciate your constant energy and excitement. To the members of Country Hills Community Church: Carmyn, Don, Bryan, Christine, Irene, Kim, and everyone else, thank you for your motivation, for understanding the tremendous time pressures I was under, and for making me feel like part of a wonderful family all the time.

To the members of the comp.graphics.apps.ulead newsgroup, thank you for reminding me of the things you needed a book to teach you.

My gratitude to you, the reader, for picking this book up and flipping through it—I hope your imagination is lit aflame by the sparks of imagination I tried to pour into this book.

Finally, and most importantly, thank you to the Creator who gave me the talent and willpower to strive for great things. VIRTUTIS GLORIA MERCES.

From Kate: Thanks to Molly Joss for the introduction, and to Andy Shafran, Hope Stephan, and Lori Jareo for smoothing my way throughout this project.

From Iacobus: All my family and friends for great support; Jason, Kate, Hope, Lori, Andy, and everyone else I may have stupidly forgotten who I worked with on this book; Diet Coke; coffee; my fluffy kittycats and the big "G."

Contents

8—Photo Editing: Advanced Special Effects 163

12—PhotoImpact Album 6.0: A Digital Photographer's Dream 269

13—Gearing Up: Printing, Sharing, and More . . . 295

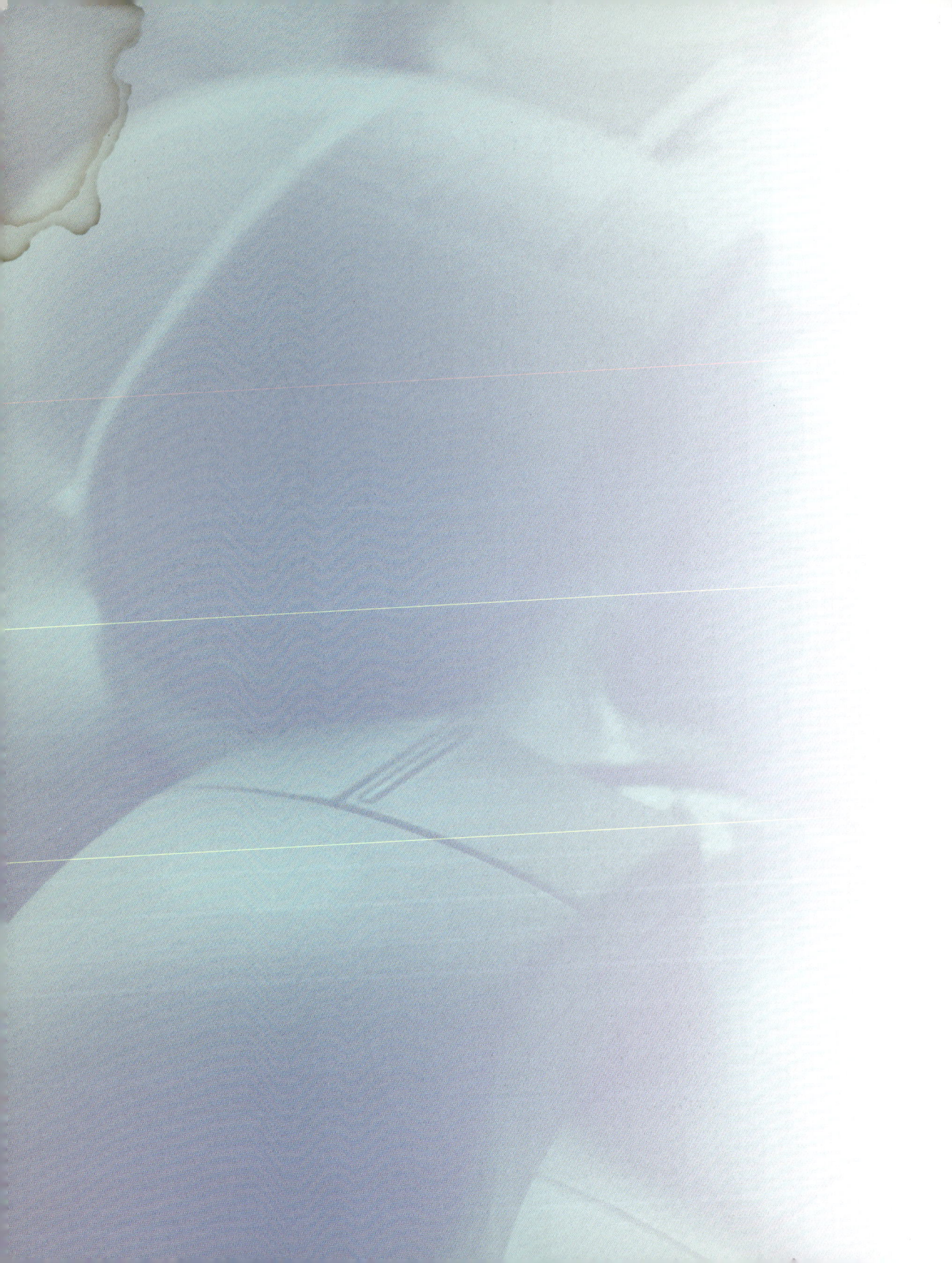

Introduction

A few years ago, there wasn't a single English-language PhotoImpact book on the market. As a regular contributor in the Ulead Usenet newsgroup, I kept seeing the same questions over and over—people needed a resource to help them really unleash everything that PhotoImpact had to offer. And one of the questions that was asked many times was "Where can I find a book that covers PhotoImpact?" It was inexplicable that people could go to a bookstore and see a dozen titles on other graphics applications, but nothing on PhotoImpact. It is, after all, an incredible tool that consistently wins industry praise and many awards for value and ease of use. So why weren't there any books? There were a variety of Web-based tutorials, but nothing central that covered the program as a whole in any great detail.

At the time, I wasn't an author yet, so I merely added my voice to the many others who were asking for a book. Over the next couple of years, I gained experience writing and editing in the technology realm, and I began to ponder the concept of writing my own PhotoImpact book. I spoke to a publisher I was working with at the time about it, but they weren't convinced there were enough PhotoImpact users out there that would be interested in a book. A short while later, another author released the first English-language PhotoImpact book. It was wonderful to see a product finally meet the needs of users, but it didn't diminish the desire to write my own book. I envisioned a thick tome of knowledge, full-color, high-gloss pages that would let people really see what PhotoImpact could do.

A few years later, my vision has become a reality (much to my surprise and delight!)

The book you hold in your hands is the result of years of hopes and dreams, but less than a month of actual writing. I poured everything I had into this book, and while I won't pretend it's perfect, I'm proud of the results. The book could easily be twice as long, but the constraints of time and budget forced me to decide the most important concepts to pass along to you. I hope you are pleased with the results, and that you find this book useful as you explore everything that PhotoImpact 6.0 has to offer. I'm confident this will be the first of many books on Ulead products and thank you for your support. I hope that at least once a chapter you'll exclaim, "Wow, I didn't know PhotoImpact could do that!" PhotoImpact is the best program in its field, and after reading this book, I hope you'll agree.

What You'll Find in This Book

The goal of this book is not to replace the PhotoImpact manual. Where necessary, we walk through an explanation of the tools to help you understand when and why you'd use them, but we try to make everything as real-world as possible. I'm not a professional writer who merely conveys information—I'm a graphic designer who loves PhotoImpact and uses it daily. The examples in the book are simple to follow but serve as an important building block for future efforts. Rather than show you how to achieve a single complicated effect, we focus on exposing you to the basic functions that, when combined with each other, result in a nearly infinite number of possibilities. More than anything, PhotoImpact is about flexibility and creativity, and in this book we try to show you that.

Who This Book is for

Although I don't pretend to be the most skilled PhotoImpact user on the planet, I think that any reader, no matter how advanced in skill, will gain something from this book. Beginners should start at Chapter 1 and read through everything in order —you'll find that we build each chapter on the basics of the previous one. Intermediate and advanced users can skip to whatever chapter they want, but I'd encourage them to read the whole thing anyway. You never know what you'll learn!

PhotoImpact is a program that anyone can learn to use in a short period of time, and it's a program that can be used for almost anything. If you're an advanced Web designer, you'll appreciate the powerful Web features like JavaScript rollovers, slicing, image optimization, and flexible image and shape creation tools. If you're just getting started in the world of Web design, the component designer and EasyPalette will be your best friends. Digital photographer? Powerful correction tools for red eye, hue shifting, and incredible batch tools will let you convert and correct images faster than you ever thought possible. And if you're just an average computer user new to the world of graphic design, this book will show you how to unlock the incredible value that PhotoImpact offers.

How This Book is Organized

PhotoImpact Solutions is divided into thirteen chapters:

▶ Chapter 1, "An Introduction to Digital Imaging Basics"—The ABCs of the graphics world. Learn about file formats, industry terms like dpi and resolution, and gain some insight into the variety of things PhotoImpact can be used for.

▶ Chapter 2, "Getting Around in PhotoImpact"—The 101 level class. How to zoom, crop, resize, open and save files, and tweak PhotoImpact's operation for maximum speed and quality.

▶ Chapter 3, "Objects and Selections: Built for Speed"—Creating, moving, copying, inserting and saving objects. Learn about how to create selections, and the wonderful world of objects.

▶ Chapter 4, "Working with Words: The Text Tools"—Creating and modifying text, applying effects to it, and making it really shine.

▶ Chapter 5, "Working with Shapes: The Path Tools"—Everything you need to know about how to create, edit, and manipulate path shapes in PhotoImpact. Learn to apply text to a path and how to use the EasyPalette with paths.

▶ Chapter 6, "EasyPalette: Your New Best Friend"—The PhotoImpact Easy Palette is the ultimate design tool. Learn how to use the incredible variety of presets, what options it gives you, and how to add your own presets to it.

▶ Chapter 7, "Photo Editing Basics: Retouching and Enhancing Your Images"—Learn to salvage even the most damaged of images using techniques and tools found in PhotoImpact. The wonders of the fill tool and corrective hue shifting are explored. Warm up that scanner!

▶ Chapter 8, "Photo Editing: Advanced Special Effects"—An eye-popping, jaw-dropping chapter showing you how to unleash the wonders of both built-in and third party plug-ins, frames, edges, the new stamp tool. Take your images to the next dimension!

▶ Chapter 9, "Graphic Design for the Web: A PhotoImpact Primer"—Before embarking on creating your first Web site, learn a little about color palettes and the rules of graphic design for the Web. PhotoImpact offers methods for you to create your own graphics from scratch, or use the built-in Component Designer.

▶ Chapter 10, "The PhotoImpact Web Design Studio"—Design an entire site within PhotoImpact? You bet! Explore the new HTML tools that come with PhotoImpact 6.0—the Image Optimizer, the Image Map tool—and learn how to create JavaScript Rollover effects.

▶ Chapter 11, "Moving Pictures: GIF Animator 4.0"—Ever wanted to know how to create those cool animated banners? This chapter will show you how—along with some important tips and tricks on using GIF Animator 4.0.

▶ Chapter 12, "PhotoImpact Album 6.0: A Digital Photographer's Dream"—Learn to organize, sort, search, and export your image collection to the Web.

▶ Chapter 13, "Gearing Up: Printing, Sharing, and More"—Learn about the power of Quick Commands, the ups and downs of printing from PhotoImpact, and the incredible quality of online printing services. Also, learn how to e-mail your images to others, and share them online with Ulead's iMira service for free!

Conventions Used in This Book

The following conventions are used in this book:

All Web page URLs mentioned in the book appear in **boldface**, as in **www.ulead.com.**

Besides these terminological and typographic conventions, the book also features the following special displays for different types of important text:

TIP
Text formatted like this offers a helpful tip relevant to the topic being discussed in the main text.

NOTE
Text formatted like this highlights other interesting or useful information that relates to the topic under discussion.

CAUTION
Cautions highlight actions or commands that can make irreversible changes to your files or potentially cause problems in the future. Read them carefully, because they contain important information that can make the difference between keeping your files, software and hardware safe and you losing a huge amount of work.

Keeping the Book's Content Current

For updates, corrections, and other information related to the content of the book, head out to:

www.muskalipman.com

1

An Introduction to Digital Imaging Basics

Welcome to the wonderful world of digital images! Ever since viewing my first digitized photo years ago, I've been enchanted by the way computers can help people save, view, and manipulate digital imagery. When I got my first grayscale hand scanner, many years ago, I sat down and scanned dozens of photos just so I could have them on my computer. Using rudimentary image editors, I'd recolor the images and explore the strange new world of image filters and effects. Nearly a decade later, using a digital camera, I work strictly in the digital realm until the final printed output. And if I'm not printing the image, then I'm mailing to my friends or loading it onto my Pocket PC.

I still have a great deal of fun experimenting with images, trying to get the image in my mind onto the computer screen. One of the greatest things about computers is that they allow users who may not have had the classic training in the arts to express themselves in creative ways with a few simple clicks. PhotoImpact is especially great for beginners because it comes with a huge set of presets, allowing anyone to create an interesting project in no time. In order to get started down the road to digital image nirvana, though, you first need to understand some of the basics.

Terminology of the Trade

Like everything else in life, the world of digital imaging brings with it some new terms and concepts that you should understand if you want to grasp the more advanced concepts. I'm going to walk you through a few of the more important terms.

Bitmap

Bitmap images, sometimes called raster images, are made up of tiny elements called pixels. A pixel is a single element of color that, when combined with thousands of other pixels, gives you the display you see on your monitor. In the case of a digital photograph, the number of pixels is defined by the resolution. A digital image that is 1536×1024 is actually 1,572,864 pixels in total (usually called 1.5 megapixels in the camera world). If you shrink that image, you'll reduce the total number of pixels. If you enlarge the image, you expand the number of pixels in the image and force PhotoImpact to extrapolate the new pixels; this usually results in a jagged or blurry image. Bitmap images are great for onscreen display but not ideal for printing. This is explained in greater detail in Chapter 13, "Gearing Up: Printing, Sharing, and More." PhotoImpact is a bitmap-only program.

Vector

Vector images, sometimes referred to as "line art," are images that are based on lines and mathematical definitions governing those lines. Rather than being made up of individual pixels, vector images are made of up single pixels and mathematical formulas defining the shape of the pixels. This allows vector-based images to scale up and down in size with perfect quality. Traditional clip art is a good example of this: You can expand the clip art as large as you want and the quality stays constant. PhotoImpact cannot create or manipulate vector-based images. An example of a program that can would be CorelDraw or Adobe Illustrator.

DPI

DPI stands for "dots per inch" and is generally a confusing subject. A 72-dpi image has 72 dots per inch on the monitor making up the detail that you see. Computer monitors are relatively low resolution devices (most people have monitors of 72 to 96 dpi), which causes significant eye strain over time. IBM and several other companies are developing new methods of increasing the dpi of LCD screens, so eventually we'll have screens that are as easy to look at as a printed page. It gets more confusing when printing is introduced, because many people use the computer term, dpi, and the printing term, lpi, (lines per inch), interchangeably. And most confusing of all, in its New Image window, PhotoImpact refers to dpi as "resolution," which is a completely different term. DPI is easiest to grasp when it's expressed in a series of simple rules:

▶ If you're scanning or creating images for display on the Web, 72 or 96 dpi will suffice.

▶ If you're going to be printing the images on a home printer, scan or create a new file at 150 dpi.

▶ If you are creating an image for, say, a CD cover that will be printed by a commercial printer, set the new image size in inches or centimeters and choose a resolution (dpi) of 300. You should, however, always ask your printer what settings to use, because he or she will know for sure. The business card templates in PhotoImpact 6.0 are set at 300 dpi, so this is a good rule of thumb to follow.

Resolution

Resolution is the measure of how many pixels are on a computer screen at one time. As I write this book, I'm in 800×600 resolution on my 19-inch monitor. This gives the computer a total of 480,000 pixels with which to create the shapes I see on my screen. My preferred resolution is 1280×1024, which is 1.3 million pixels—more than twice the number of pixels. This means a greater level of detail in everything I look at. Images look smoother and sharper, and I can see more of everything at once (larger images don't need to be scrolled). The ideal resolution depends on your monitor size and eyesight, but reasonable resolutions are 800×600 on a 15-inch monitor; 1024×768 on a 17-inch monitor; and 1280×1024 on a 19-inch monitor. Setting your computer resolution is discussed more in Chapter 2, "Getting Around in PhotoImpact."

Color Depth

The number of colors your computer displays on the screen has a dramatic impact on the quality of what you see. Every new computer on the market is capable of displaying 16-bit or higher color, resulting in true-to-life color images. Color depth is calculated via a simple mathematical formula: 8-bit color is really 2^8—256 colors. Using that formula, 16-bit color gives you 64,000 colors, 24-bit color gives you 16.7 million colors, and 32-bit is an incredible 4.2 billion colors. If you're stuck in 8-bit color, digital images will look ugly and browsing the Web will be a less-than-optimal experience for you. Setting your computer color depth is also discussed more in Chapter 2.

Important File Formats

Choosing the right file format for saving your image is at the heart of any design, because every file format has a trade-off between size, quality, and compatibility.

▶ **GIF**—GIF is short for Graphics Interchange Format and is usually pronounced "jiff," though some people pronounce it with a hard "g." The GIF format was a creation of CompuServe Information Service in the 1980s during the boom period of the Bulletin Board System (BBS). This format is an 8-bit, 256-color file type that supports animation, transparency, and interlacing (which enables viewing during downloads). GIF files can be made very small by limiting the number of colors contained in the image; this is easily controlled in Image Optimizer, which is covered in detail in Chapter 10, "The PhotoImpact Web Design Studio." GIF is the ideal format for line art, buttons, and any other image form that is not photographic in nature and doesn't require thousands of colors for high visual quality. It's readable in all Web browsers and is a staple of Web image display.

▶ **JPEG**—The current standard for 24-bit photographic images, JPEG uses a lossy compression for saving data. What this means is that the file discards data that the human eye can't see at low levels, but the higher the compression is cranked, the more obvious the data loss becomes. Compression levels are explained in more detail in the Image Optimizer section in Chapter 10. JPEG does not support transparency or animation, but progressive JPEGs function like interlaced GIFs in that users can see low-resolution versions right away and these become clearer as the download progresses. JPEG is readable in all Web browsers and is a staple for Web image display. The file format is short for Joint Photographic Experts Group and is pronounced "jay-peg."

▶ **PNG**—A powerful hybrid of GIF and JPEG, PNG (pronounced "ping") supports 48-bit color, transparency, and lossless compression (meaning no data is lost when the file is saved). The file sizes are much smaller than TIFF or BMP, but because of the lossless compression, the quality is just as high. PNG is the perfect file format for image archiving: It's a blend of small file size and perfect quality. Although it may someday replace both GIF and JPEG as the dominant Internet file format, currently the browser support for PNG is spotty at best.

▶ **TIFF**—"TIFF" is an acronym for Tagged Image File Format. An older format, TIFF is still the standard in the print world for photographic images and images requiring a clipping path (an edge that allows designers to knock out backgrounds). TIFF supports 24-bit color and lossless compression, but the file sizes will be enormous. TIFF support is important for PhotoImpact to have, but I don't recommend using this format for saving your images unless you plan on passing them to a commercial printer.

▶ **BMP**—The standard image format for many Windows images, BMP is a format that any Windows computer can open and view. BMP, usually called "bit-map," supports 24-bit color, but no animation or transparency. It has no compression, so file sizes will be huge. (BMP is the format for Windows desktop wallpaper.)

▶ **UFO**—The Ulead File for Objects is a file format specific to PhotoImpact. It supports up to 48-bit color, objects, embedded HTML content, lossless compression, and more. I haven't seen a specification for the format (it's a proprietary format, after all), but it's your only option for saving multi-object images. I keep a UFO source file for all my work in case I need to go back and modify it later.

▶ **ICO**—I was a little surprised when I first realized this, but PhotoImpact can read and write Windows icon files. This means you can create custom program icons or edit current icons. While PhotoImpact doesn't have support for all the ICO attributes (like 16-bit color icons), it will work for basic icons.

PhotoImpact: Where It's Been and Where It's Going

Would you be surprised if I said that Ulead, the creator of PhotoImpact, was entering its second decade of making photo manipulation software? It all began with a product called Photo Styler, first launched in 1990. This was Ulead's first product, and it was the first true-color image editor for the Windows platform. Six years later, Ulead launched PhotoImpact 3.0 and it was the first true version of the product we know and love. (It was also the first product to come bundled with Web-specific tools like GIF Animator and SmartSaver.) A couple of years would go by before Adobe released its program for Web designers.

In 1997, the Web was exploding with content and designers, and Ulead released what I believe to be its first truly killer Web product: PhotoImpact 4.0. In this version, new Web tools were introduced, along with vector/path tools, special effects (like particles and type effects), and an enhanced EasyPalette. I remember seeing this in CompUSA while I was vacationing in Phoenix, Arizona, and buying it because it seemed to have a lot of value to me as a Web designer. A year later in 1998, Ulead released an interim update in the form of 4.2. This fixed a few problems and added minor new features.

Version 5.0 of the PhotoImpact line came out in 1999, and offered an increased focus and refinement of the Web tools: JavaScript rollover effects, image slicing, and integrated component design. The EasyPalette was a refined tool with hundreds of presets, and the Quick Commands truly became a power-user's dream.

And in late summer of 2000, Ulead launched the latest version of its image-editing powerhouse application: PhotoImpact 6.0.

New in Version 6.0

PhotoImpact 6.0 introduces quite a few significant advances over 5.0. It's an evolutionary upgrade, rather than a revolutionary one, but after using it, I was hooked. Here are some of the new things that version 6.0 has:

► True Web page creation tools with HTML text objects

► Advanced Web object linking

► Transparent Web backgrounds

► Component Designer Objects that can be edited and exported as objects

► Templates for Web pages, business cards, certificates, and more

► Animation Studio with powerful presets for animation

► Animated type effects

▶ Single-character text formatting

▶ Text to Path

▶ Improved text controls, including line spacing, character spacing, and baseline shifting

▶ Spline path drawing tools

▶ Colorize Pen

▶ Color Replacement Pen

▶ Enhanced screen capture

▶ …and a whole lot more

The PhotoImpact 6.0 package you purchased contains 1790 web components, 2000 photos, 1000 pieces of clip art, 700 textures, 55 new templates, 30 new fonts, and an incredible 2200 EasyPalette Samples & Presets. This is in addition to the programs you're already aware of: the core PhotoImpact program, GIF Animator 4.0, and PhotoImpact Album 6.0. In a nutshell, you're getting a lot of value for your money. As someone who used to purchase the very expensive Adobe applications, I'm consistently pleased at the value that Ulead crams into their products.

What's Next for PhotoImpact

This is pure speculation on my part, but PhotoImpact is clearly taking steps to make its application into a Web designer's toolkit. The new HTML tools are fairly basic when compared with something like FrontPage 2000, but I would expect this to change in 7.0 and beyond. I can see richer HTML support coming down the pipe, with perhaps some frames support and a way to edit the code directly in the program.

The company has also introduced a new series of templates (Web pages, business cards, flyers, and more), which I imagine will continue to expand. Although I've never used PhotoImpact as a print design and layout tool, the templates I've seen are quite compelling. By bumping up the image dpi, you can get decent print quality, so if Ulead continues to release more templates, I can see version 7.0 of PhotoImpact taking some territory away from the template-heavy Microsoft PhotoDraw 2000.

Using PhotoImpact Images

What can you use PhotoImpact for? Well, it might be better to ask what you *can't* use it for—PhotoImpact is very flexible. If you work on CMYK images in a prepress environment, PhotoImpact isn't the right tool for you. But if you're a Web designer (amateur or professional), a digital photographer, or just interested in computer graphics, PhotoImpact is one of the best tools on the market. Let's explore some of the possibilities, and these really are only *some* of them:

PowerPoint

Aside from the skill of the presenter, the difference between good and great PowerPoint presentations is the quality of the graphics in the presentation. Whenever I create a PowerPoint presentation, I strive to make it unique and graphically compelling because the design conveys my message to the audience. PhotoImpact is a perfect tool to do this; there are presets for any sort of design I can come up with, and the effects I'm able to generate with it are impressive when projected onto a 20-foot screen. The image seen in Figure 1.1 shows an example of this: The multi-colored background is a texture I found on the Internet, while the text and images were all created, resized, shadows added, and tweaked in PhotoImpact. PhotoImpact's button tools and Component Designer are also excellent for making unique bullet graphics.

Figure 1.1

A PhotoImpact image in a PowerPoint presentation.

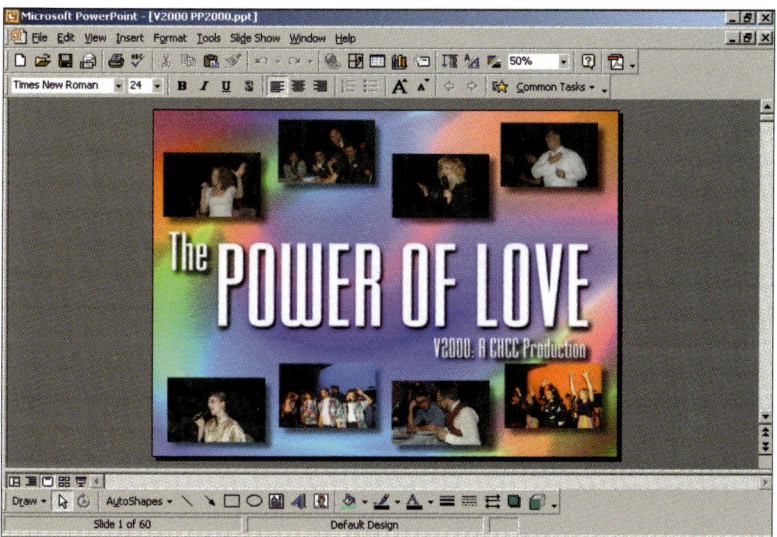

Desktop Publishing (DTP)

Although the Web has overshadowed the desktop publishing realm in recent years, designing attractive brochures, flyers, and print pieces is still an important part of day-to-day business, whether you're a small business or a church office. I personally find Microsoft Publisher 2000 to be the best program for desktop publishing; it's fast, simple, and reasonably flexible in accommodating my needs. Let's face it, though—most clipart is lame. Using PhotoImpact, I created the title image in Figure 1.2, and by using the Fire Type preset, I saved myself the time of manually creating the fire effect. If the dpi in your image is high enough (300), you can create logos for business cards, letterheads, and more.

Figure 1.2
Logos designed in
PhotoImpact can be
used in almost any
desktop publishing
application.

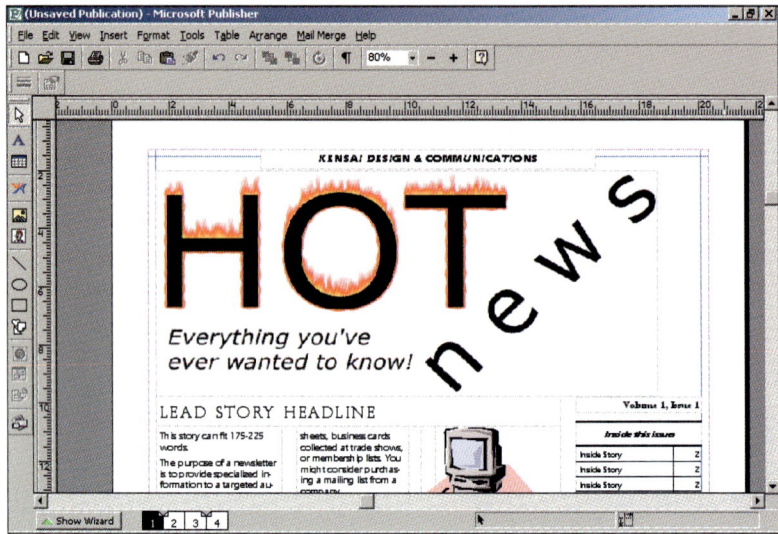

Web Sites

Web graphics are where PhotoImpact really shines. In Chapters 7 through
10, we'll explore the ways you can prepare photos for Web display or
create entire Web sites from scratch with rollovers, sliced up images, and
many other things. PhotoImpact 6.0 is first and foremost a Web graphics
design tool, and nearly every aspect of the program has been designed
with that in mind. Figure 1.3 shows a Web site I designed with an earlier
version of PhotoImpact. The buttons are shapes drawn with the Path
Tools, while the overall design was tweaked to match the client's
corporate colors.

Figure 1.3
A Web site designed
with PhotoImpact.

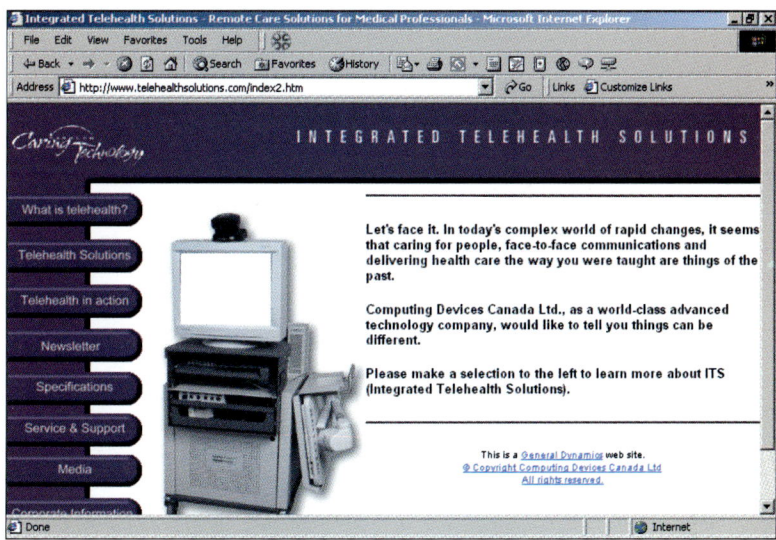

Portable Computers

Although relatively unknown to many people, handheld computers are
becoming increasingly popular. When I'm not writing about PhotoImpact,
I'm writing about Windows Powered Pocket PCs, and I'm constantly
finding reasons to use them together. The screen size of a Pocket PC is half-
VGA: 240 pixels wide and 320 pixels high, so most regular images don't fit
on the screen. I like to carry images of friends and family on my Pocket PC
(a virtual photo album), so I use PhotoImpact to resize and sharpen the
images before putting them on the Pocket PC as optimized JPEG files. I also
use it to design custom graphics for the device. Figure 1.4 shows a banner
I designed for Lockergnome users (**www.lockergnome.com** is a daily
technology newsletter). This was done in PhotoImpact, using graphics I
took from the official Web site, plus some creative color sampling. The
banner is actually two pieces, so using the Image Slicer to crop exactly 20
pixels off the top was critical to making this file work.

Figure 1.4
The banner was
designed with
PhotoImpact.

Desktop Wallpaper

I believe computers should be customized to match the user's interests. Changing your desktop wallpaper is a great way to do this! PhotoImpact is a powerful tool for making desktop wallpaper. If you're into cars, people, or space landscapes, PhotoImpact is the perfect tool for resizing and tweaking the image to fit your desktop. Want to spice it up a bit? Add a frame or edge effect to your image, a soft vignette, or any number of other special effects. If you want to create a completely custom wallpaper, you can use the Background Designer or a third-party plug-in like Flaming Pear's Solar Cell. Figure 1.5 shows the desktop wallpaper I created using that tool. Anything is possible!

Figure 1.5

Custom desktop wallpaper designed in PhotoImpact 6.0.

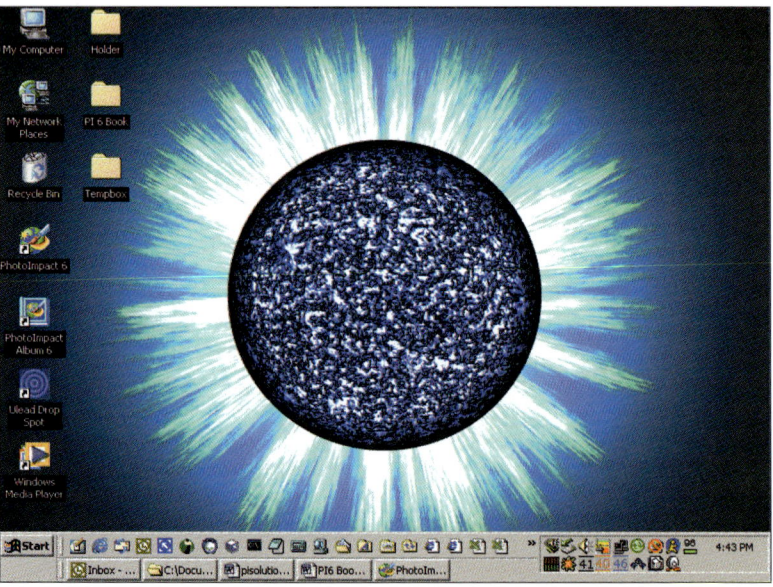

2

Getting Around in PhotoImpact

Like most Windows-based programs, PhotoImpact 6.0 follows a series of standards whose consistency makes the software easier to use. For example, under the File menu of every program, you can expect to see the standard functions of New, Open, Close, Save, Save As, Print, and so on. Right-clicking on any part of the screen will produce options for you to choose from, and this becomes especially useful when you're dealing with objects. (See Chapter 3, "Objects and Selections: Built for Speed.") One of the reasons why I like the way PhotoImpact works is its pedigree. It's 100 percent PC-based, never having evolved from the Apple platform like so many other programs. When using Adobe Photoshop on the PC, for example, there are dozens of Mac-like quirks that simply don't exist in the PC world. But PhotoImpact works the way I do!

A Brief Visual Tour of PhotoImpact 6.0

In this section, we're going to look at the toolbar, which is one of the core elements of PhotoImpact and what you see when you first start up the program. Almost all functions begin with an option from the toolbar, so it's important to get to know the names of the tools and how to find them.

What You See on Your Screen

After you've installed PhotoImpact and start it up for the first time, you'll see a screen that should resemble Figure 2.1. Your screen may vary depending on the resolution of your monitor. For this book, my resolution for screenshots was set at 800×600. I normally work in 1280×1024 resolution and have all panels active. By default, the EasyPalette and Brush Panel are activated, while the Quick Command panel is not. You can activate or deactivate the panels as you wish (see the following Tip).

Figure 2.1
A typical PhotoImpact window when first loaded.

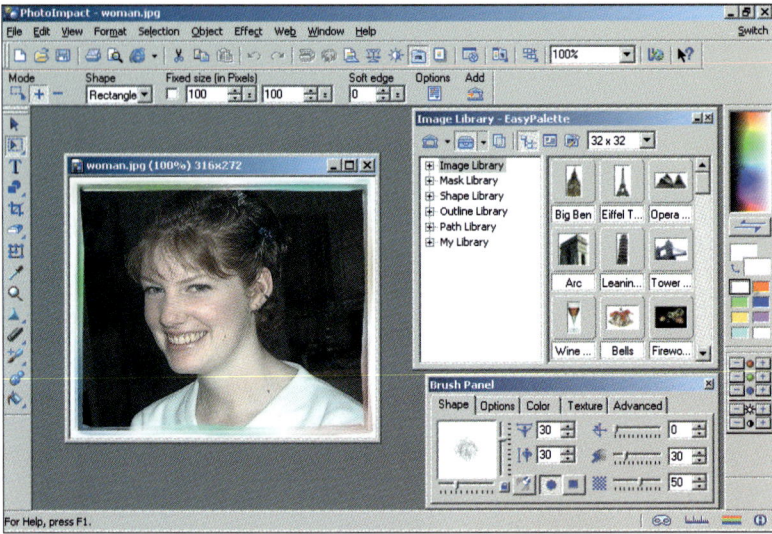

TIP

If you want to make the EasyPalette more compact, change the size of the preview images. By default, it's set at 64×64. Using the drop-down menu, you can change this to 32×32 and save screen space.

The menus in PhotoImpact are "smart." If you don't have an image file open, they won't display nearly as many options. For instance, there is no Effect menu if there is no file open. Once you open or create a file, the proper menus will be added (as Figure 2.1 shows). The reason for this is simple: Everything other than the basic File/Edit/View/Web/Help menus all modify images or objects. PhotoImpact keeps things simple.

NOTE

If you're running your screen resolution at 1024×768 or higher, you may wish to enable the Quick Command Panel. Go to View > Toolbars & Panels > Quick Command Panel, or press Ctrl+F2.

Conversely, if you're running in 800×600 resolution or even in 640×480 resolution, you may want to deactivate all of the floating panels. You can do this by deselecting the EasyPalette and Brush Panel under the Toolbars & Panels section of the View menu (or by pressing Ctrl+F1 and Ctrl+F3).

Getting to Know the Tool Panel

There are certain parts of PhotoImpact 6 that you'll get to know very well as you use the program, so I'll introduce them early on. One of the most important is the Tool Panel (shown in Figure 2.2), because it contains the most frequently used tools in PhotoImpact. In order from top to bottom, these tools are:

Figure 2.2
The PhotoImpact
Tool Panel.

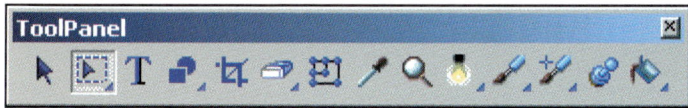

▶ **Pick**—Used for selecting objects, masks, text, and essentially any other item that can be moved. You can also use this tool to move selections without converting the selection to an object.

▶ **Selection**—Used to create and manipulate selections (we'll discuss this in detail in Chapter 3, "Objects and Selections"). If you click and hold your left mouse button while hovering over this tool, a menu appears that shows the different settings this tool has:

—**Standard Selection**—Used for making regular selections in a click-and-drag motion, with options for fixed sizes and shapes.

—**Lasso**—Used for making irregularly shaped selections by drawing a path with selection points and then closing the path.

CHAPTER 2

—Magic Wand—Used for selecting areas of an image based on similarity of color or shade.

—Bezier Curve—Used for irregularly shaped or artistic selections by drawing a curved path and closing it.

▶ **Text**—Used to create new text or to edit text currently in your image. We'll delve into text issues in Chapter 4, "Working with Words: The Text Tools."

▶ **Path**—Used for creating and manipulating paths. (You'll learn about paths in Chapter 5, "Working with Shapes: The Path Tools.") Click and hold on this tool to see the following options:

—Path Drawing—Used for creating path shapes.

—Outline Drawing—Similar to the Path Drawing tool, but the shapes are outlined instead of filled in.

—Line and Arrow—This has lines and arrows galore!

—Path Edit—This is what you'll use if you want to edit a path that's already been created.

▶ **Crop**—Performs the function of cropping, which is the trimming of an image.

▶ **Eraser**—As the name suggests, this is for erasing parts of your image. It has two modes:

—Object Paint Eraser—Neatly erases inside an object without touching the surrounding area.

—Object Magic Eraser—Used for area-based erasing of an object, using color similarity.

▶ **Transform**—A powerful tool that lets you adjust a variety of size and perspective characteristics.

▶ **Eyedropper**—Allows you to sample colors from anywhere in your image. This is useful when you need to color-match a background with the dominant color in a logo.

▶ **Zoom**—Zoom in and out from your image with this tool.

▶ **Retouch**—Actually a flexible set of tools that provides quick access to a variety of image retouching and enhancing tools. You can find more about this in Chapter 7, "Photo Editing Basics: Retouching/Enhancing."

—**Dodge**—Based on classic photography darkroom techniques, "dodging" is the art of lightening up parts of an image.

—**Burn**—Another darkroom technique, "burning" involves darkening part of an image.

—**Blur**—Fine control over blurring parts of an image. You "paint on" the blur—it's great for those witness protection program photos!

—**Sharpen**—Fine control over sharpening. As you paint with this tool, you sharpen the image.

—**Tonal Adjustment**—With this tool, you can adjust the tones of colors in an image, such as highlighting and darkening, by painting them on.

—**Smudge**—As the name suggests, this smudges part of an image. With a small brush size, you can have razor-sharp control over this tool, using it to fix cracks and erase wrinkles.

—**Saturation**—Resaturate images by painting on the effect. This is works well on faded images or washed-out skin tones.

—**Warping**—You can stretch parts of an image with this tool.

—**Bristle Smear**—This is an artistic smearing effect, as if you were to take a stiff, wired brush to wet paint.

—**Remove Red Eye**—Just like the name says, it removes that glared, red light in your subject's eyes.

—**Remove Scratch**—A variation on the Blur Tool, this helps you remove scratches from scanned images.

—**Remove Noise**—Perfect for removing "noise" or "static" from an image, such as background speckles and garbage that detract from the focal point of the image.

—**Color Transform Pen**—Replace one color with another using this tool.

—**Colorize Pen**—Add some color to those black-and-white images with this classy tool.

CHAPTER 2

▶ **Paint**—One of the core elements of every image editing program, the Paint Tools in PhotoImpact offer a variety of presets: Paintbrush, Airbrush, Crayon, Charcoal, Chalk, Pencil, Marker, Oil Paint, Particle, Drop Water, Bristle, and Color Replacement Pen. See Chapter 7 for more on painting.

▶ **Clone**—You have a wide variety of brush styles to choose from when performing the cloning function: Clone-Paintbrush, Clone-Airbrush, Clone-Crayon, Clone-Charcoal, Clone-Chalk, Clone-Pencil, Clone-Marker, Clone-Oil Paint, Clone-Bristle. Chapter 7 delves into cloning.

▶ **Stamp**—Stamps are new to version 6.0, and you can explore this fun feature in Chapter 8, "Photo Editing: Advanced Special Effects."

▶ **Fill**—A myriad of different fills can be performed with PhotoImpact, all based on four distinct settings:

—**Bucket Fill**—This does straight, solid fills, from one color to another.

—**Linear Gradient Fill**—This does fills that gently transition from one color to another, along a straight line that you define.

—**Rectangular Gradient Fill**—This is similar to the Linear Gradient Fill tool, only the fill flows in a rectangular pattern.

—**Elliptical Gradient Fill**—This also is similar to the Linear Gradient Fill tool, only the fills flow in an elliptical pattern.

And there you have it—the PhotoImpact Toolbar! The functions on the toolbar will be used time and time again, so be sure you know what each function looks like before you continue.

The Value Slider

A new feature of PhotoImpact 6.0 is what I call the "Value Slider." In many parts of the program, there are boxes where you can insert numerical values such as for the size of an image or the dimensions of a crop box. You can enter a specific value in the box, use the small up and down arrow keys (also called the spin buttons), or click and hold on the small drop-down arrow and slide your mouse left or right. You'll see the value change rapidly or slowly, depending on how quickly you move your mouse. This is great for speed, but not for accuracy. If you have a specific value you need in the boxes, it's best to type in the number yourself. See Figure 2.3 for a better look.

Figure 2.3
The Value Slider.

Working with Files

Knowing how to work with your files properly is critical in PhotoImpact. Developing good techniques for file management will help you work faster and smarter. It may even save you some hassle along the way.

Creating a New File

Creating a new image file in PhotoImpact is simple. Either click the New icon or go to the File menu and chose New. Either way, you'll end up with the New File window, as shown in Figure 2.4.

Figure 2.4
The New File window.

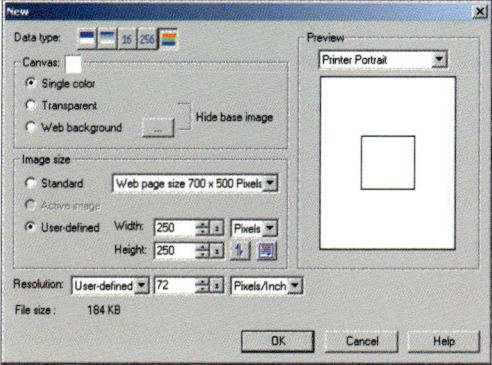

There are several things to be aware of when you look at this window:

▶ **Data type**—This is the bit depth, or number of colors, that your image will have. Your choices here, from left to right, are Black and White, Grayscale, 16 Color, 256 Color, and True Color. Unless you specifically need one of these other modes, always start in True Color. Even if you're planning on ending up with a black-and-white image in the end, many filters don't work on anything other than 24-bit color images. Remember, you can always scale down your color depth later.

▶ **Canvas**—This is the color of your background. In most cases it's safe to leave this as white, because you can always fill in the background later. If you're planning on using the image on a Web page, you may want to choose the Transparent option so you can see how the image will "float" on your background transparently. The last option is Web Background, which is part of the new Web site design tools in PhotoImpact 6.0. This option allows you to create the background you want your Web site to have. It has many options, and we'll explore them fully in Chapter 9, "Web Graphic Design."

▶ **Image size**—As you might imagine, these settings allow you to set the size of the image you want. There are more than two dozen choices in the Standard selections, all measured in pixels, and these

CHAPTER 2

are great for starter projects. If you need to create Web banners or micro buttons (sometimes called "badges" on a Web site), the templates are here. Active Image creates a new blank image with the same dimensions as the current image. This is useful when you want to closely match a current image by size. Lastly, User-defined allows the user to pick a specific image size in pixels, inches, or centimeters.

TIP

If you have a specific size of image that you're constantly using, you can add it as a preset to the **User-defined** section. To do this, set the size you want and click on the Add button (circled in Figure 2.5). You'll then be prompted for a name for the preset, and it will reside in the menu permanently. Perfect for those large jobs where speed counts!

Figure 2.5

Adding a user-defined image size for fast access later.

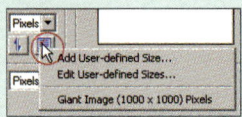

▶ **Resolution**—This is where you can choose the resolution of your new project. If you're doing Web work, leave it at 72 dpi. If you're designing a logo or something for printing, you should bump it up to 300 dpi or so. The final number depends on what kind of printer you have. Experiment a little if you plan on doing a lot of printing.

▶ **Preview**—The Preview feature allows you to see the relative size of your image based on the selected resolution. This can give you an idea of how large your image will be on the user's screen. This can be particularly valuable if you're running in a high resolution, 1024×768 or greater. When running at a high resolution, I often forget how big my images are on the screens of users with lower resolutions. If you're creating a Web logo, preview the proposed size on the 800×600 setting. How much screen space does it take up? Too much, too little? Put yourself in your visitors' place and all your Web graphics will be better for it!

Cropping

Learning to crop is a critical skill when working with graphics, because cropping helps you reframe the photo and can improve any image. Cropping is defined as removing everything in an image except what was selected. If you had an image of an apple on a table, and wanted to draw attention only to the apple, you would draw a selection around the apple (selections are discussed in Chapter 3, "Objects and Selections") and crop out everything else.

Especially in the realm of digital photography, cropping is critical. The difference between good and bad photography often comes down to framing the image. Where is the subject in the photo? In the center or off to the side? Is the subject the focus of the image, or are distracting elements coming in from the side to create visual confusion? Cropping can often make a poor photo into an acceptable one and gives you some interesting composition options. Examine Figure 2.6.

Figure 2.6
Our image prior
to cropping.

In Figure 2.6, we have an image taken with a digital camera. The framing of the subject in the photo is quite good—the subject is firmly in the middle and there are no distractions in the background or sides. But what if we wanted to get a closer shot of the girl in the photo, with less distraction from the background? Cropping tools come to the rescue in Figure 2.7.

Figure 2.7
The Crop
Tool's options.

Before we start, it's important to understand some of the options the Crop Tool gives us. First, by entering values or dragging the value slider, we change the location of the crop box in relation to the left or top part of the image. We can also set the exact size value, and, if you have a crop that you'll be performing on a series of images, you can add your crop as a preset to the EasyPalette by using the Add button on the Crop Tool's Attribute Toolbar.

CHAPTER 2

In order to crop, follow these simple steps:

1. Click on the Crop Tool.

2. Draw the crop box around the part of the image you want to keep (see Figure 2.8).

Figure 2.8
Drawing our selection
for cropping.

3. Adjust the crop box. You can move it around or change any of its dimensions by either adjusting the numerical values or dragging the handles of the box (see Figure 2.9).

Figure 2.9
Adjusting the
crop box.

4. Click the Crop button to see the final image as shown in Figure 2.10.

Figure 2.10
Our final
cropped image.

5. If you're unhappy with the crop, press Ctrl+Z twice and try it again.

Another interesting use of cropping is to crop specific parts of an image to achieve a certain effect. In Figure 2.11, I've cropped the image so that the focus of the image, the girl, is off to the right while there is open space to the left. If I put text in the open area to the left, it would make an interesting banner! Remember that the difference between good and great photography is how you frame the subject. Experiment with the cropping tool and make your photos shine!

Figure 2.11
Different cropping
styles can produce
interesting results.

TIP

If you're looking for the fastest way to crop, try this method that I use: Create a selection using the Standard Selection tool, then press Ctrl+R on the keyboard. You're done!

NOTE

PhotoImpact uses handles for adjusting certain effects and selections. A handle is denoted by a small box that can be adjusted by clicking and dragging the mouse (see Figure 2.12). The mouse cursor will change to small arrows showing you the direction you can adjust the handle. And if you hold down the Shift key while adjusting the handles, you can constrain the aspect ratio. This means that all the sides will be even, allowing you to make a perfect square.

Figure 2.12
Adjusting handles.

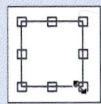

TIP

You may also incrementally adjust the border of the crop box pixel by pixel by clicking and holding a particular handle and using the cursor keys on your keyboard.

CHAPTER 2

Zooming

Zooming is simply the function of telling the program to make the image larger or smaller, showing you more or less detail. This function is useful for a few different purposes:

▶ Zooming in on an image to find things that you can't see at regular zoom.

▶ Zooming out to see more of a large image so you can crop it.

▶ Zooming in on an image to correct flaws, such as red eye or background flaws.

▶ Zooming out to see what an image would look like smaller (useful for Web design).

In the movies and on TV, zooming is a magical thing. The camera zooms in 500 percent and the quality is still fantastic. In real life, things are a little different! When zooming in, you're looking at the same pixels as before, but they're enlarged. So the more you zoom in, the more pixelated the image will look. And, despite what the media would have you believe, you can't click the magic "enhance" button and have it look perfect.

When you click on the Zoom Tool, the toolbar will load and you'll see the following Zoom Tool's Attribute Toolbar as in Figure 2.13:

Figure 2.13
The Zoom Tool's
Attribute Toolbar.

The Zoom Tool's Attribute Toolbar offers a few simple options:

▶ You can use the Zoom Level slider to choose a zoom level, or you can enter a specific value in number box.

▶ The three View options allow you to show the image at a 1:1 ratio (100 percent real size), show as much of the image as your screen size will permit, or restore the last zoom setting.

▶ By clicking and checking the Adjust Window box, PhotoImpact will automatically adjust the window size to fit the absolute edges of the image as you zoom in and out.

▶ You can also add a custom zoom setting to the EasyPalette by using the Add button.

To see zooming in action, let's take a look at a high resolution image that I took. The image is 1536×1024 in size, and since I'm running in 800×600 resolution while writing this book, I can't see the entire image at 100 percent zoom. By zooming out to 25 percent (Figure 2.14), I can see the entire image. By moving up to 100 percent zoom (Figure 2.15), I can see much more of the detail that the camera captured. I can make out some of the details on the red car in the image. Since I'm really curious about that car, I'll zoom in to 500 percent (see Figure 2.16) to see if I can make out the license plate…no such luck! It's just a white blob of pixels. I bet Fox Mulder from *The X-Files* could do it!

Figure 2.14
A high resolution image at 25 percent zoom.

Figure 2.15
The same image at 100 percent zoom—its true size.

Figure 2.16
The same image at 500 percent zoom.

TIP

If you have a mouse with a scroll wheel, hold down the Control or CTRL key on your keyboard while scrolling, and you can zoom in and out very quickly! If you don't have a scroll wheel on your mouse, you can press Ctrl+Left click to zoom in and Ctrl+Right click to zoom out.

Moving Objects, Selections and Text

A wide variety of items can be moved in PhotoImpact; anything that isn't merged with the base layer can be moved. Objects, text, and even selections can be moved. The key to figuring out what can be moved is to watch for the cursor change, as Figure 2.17 shows.

Figure 2.17
Moving objects is easy— look for the cursor to change over what you can move.

If you want to move an item, first select the Pick Tool and then select the item. When your mouse cursor moves over the item, as you see in Figure 2.18, the cursor changes to the movement tool.

Figure 2.18
The movement tool.

I Left-click on the object and, while holding down the mouse button, drag the item to its new location. Release the left mouse button and the item has been moved.

The procedure is exactly the same for moving selections, masks, and text. In the case of moving selections and masks, the program will also display the selection or mask in its current position as well as the position you're dragging it to. Figure 2.19 illustrates this feature.

Figure 2.19
Moving a selection.

Resizing

Resizing images is one of the most common tasks in PhotoImpact. I take a lot of photos in the high resolution mode on my digital camera (1536×1024) and, as such, I need to make them much smaller if I want to post them to a Web site. You may also run across images that are too small and need to be made larger—thus, the resizing tool is the ticket.

There are two ways to resize: Bring up the Dimensions window to resize your image. You can look under the Format menu, and choose Dimensions. You can also press CTRL+G on your keyboard. I prefer the keyboard method for speed purposes. You should see a window load that matches Figure 2.20:

Figure 2.20
The Dimensions window.

CHAPTER 2

There's a lot of important information in this window, so take note:

▶ **Active image**—This information tells you the current size of the image. This is useful for guessing how much smaller to make the image.

▶ **New image**—The choices here are all related to how much bigger or smaller you want your image to be. The Standard choices offer all the choices you have when creating a new image (discussed above), while the User-defined settings can be whatever you want them to be. You should normally keep the box checked off for Keep aspect ratio, unless you want your image to look distorted. Unit options include Pixels, Inches, Cm (which is centimeters), and Percent. In most cases, choose Percent—it's easier to gauge visually.

▶ **Resample method**—This method offers three choices: Nearest Neighbor, Bilinear, and Bicubic. Always choose Bicubic, because this offers the highest quality of resizing, although it may take slightly longer to finish. The other two will sometimes make your image look jagged when resized smaller.

▶ **Apply to**—This function serves to give you a choice of which part of your image to resize: the Base Image, the Selected Object, or all Images and Objects. Choose the one that works best for you. Unless you have multiple objects in your image, only Base Image will be available as a choice.

▶ **Preview**—This gives you an idea of how your image will look when printed or when displayed on a computer screen at various resolutions. This is the same preview you get when creating a new image.

TIP

If you have a lot of images to resize, don't do it manually! In Chapter 13, "Gearing Up: Printing, Sharing, and More," I'll tell you about Quick Commands. They'll make resizing many images a breeze!

TIP

Images at 256 color (8-bit) don't resize with the same quality as 24-bit images—trying to resize an 8-bit color image results in jagged edges and extremely poor quality. The solution is to change the data type to 24-bit, perform the resize, then change it back to 8-bit, or use the Image Optimizer to export the image as a GIF.

Data/Image Type

Images are digital data, and there are various ways of displaying the data. In addition to image resolution, image type is what controls how the colors of the image look on the screen. Image type is also referred to as data type, color depth, or bit depth. The options PhotoImpact gives you include 8-bit Grayscale, 8-bit Optimized Indexed 256-color, 8-bit Web Optimized, 24-bit RGB True Color, 8-bit Indexed 256 Color, 16-bit Grayscale, and 48-bit RGB True Color (sometimes used by newer scanners).

Changing the data type of an image in PhotoImpact is a quick, two-click process.

1. In the bottom right corner of the PhotoImpact program window, click on the Image Type Icon.

2. A menu will open, allowing you to select between a variety of image types (see figure 2.21). Choose the appropriate type for your image, and a new image will be created in this format.

Figure 2.21
The Image Type menu.

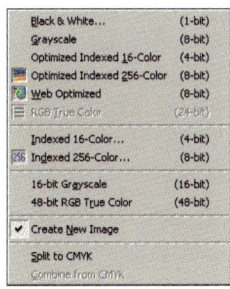

TIP

If you don't want a new image to be created when you choose a new Image Type, uncheck the Create New Image box on the Image Type menu.

TIP

Although it might seem like the easiest way to get a black-and-white image is to select 16-bit Grayscale from the Image Type menu, you can't apply any special effects to grayscale images. A better way is to choose Effect > Special > Monochrome. This gives you a B&W image, but with full access to all effects and plug-ins.

CHAPTER 2

Tweaking PhotoImpact for Maximum Quality and Performance

PhotoImpact is a flexible tool. It offers power users several nice options for tweaking the program to work the way they want. The goal of this section is to show you a few of the most important options. Feel free to explore the rest on your own!

Making Sure You Have the Right Hardware

Before we get into the PhotoImpact settings, it's important to make sure your computer is set up properly to run the program. The system requirements state that any Pentium computer with 32 megabytes (MB) of RAM and 270 MB of hard drive space can run the program. However, unless you have a great deal of patience, you'll want more than this. The larger the image you're working with, the more CPU and RAM you'll want. A decent machine for using PhotoImpact would be a 350MHz or faster CPU, 64 MB or more of RAM, and at least 500 MB of free storage space (you'll need space for all the wonderful creations you're going to make!). Of all the hardware, RAM is the most important for speed—buy as much as you can reasonably afford. The system I use has 384 megs of RAM and sometimes even that doesn't seem enough. If you want to make it hum, 128 megs of RAM or more on a Windows 98 or Windows 2000-based system should do the trick!

If you're planning on doing a fair amount of graphics work, spring for at least a 17-inch monitor or a 19-inch monitor if you can afford it. You'll love the ability to run at high resolutions and see more of your images!

Setting Resolution and Color Depth

To change your resolution, right-click on your desktop, select Properties, and go to the Settings tab. Depending on your operating system version, it will say "Resolution" or "Screen area." If you have a 14- or 15-inch monitor, try 800×600 (if your monitor supports this). If your monitor is 17 inches, try 1024×768, and if you're lucky enough to have a 19-inch or larger monitor, try 1280×1024. The higher the resolution, the smaller everything is, and so the more you can fit on your screen at once. The most important thing to remember is that the higher resolutions are better only if you can see everything properly. As for color depth, this is on the same Display Settings tab and will likely be called Colors. Your choices will vary depending on your hardware, but try to set it at a minimum of 16 bit (64,000 colors). If you can set it at 24 bit (16.7 million colors), or 32 bit (4.2 billion colors) and still run in your favored resolution, do so.

Customizable Settings In PhotoImpact

Under the File menu, you'll find an item called Preferences (Figure 2.22). And from that item you'll see three options: General, Customize Standard Toolbar, and Color Management. As you might imagine, the latter two are for making your own toolbars in PhotoImpact and setting up color matching for on-screen display and printing. The most important options are in the General settings (also directly accessible using F6 on your keyboard), so we're going to look at some of those now.

Figure 2.22
The General
Preferences window.

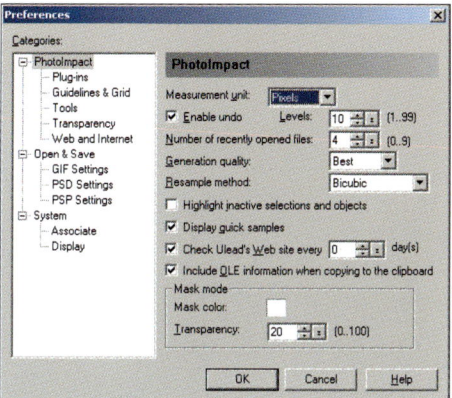

Setting Undo Levels

An important feature in PhotoImpact is its ability to undo and redo functions. By default, it's set at ten levels of undo. You can set this number to a maximum of ninety-nine, but the practical number depends on how much system RAM you have. Each level of undo is stored in RAM, so you'll need a lot of RAM if you plan on keeping ninety-nine versions of your graphic in memory! A safe setting for an average machine is twenty-five.

Setting Generation Quality

Certain filters and settings require PhotoImpact to regenerate the image. This setting affects the speed and quality of that regeneration. I always set mine on Best because there's no substitute for quality!

Setting Resample Method

There are three options available: Nearest Neighbor, Bilinear, and Bicubic. Bicubic produces the best overall quality; make sure you choose this method. For more on this, look earlier in this chapter under "Resizing."

CHAPTER 2

Setting Your Scratch Disk

A Scratch Disk, also called virtual memory, is the location where your temporary files are stored as PhotoImpact executes your commands to resize, enhance, and so on. Depending on the size of images you're working with, you may want to set this on a drive where you have a great deal of space. For the average user, as long as you have at least 200 megs free on your main system drive, you'll be fine. To be on the safe side, however, I always set mine to another partition with plenty of space. You can't be too careful! (See Figure 2.23). Other options on this screen include limiting hard disk usage and limiting RAM usage, but these are advanced settings that work well at their current defaults.

Figure 2.23
The System
Preferences window.

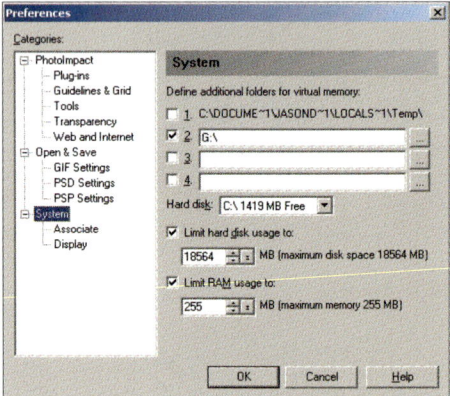

Setting the Plug-in Folder

Plug-ins (also known as "filters") are basically mini-programs that can do as little as a simple effect (such as create a kaleidoscope image) or as much as an entire 3D landscape (Kai's Power Tools 6). There are many freeware and commercial plug-ins available on the Internet (a good start is **www.plugins.com**). Many of my favorites are made by Flaming Pear Software (**www.flamingpear.com**), and we'll discuss these in Chapter 8. When you're looking around the Net for plug-ins, don't be surprised if you don't find any made specifically for PhotoImpact. The dominant graphics app in the market right now, although definitely not the best for the Web, is Adobe Photoshop. Many plug-ins are designed for Photoshop, but nearly all will work in PhotoImpact. Experiment and find out!

This setting in PhotoImpact controls where the program should look for these plug-ins. It's often best to keep them in a separate folder, away from PhotoImpact, so you can organize them better. PhotoImpact will automatically drill down through subfolders to look for all available plug-ins, so you need only set up the main folder, as shown in Figure 2.24.

Figure 2.24
The Plug-in
Preference window.

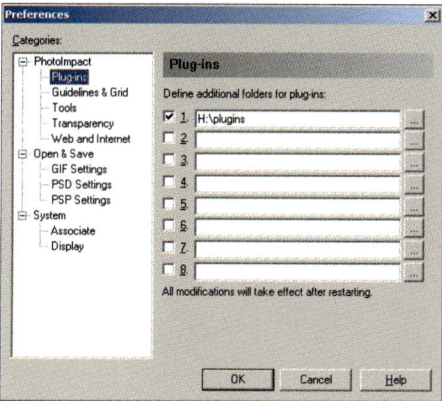

File Associations

PhotoImpact allows you to have complete control over which types of files it will open for you (see Figure 2.25). This long list of files contains nearly every graphics format imaginable, and PhotoImpact can open all of them. Remember, though, that PhotoImpact is a large program and takes several seconds to load (depending on your computer speed).

Figure 2.25
The File Associations
window.

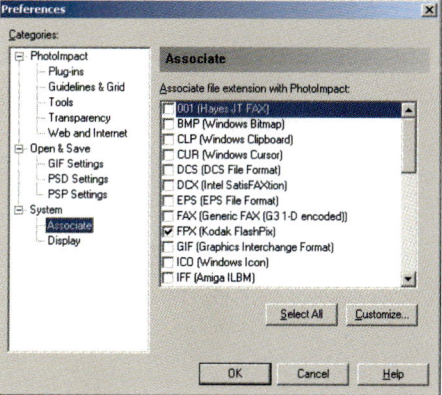

CHAPTER 2

Photoshop and Paint Shop Pro File Settings

PhotoImpact is a versatile program, and part of its strength is its ability to work with a wide variety of file types. Two of the most critical in the business world are PSD (Photoshop's native format) and PSP (Paint Shop Pro's native format). When I design Web pages for my clients, I often need to get a high-resolution version of their logo from the graphic designer who created it. More often that not, it's from a Mac user who's using a version of Photoshop. Being able to read these files is critical! The settings here and on the PSP Settings window are usually fine at their default value (see Figure 2.26), but it's important that you know they are here.

Figure 2.26
The PSD Settings window.

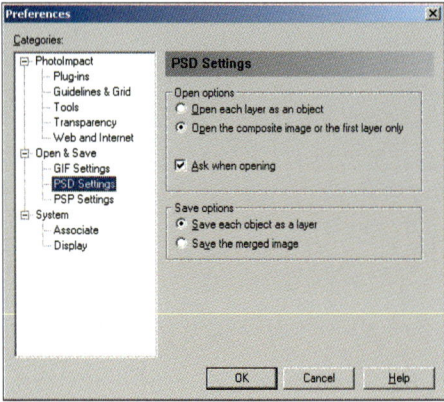

3

Objects and Selections: Built for Speed

Most of the major graphics applications on the market today are layer-oriented. What that means is that when you're putting together an image with different components (text, multiple images), each component is on a different layer. In order to move one component, you need to first select the layer it is on, and then you can move it or edit it. I always found this to be frustrating when working with Photoshop, so when I started using PhotoImpact for Web design (back in version 4.0) I was very pleased with the way it dealt with multiple-component images: Everything was an object. Objects are, of course, very easy to work with. Figure 3.1 shows a multi-object image.

Figure 3.1
Every item in this image is a unique object.

To me, the two most important elements of any graphics program are ease of use and speed of use, which are usually tightly bound together. Designing Web sites for clients usually means two things: lots of repetitive work and tiny modifications to meet specifications. It's critical that whichever graphics app I'm using allows me to work quickly, and that's exactly what objects allow me to do. In Figure 3.1, you can see a quick image I tossed together using some of the built-in images PhotoImpact has. Each item in that image is a separate object: the Eiffel Tower, the heart, the glass of wine, the two pieces of text. Each of these can be moved, changed, or deleted using the Pick Tool.

CHAPTER 3

There's no need to move over to a layer manager to first select the layer that the object resides on. Also, because PhotoImpact has extensive right-click support, you can make changes very quickly to the object. We'll discuss this in more detail later, but if I wanted to add a drop shadow to the text, it's literally a three-click process, and I never have to leave my object to go up to the system menus. Now that's speed!

TIP

If you've used PhotoImpact 5.0 before, you may notice one new feature in 6.0 right away: A green selection box is around all objects in your image at all times. I find this very distracting, so I turn it off by pressing CTRL+SHIFT+Q on the keyboard. It may also be turned off by looking under the View menu and unchecking Show Box around Object.

Creating and Inserting Objects

In Chapter 6, "EasyPalette: Your New Best Friend," you'll learn about the EasyPalette and all the options it gives you. One of my favorite things about the EasyPalette is the way you can use it to build up your own set of object resources. For instance, when I was working on my own personal Web site (which never quite seems to get done), I wanted to put up some of my favorite photographs. Because they were my photos, I wanted to put my e-mail address on them. I created my text object and added it to the EasyPalette. Then, with a simple double-click, I was able to add my e-mail address to each image. Fast and easy!

Creating Your Own Objects

Creating objects in PhotoImpact is a fairly simple matter. Whenever you create text or a path or paste in an image from the clipboard, you've created an object. You can tell something is an object when you've selected the Pick Tool. If you then click on something, it will draw a selection around the object and turn your cursor into the four-way moving cursor. You can see this in Figure 3.1. These objects can be moved, copied, deleted, and manipulated in many ways, all without affecting other objects around them. That's another beauty of objects: They're totally isolated from other objects, so you can do anything to them and still have the rest of your image remain the same.

We'll go into detail about creating text objects in Chapter 4, "Working With Words: The Text Tools," and paths in Chapter 5, "Working With Shapes: The Path Tools." But I'll tell you now that one common way of introducing new objects into a composition is to use the Paste command. The Paste command has three ways of being accessed: CTRL+V, right click and choose Paste, or, choosing one of the Paste options listed under the Edit menu.

Let's say you are browsing through a Web site and find a photograph of a car that you want to use in one of your images. After making sure you are allowed to use the image, follow these steps:

1. In Microsoft Internet Explorer, right-click on the image and choose the Copy command (see Figure 3.2). This copies the image to your system clipboard and from here you can paste it into almost any application.

Figure 3.2
Copying the image
to the clipboard.

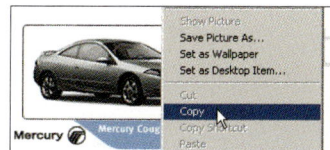

2. Go to your PhotoImpact image (in this example we're assuming you've already created a new image), right-click somewhere inside your image and choose Paste, as shown in Figure 3.3.

Figure 3.3
Pasting the new image
into an existing image.

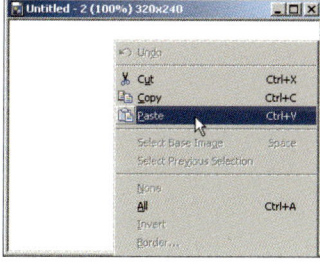

3. You'll see your new image appear in the PhotoImpact image window (see Figure 3.4). You've just created an object! If you right-click on the object, you'll see a variety of options for your object.

Figure 3.4
Our new object.

Later in this chapter you'll learn how to apply special effects such as drop shadows and fire effects to your object.

Inserting Objects from the EasyPalette

You'll learn more about using the EasyPalette in Chapter 6, but for now, let's talk about how the EasyPalette works with images and how you can insert images from it. Think of the EasyPalette as a desktop organizer with lots of little compartments with something different in each. Some compartments have tools (pens and erasers), some have materials (paperclips and staples). In the same way, the EasyPalette has Galleries with different tools and effects; it also has Object Libraries with objects for you to use in your images.

Inserting an object from the EasyPalette is fast and simple. Just follow these steps:

1. Because objects reside in the Object Libraries, make sure the EasyPalette is displaying Object Libraries. Click the second icon in from the left, as Figure 3.5 shows.

Figure 3.5
The EasyPalette displaying the Image Library, which contains a number of ready-to-use objects to use in your compositions.

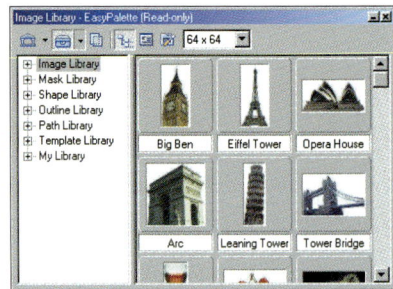

2. Scroll through the images, masks, shapes, outlines, or paths and choose the item you want to insert. Click and hold on the item, then drag the cursor over to your object. When you are over your image, the cursor will change to look like this:

I've dragged over the "opera" object.

3. The object will appear in your image, as Figure 3.6 shows.

Figure 3.6
The object has been
inserted into our image.

TIP

An even faster way of inserting objects from the EasyPalette is to double-click on the object. It will drop into the middle of your active image. Or you can right-click on the object in the EasyPalette and select the Copy Object to Image command or the Copy Object to New Document command if you want to create a new image from the object.

Adding Your Own Objects to the EasyPalette

Now that you know how fast you can take objects from the EasyPalette and put them into your own images, you can imagine how useful it is to have your own objects in there. Input your company logo, a personal watermark to identify your images, or anything else you can imagine. Any object can be placed in the EasyPalette—text, images, and so on.

Using the example I talked about above, I've created a text object that has my name and e-mail address on it, and I want to insert this into every image I'm posting on my Web site. First, I need to add it to the EasyPalette!

1. I've created a text object with an ellipse around it (see Figure 3.7) and grouped these items into one object (we'll discuss how to do this later in this chapter).

Figure 3.7
An object created for
use on all my photos.

2. Next I'll drag and drop the object onto the EasyPalette and I'll be presented with an Add to EasyPalette window with a few options (see Figure 3.8). Picking a good sample name can be important, especially if your object is hard to recognize at small sizes. You can also choose which Gallery or Library to add it to. In my case, I want to add this to the My Library group (this group is already created for you by default).

Figure 3.8
The Add to
EasyPalette window.

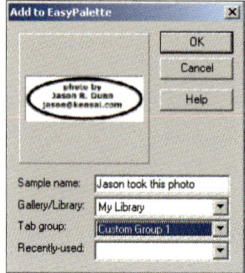

3. My image has been added to the EasyPalette and I can very easily add it to any image I'm working on (see Figure 3.9).

Figure 3.9
My object is part of the
EasyPalette now.

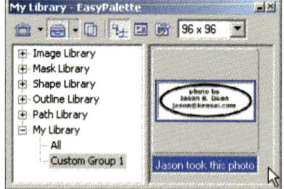

Photo-Objects from Hemera

Hemera Technologies (**www.hemera.com**), a rapidly-growing company in eastern Canada, makes some software that is so incredibly useful to me that I wanted to mention it here. I'm sure you're familiar with clip art—you can't go into a software store without seeing collections of "10,000,000 clipart images." Most clip art is, quite frankly, utterly lame for Web purposes. The Web is all about high-quality images and photographs, not cheesy looking clip art. The searching tools in all the packages I tried were also horrible, and it took forever to find the image I wanted.

There are online photo resources like PhotoDisc (**www.photodisc.com**) that offer thousands of high-quality and very distinctive images. But I found these to be very expensive—$24.95 for a single image. This is pricey when you need many of them, especially when you're working on sites for non-profit companies. What's a Web designer to do? Hemera has the solution!

What Hemera has done is create large collections of very high quality photographs that already have the backgrounds removed (see Figure 3.10), all for a very affordable price (under $90 for their current 50,000 photo object collection). This makes them ideal for Web and print work, because you can just drop them into your image and they look fantastic. A quick-right click in PhotoImpact adds a drop shadow. And a quick EasyPalette setting changes the way the image looks. The images can be exported in a variety of formats for use in different programs and at variable dpi settings (72 dpi for screen work and 300 dpi for print work).

Figure 3.10
The Hemera search tool in action.

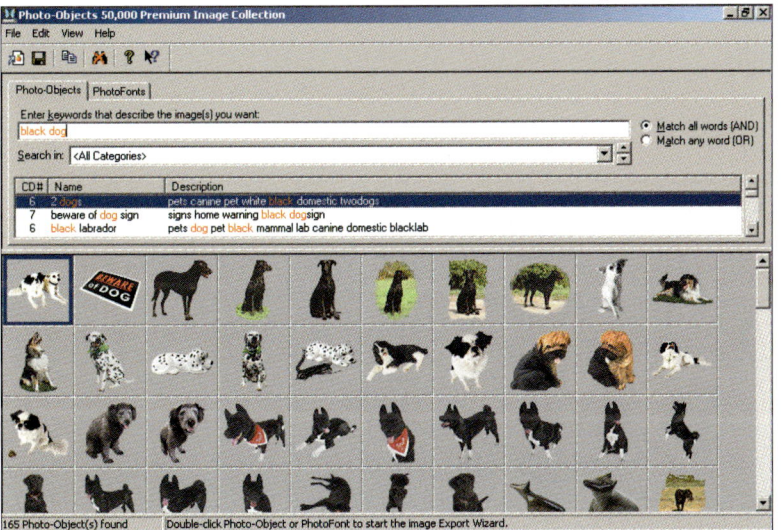

The search tool is one of the most valuable parts of this package. Imagine typing in a few terms and, as you type them, the images display. The more terms you type, the more specific the images get. You don't even need to click a search button! The above illustration shows the way the search tools work and the results that are displayed for the terms "black dog"—165 images in total! I can't recommend this product enough.

CHAPTER 3

Manipulating Objects

Objects are easy to create and manipulate. You can perform a variety of actions on objects, all with simple commands that are listed on the right-click menu of an object. Below is a list of the commands you have available to you with the object right-click menu and what they do (Figure 3.11 shows the menu that these commands come from).

Figure 3.11
Right-click options
for objects.

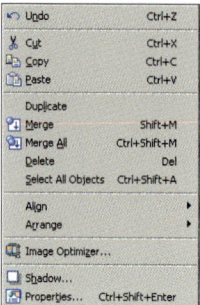

▶ **Cut, Copy, Paste**—These commands are self-explanatory. Cut removes the object from your image and puts it on the clipboard for pasting into another image, while Copy does the same thing without deleting the image. Paste is an option only if there's already an object on the clipboard. If there isn't, it will be grayed (or "ghosted") out. Remember that using the Paste command doesn't clear the clipboard, so if you want to make multiple copies of something, you can keep pressing CTRL+V to make copies.

▶ **Duplicate**—The Duplicate command will simply make a clone of your object, offset by a few pixels so you can see that it was duplicated.

▶ **Merge, Merge All**—These two commands are related. If you select Merge, it will merge the object with the background, effectively making it a permanent part of the background (also called the *Base Image* in PhotoImpact). Once an object is merged, it cannot be selected or moved in any way. And, unless you use the Undo function (or CTRL+Z on your keyboard), the merged object can never be easily separated from the background. Similarly, Merge All will take every object in the image and merge it with the background (Base Image), making your image "flat". This is usually the final step in creating Web graphics before you export them as GIF or JPEG images. Never merge an image and save it as your only copy. You may need to make adjustments later, so be sure to keep an unmerged UFO file (PhotoImpact's proprietary file format) around for later use.

▶ **Delete**—This command is also self-evident. You can use Undo or CTRL+Z on your keyboard to undo the delete action.

▶ **Select All Objects**—This command selects all objects, but not the background. Once selected, objects can be manipulated en masse. This is useful when you need to move everything at once, delete everything at once, or even copy all your objects to the clipboard as one group. You may alternatively use CTRL+SHIFT+A on your keyboard to select all objects in the composition.

▶ **Align**—There are a variety of ways you can align your images, but all have the same starting point. You need to select the multiple images you want to align. A fast way to do this is by holding down the CTRL key or the SHIFT key as you click on the images. Once you've selected your images, you can align them from the top, bottom, left, or right. You can also center them horizontally or vertically (or both at once), and you can even space the objects evenly by any pixel amount. My personal method of aligning objects is to first align them on the vertical or horizontal axis (depending on my image) and then right-click the group of objects and use the Align > Space Evenly command. (This is a good command to experiment with.)

▶ **Arrange**—This command controls the depth placement of the object in relation to other objects. If you want your object to be up front and on top of other objects, this is one place where you set it.

▶ **Image Optimizer**—This is the tool you use for exporting your images to the Web. We'll cover this in detail in Chapter 9, "Graphic Design for the Web: A PhotoImpact Primer."

▶ **Shadow**—This command creates quick and easy shadows. This topic is covered in the next section, Object Effects.

▶ **Properties**—This command provides fine control over your object properties and is covered later in this chapter.

TIP

If you want to copy an object quickly using the keyboard, remember that all the regular keyboard commands still apply: CTRL+C for Copy, CTRL+X for Cut, and CTRL+V for Paste.

TIP

If you click on an object and drag it while holding down the CTRL key on your keyboard, it will be copied. And if you hold down the SHIFT key while dragging an object, it will snap to invisible guidelines that run vertically and horizontally inside the image. This helps you move your object precisely.

CHAPTER 3

Object Effects

As I explained in the introduction to this chapter, one of the beauties of objects is that they are isolated from the rest of the image but can be accessed quickly without having to switch to different tools or layers. There are some common object effects you may wish to use and some guidelines to keep in mind when using third-party plug-ins on your objects. See Figure 3.12.

Figure 3.12
A purple-flamed, lightning-bolt-infused, drop-shadowed lightbulb—all in less than two minutes!

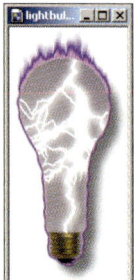

Adding a Drop Shadow

Drop shadows are a simple yet effective way to enhance many images. Although many designers avoid them now because they feel the effect has been overused, I think they add a touch of dimension to any image and encourage you to use them (with restraint). To create a drop shadow effect on any object, follow these easy steps:

1.   Right-click on your object, and choose Shadow from the menu.

2.   The Shadow settings window will come up (see Figure 3.13). This is the control center for all shadow functions. From this window, you can control the color of the shadow, the direction of it, X and Y axis offsets (the higher the value, the more it looks like the image is lifting off the page or screen), transparency, the overall size of the shadow, and how soft the edges look. The default values are usually fine for most circumstances, but there is a lot of room for experimentation here. Play around with the settings and see what you can do!

Figure 3.13
The Shadow settings window.

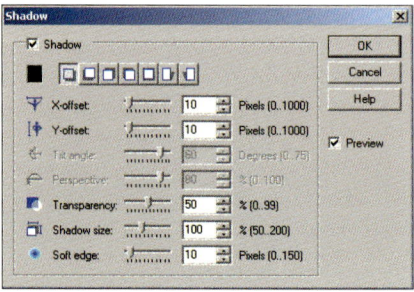

3. As you make changes to this screen, the effects can be seen immediately on your image. Once your shadow looks the way you want it to look, click OK. You're done!

> **TIP**
> The smaller the text size, the less of a shadow effect it should have. Ten-point text with a default shadow (offset of 10 pixels) looks unrealistic—an offset of 2 pixels looks much better.

Adding a Fire Effect

Fire effects in PhotoImpact are very simple to do; you'll be surprised how quickly you can create them. Fire effects look great on logos or Web graphics or can get your print pages noticed. Remember, like all special effects, don't overexpose your user to the effect or it will no longer be visually exciting. In this example, we'll start with a simple black circle created with the path tools (see Figure 3.14). You can substitute text and use the same steps to get flaming text.

Figure 3.14
We start with a simple black circle.

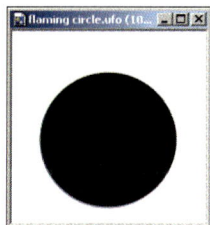

1. Select the circle, then right-click on it and select Duplicate. The circle will duplicate itself, creating a copy that is offset by a few pixels (as Figure 3.15 shows). The reason we're creating a duplicate is that the flame effect will create an outline of our original image and we want to have both the flames and our original shape for our final composition.

Figure 3.15
Duplicating the circle.

CHAPTER 3

2. Look at the EasyPalette and, under the Type Gallery, look at the Fire settings (see Figure 3.16). I've chosen the blue preset for a "cold fire" effect. Any of the fire effects listed would work here.

Figure 3.16
The EasyPalette
Fire presets.

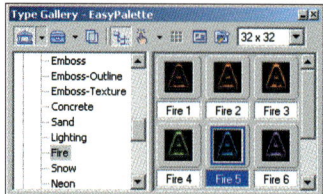

3. By double-clicking on the preset it is applied to the target object as shown in Figure 3.17 (remember that you need to have an object selected before an effect can be applied to it).

Figure 3.17
Applying the cold
fire effect.

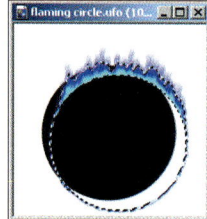

4. Using the arrow keys, adjust the fire effect until it's positioned closely around the source image as in Figure 3.18. The key is to make it look like it's one object. Once you like the way it looks, you're done!

Figure 3.18
The final image—a
"cold-fire solar eclipse."

TIP

If you're having trouble seeing borders to active objects when aligning due to the animating marquee, you can toggle the animating marquee on and off using SHIFT+Q on your keyboard.

NOTE

Almost every preset in the EasyPalette has variable settings that can be controlled. Right-click on a preset and if you see Modify Properties and Apply, this means the preset has a setting you can modify (the exceptions to this rule are some of the frames). In the case of our fire effect here, I could have modified any of the three flame colors or controlled the intensity of the flame. Experiment and have fun with it!

CAUTION

Remember that in order to apply a plug-in or preset to an object, you need to have that object selected. If you don't, you'll see an error like that shown in Figure 3.19.

Figure 3.19
The error message when there's nothing to apply the preset to.

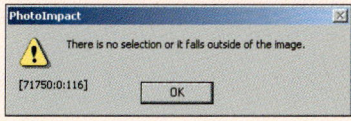

Applying Plug-ins and Filters to Objects

PhotoImpact 6.0 has dozens of special effects filters. There are many third party plug-ins that you can use to create striking images, and nearly all of them can be applied to objects without any difficulty. Just as in the fire effect described earlier, first select the object, then select the effect, and the effect will be applied to the object. You can also apply the effect to multiple objects at the same time. In Figure 3.20, I've selected all the objects at once. I then chose Effect > Creative > Particle on the text toolbar and then selected Bubble as the special effect. Thus, I've created an image that takes on a whole new look.

Figure 3.20
A series of selected soccer ball objects.

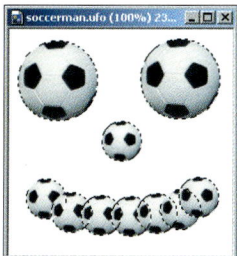

Figure 3.21
The same objects after the bubble particle effect.

Object Properties

Each object has its own set of properties that can be specified, such as name, transparency value, and so on. Some of these settings can also be set from elsewhere, but if you're working on a complex, multi-object image, it pays to keep track of all the little details. The properties for an object are accessed by right-clicking on the object and choosing Properties (see Figure 3.11 earlier in this chapter). Object Properties, as shown in Figure 3.22, is what comes up.

Figure 3.22
The General tab of the Object Properties window.

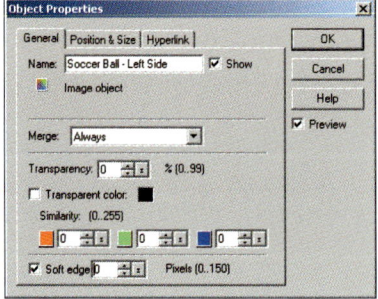

There are several properties for each object, but the most important ones are:

▶ **Name**—The name of the object; this is important when you have many objects!

▶ **Show**—If this box is unchecked, your object will be hidden. This is the equivalent function of "hide layer" in some other graphic design programs.

▶ **Transparency**—The higher the value, the more transparent the object. You can use this to achieve interesting special effects.

▶ **Transparent color**—You can indeed knock out colors with this setting, but if you're planning on making transparent GIFs for the Web, it's better to use the Image Optimizer tool (more on this in Chapter 9).

- ▶ **Soft edge** —Cyber artists can crank this up to around 30 to give the object a soft-focus effect. Set it to 50 and higher and it functions as a fade-out effect. Experiment with it!
- ▶ **Position & Size tab**—You can specify, down to the pixel level, the exact size and position of your object.
- ▶ **Hyperlink tab**—There are a lot of options here for Web design, and we'll deal with all of them in Chapter 10, "The Web Design Studio inside PhotoImpact."

TIP

If you're looking for a fast way to get to an object's properties, try double-clicking on it. Fast!

Saving Objects

The one critical thing to understand about saving objects is that only one file format supports objects: Ulead File For Objects (UFO). Any other format (JPEG, TIFF, and so on) will merge your objects into one, making them impossible to manipulate again. So it's important to choose the UFO format when using the Save feature (found under the File menu) to maintain your original objects' properties without merging.

If you want to save your objects in another format, say the GIF or JPEG formats for the Web, you can right-click and select Image Optimizer. I'll go into detail on how this works in Chapter 10. For now, however, you should understand that it's very simple to save individual objects in whichever format you need.

Lastly, if you want to save an object in a format like TIFF or BMP, but don't want to affect your original image, drag the object out of the image window while holding down the Control key. This will create a copy of your object in its own file, and you can right-click to Merge All and then save it in whichever format you wish.

TIP

You can make an exact duplicate of your current active and open composition within PhotoImpact by using CTRL+D on your keyboard. This will make a duplicate of everything—any floating, unmerged objects and the Base Image itself will be included. This is great if you want to experiment on an exact copy but don't want to affect the original image.

CHAPTER 3

Selections

Selections are closely related to objects, because at some point in time many objects were once created using selections. The easiest way to understand what selections are is to understand that when something has a selection around it, whatever you do will be done only inside the boundaries of that selection. For example, in Figure 3.23, I've created a selection that covers most of the wall and some of the window. You can tell it's a selection because it has the staggered blue line (called the Marquee) around the edge. Let's say I wanted to fill that selection with yellow. By pressing CTRL+F and selecting yellow, I get the hideous mess in Figure 3.24. No one said PhotoImpact would give you good taste!

Figure 3.23
A selection in action.

Figure 3.24
Post-fill results.

So how do you make selections? There are four tools in PhotoImpact for making selections, and I'll give you some information about each tool. Making accurate selections is something that takes experience, so although I can give you information about how the tools work, it's important to practice using them.

Standard Selection Tool

The easiest to use of all the selection tools, this tool allows you to create selections based on either a click-and-drag motion or a fixed size. When you click on the tool, its corresponding Attribute Toolbar will load (see Figure 3.25), giving you a few options.

Figure 3.25
The Standard Selection's
Attribute Toolbar.

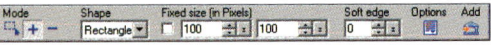

> **Mode**—There are three modes for all selection tools. From left to right, they allow you to make a new selection (removing whatever selection was already there), add to a current selection, or remove from a current selection.

> **Shape**—You first pick the shape, and then you draw your selection either as a rectangle, a square, an ellipse, or a circle. This can be useful when trying to accurately isolate part of an image.

> **Fixed size** —By checking this box and specifying a value, clicking on your image will yield an exact pixel-by-pixel selection based on the dimensions you chose. This can be useful in a variety of situations. Although the Crop Tool is usually a better choice for things like this, this is the way to do it if you need to prep some still images for insertion into a digital video project and need to make sure they are exactly 640×480.

> **Soft edge** —This is exactly as described under the Object Properties section above. When used with selections, it's great for the soft-edge vignette effect.

> **Options**—This includes Draw from Center (for more precise selections), Preserve Base Image (which leaves your Base Image alone rather than have the selection destroy the Base Image wherever the selection was made), and Anti-aliasing (which smoothes the edges of a selection).

> **Add**—If you have a selection you make on a regular basis, you can add the selection to the EasyPalette for future use.

Lasso Selection Tool

The Lasso Tool is ideal for hand-drawing a detailed selection around an object. You use this tool by clicking selection points around the edges of the object you want to "lasso." When you've gone around the entire perimeter of the object and end up at the starting point, a quick double-click will turn it from a lasso into a selection. Figure 3.26 shows the lasso tool in action.

Figure 3.26
The Lasso Tool's
Attribute Toolbar.

The toolbar that loads when this tool is selected has two unique options:

▶ **Snap to edges**—When this option is selected, PhotoImpact will attempt to find the edge of the object you're selecting and try to "snap" to the edges. Depending on the complexity of the object edge it's trying to snap, this can have varying degrees of success.

▶ **Sensitivity**—The value of this setting determines how PhotoImpact detects the edges of your object. See Figure 3.27.

Figure 3.27
The Lasso tool
in action.

TIP

Sometimes it's easier to create a selection around what you *don't* want and invert it in order to get a selection of what you *do* want. For instance, if the subject in your photo is standing in front of a white wall, rather than drawing a selection around the subject, use the Magic Wand tool to select the background, right click on the selection and choose Invert. Your selection will be inverted! I frequently use the Invert function because it's such a great time-saver.

Magic Wand Tool

The Magic Wand Tool (see Figure 3.28) is another selection tool that happens to be one of my favorites. It allows you to select large areas of an image based on the coloring of an image. If you have an image with a dark background, the Magic Wand Tool can be used to select large pieces of it with one click. And with a few adjustments to the Similarity setting, you can fine-tune the selection even further.

Figure 3.28
The Magic Wand Tool's
Attribute Toolbar.

This tool has two options that are worth mentioning:

▶ **Select by Line or Area**—This option allows you to control how the selection is being made. I've found that it's a good idea to try both options and see which one gives you a better selection.

▶ **Similarity**—The higher this number, the more of a color range it has. In Figure 3.29, if I wanted to select more of the purple backdrop with one selection, I should have cranked up the Similarity to around 50.

Figure 3.29
The Magic Wand
in action.

Bezier Curve Tool

The Bezier Curve Tool is an interesting tool, because it allows you to create selections using a curved tool that is essentially a path. This is a fairly advanced tool that is less useful (in most cases) than the other selection tools, but it can be used to create some beautiful sloping selections that would make interesting visuals. (You can see this in Figures 3.30 and 3.31.) The two most important options for this tool are:

▶ **Shape**—You can create your own curved shapes with the Free Path option (the default), or you can select one of the other shapes (they are the same as the Standard Selection Tool).

▶ **Draw new path** or **Edit existing path**—As the name suggests, you can either draw a new path or edit one that already exists.

Figure 3.30
The Bezier Curve Selection's Attribute Toolbar.

Figure 3.31
The Bezier Curve Tool in action.

NOTE

The EasyPalette includes a Mask Library with dozens of preset selections. Masks are essentially complex selections that, when applied to your image, can be used for a variety of edge effects. The Soften Masks are among my favorites, because they allow for fast and easy vignette effects. To use a mask, double click on it in the EasyPalette, switch to the standard selection tool, and the move the mask—you'll see your image with the mask applied, and by dragging it out of the image, you can create a new image with only the mask effect.

4

Working with Words: The Text Tools

If a picture is worth a thousand words, what's it worth to be able to combine pictures *and* words? Quite a bit—and sometimes doing just that is more than an option. It becomes a necessity. Whether you're creating logos, adding captions to images, or designing text-based buttons for a Web site, you can use PhotoImpact's Text Tool to add text to your images in a multitude of styles that you can change with the click of your mouse.

In this chapter, you'll learn how to create text, how to apply various styles to it, and how to convert it other object types. By converting text into a path, you can edit the shapes of individual letters. Using The EasyPalette Type Gallery, you can apply various special effects meant especially for text objects as well, without converting the text into another object type.

Fonts

Before you can have text, you need fonts—the computer software needed to display different typefaces. Your computer comes with dozens of fonts. Many application programs automatically install more fonts. If you don't have just the typeface you need, though, there are thousands more available, both free and commercial.

Font and Typeface Terminology

Most Windows fonts are TrueType fonts, which will display and print at high quality in any size. Windows can also use PostScript fonts, which work the same way but are usually more expensive. In addition, bitmap fonts can be used, but these are intended just for use on-screen, rather than in printed text or in high-resolution graphics.

Each font contains just one face, whether that's a plain (or *roman*) version, an *italic* one, a **bold** one, or a ***bold italic*** one—so an entire typeface family is composed of several individual fonts. You can use only the fonts that are installed on your computer, so if you want to create type in a different typeface, you'll need to locate a typeface that looks the way you want.

Here are a few special terms that describe type (see Figure 4.1):

Figure 4.1
Typography has its own special language that helps designers describe type and its various parts.

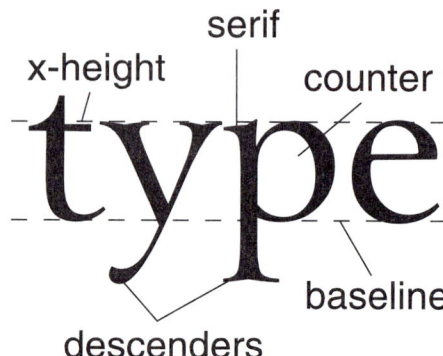

- **Roman**—The plain version of a typeface is called roman; it's also sometimes called regular or book. For example, the typeface this text is set in is Melior Roman.

- **Italic**—Book titles and some other terms are set in *italic* type. It's a slanted, somewhat "script" version of a roman face.

- **Bold**—A heavier version of a roman face is called **bold.**

- **Black**—Extra-heavy type is often referred to as **black.**

- **Baseline**—The baseline is the imaginary line that runs along the bottom of a line of type; most letters, such as the letter "b," sit right on the baseline.

- **X-height**—The height of most lower-case letters, including "x," is the x-height.

- **Ascender**—An ascender is the part of a lower-case letter, such as in the letter "d," that extends above the x-height.

- **Descender**—A descender is the part of a lower-case letter, such as in the letter "g," that extends below the baseline.

- **Counter**—A counter is a hole within a letter shape, such as the middle of an "o."

- **Serif**—Serif typefaces have small extensions called serifs at the end of each long stroke. This paragraph is set in a serif typeface.

- **Sans Serif**—Sans serif typefaces don't have serifs. The heading on the first page of this chapter that says "Fonts" is set in a sans serif typeface.

Different typefaces are useful for different purposes. For example, a large, bold sans serif typeface is easy to read—that's why the "STOP" on a stop sign is set that way. For smaller text, serif typefaces tend to be easier to read, because the serifs provide our eyes with extra "clues" to determine what each letter is as our brains process the letters into words. You can use different typefaces to create contrast between different areas of text, such as headings and body text.

Installing and Viewing Fonts

Windows stores all your fonts in one place, so it's easy to see which fonts you have, view them, and install new ones. Each font file contains a sample of how it will look when you use it in a document. Here's how to view the fonts installed on your computer:

1. Choose Start menu > Settings > Control Panel.
2. In the Control Panel, double-click on the Fonts folder.
3. Double-click on a font file to see a sample of it, along with some information about its manufacturer (see Figure 4.2).

Figure 4.2
Windows' built-in font sample display gives you a good idea of how a typeface will look at different sizes.

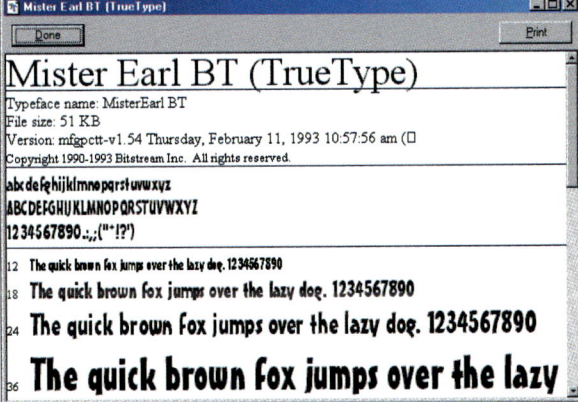

TIP
It's often useful to have a printed notebook of type samples that you can flip through quickly. To print a typeface sample, double-click on the font file and then click the Print button.

CHAPTER 4

The number next to each different type size in the sample window shows the point size of that line of type. Type is measured in points, with 72-point type being a little less than one inch tall. Different typefaces may not look as though they are the same size, even when you set them at the same point size, because of their different designs (see Figure 4.3).

Figure 4.3
These two type samples are both set in 72-point type; the left-hand face is Arrus, and the right-hand face is Colonna.

When you add to your font collection, you can install new fonts through the Fonts folder as well. To install new fonts in Windows:

1. Choose Start menu > Settings > Control Panel.

2. In the Control Panel, double-click on the Fonts folder.

3. In the Fonts folder window, choose File > Install New Font to bring up the Add Fonts dialog box (see Figure 4.4).

Figure 4.4
Installing new fonts is as simple as telling Windows where to find them.

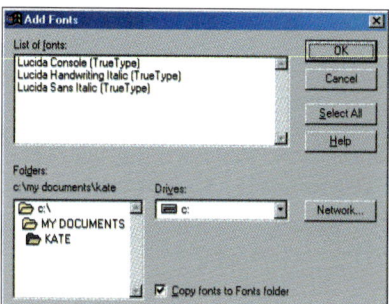

4. Navigate to the folder containing the fonts, then shift-click to select the fonts you want to install.

5. Click OK.

Getting New Fonts

Free fonts abound on the World Wide Web, and mail order companies have piles of CD-ROMs containing inexpensive fonts. Here's a short list of free font archives that will get you started in adding to your collection:

▶ **http://www.mediabuilder.com/fontlibrary.html**—This collection of free fonts is divided into both standard categories and more descriptive ones; you can look for serif or sans serif typefaces, but you can also choose from Scary, Crazy, and Historical fonts.

CHAPTER 4

▶ **http://desktoppublishing.com/fonts.html**—Located within a huge archive of desktop publishing information and links, this font source has free and shareware fonts as well as links to commercial type foundries, font utilities, and information about fonts and typefaces.

▶ **http://www.astigmatic.com/aoeff/freefonts.html**—Here you'll find a small but interesting collection of fonts, many of them dingbat fonts—typefaces with pictures instead of letters. Our favorite is DoggiePrint, which contains twenty-six dog heads in different breeds instead of the twenty-six letters of the alphabet.

▶ **http://www.fontfile.com/**—All the FontFile people want in exchange for free access to their extensive font archive is a link to their site from your own Web site.

▶ **http://www.fontfreak.com/**—This site features free fonts for both Windows and Mac users—tell your Mac-loving friends!

One warning for font-hounds: With fonts, you may find that you get what you pay for. Commercial fonts usually contain special characters that may not exist in free fonts. Examples of these characters are "curly" quotation marks and ligatures, which are two- or three-letter combinations that look cleaner than the original letters do when placed side by side. Spacing is likely to be better in commercial fonts, too.

Creating Type

Now it's time to get down to it and actually create some type. The technique is simple, but the options for formatting text in PhotoImpact are myriad, so feel free to experiment. First, make sure that the Tool Panel is visible by choosing View > Toolbars & Panels > Tool Panel. Then, to add type to an image:

1. Switch to the Text Tool.
2. Click anywhere in the image window to bring up the Text Entry Box (see Figure 4.5).   *Click on [4] to get blank page*

Figure 4.5
You can set text attributes at the same time as you enter text in the Text Entry Box.

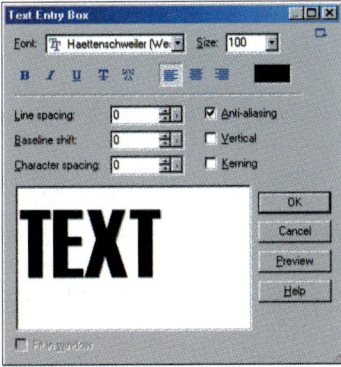

3. Type in the text you want to create.

4. To see a preview of the text in the image window as you type, click the Preview button.

5. When you're done, click OK.

As long as the type you've created stays a text object rather than an image object, you can edit it at any time by choosing the Text Tool and double-clicking on the text to reopen the Text Entry Box. You can also access the Text Entry Box by clicking to select the text and then right-clicking to display a contextual menu—the first option in the list is Edit Text.

TIP

When you want to select or edit existing text, watch the cursor to make sure that double-clicking will reopen the Text Entry Box—there should be a small "T" inside the arrow. If you double-click with the regular Text Tool cursor, which shows a text insertion bar next to the arrow, the click will open a new, blank Text Entry Box.

Table 4.1 shows some keyboard shortcuts that you may find helpful when you're working in the Text Entry Box.

Table 4.1
Text entry box
keyboard shortcuts

Text Entry Box Keyboard Shortcuts	
Start a new line of text	CTRL+ENTER
Update the image window preview	ALT+P
Copy the selected text	CTRL+C
Cut the selected text	CTRL+X
Paste text from the Clipboard	CTRL+V
Undo the change you just made	CTRL+Z

Each time you click with the Text Tool, PhotoImpact uses the appearance settings from the last text object you worked with. You can change some of these settings in the Text Entry Box, or you can leave them as is and then change them later using the Attribute Toolbar. The controls in the Text Entry Box and those in the Attribute Toolbar overlap somewhat, but each place has controls not found elsewhere. The following sections describe the different settings you can apply to text, along with where you can find the controls for those settings.

NOTE
If you don't see the Attribute Toolbar, choose View > Toolbars & Panels > Attribute Toolbar to display it. And if you don't see any type style controls in the Text Entry Box, click the button in the upper right-hand corner of the box to display the controls. You can save screen space by clicking again to hide them until you need them.

Font

The Font menu is the first control both on the Attribute Toolbar and in the Text Entry Box. As you scroll through the menu options, PhotoImpact displays a sample of each font to the right of the menu (see Figure 4.6). If you want to add fonts to the Font menu, see "Installing and Viewing Fonts."

Figure 4.6
As you scroll down the Font menu, PhotoImpact shows you a sample of each font.

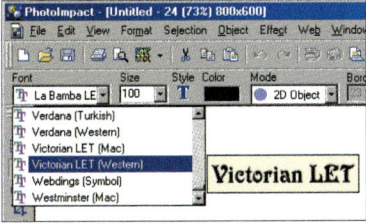

Size

You can set the size of text in several ways. The simplest is to choose an option from the Size menu, which is the second menu in both the Attribute toolbar and the Text Entry Box. The Size menu lists point sizes from 1 to 128 in one-point intervals. Because it can get tiresome scrolling through all those sizes, you can also just click in the Size field at the top of the menu and enter a number between 1 and 4096. If you enlarge the type enough that it doesn't fit in the image window, it will just extend off the edge. You can move it around to see the rest of it, and if you reduce the size again, all of the text will still be there.

The third way to resize type is to transform it using the Transform Tool (see Figure 4.7), which is useful for creating type to fit in a particular area of your design without trying to figure out what point size will work. To transform type, switch to the Transform Tool and click on the text, then drag on any of the side or corner handles. Hold down the SHIFT key on your keyboard as you drag if you want to maintain the proportions of the letters. When you're done resizing the type, click anywhere else in the image window to complete the transformation. To see what point size the transformed type is, switch back to the Text Tool and click on the transformed type. The size is displayed in the Size field of the Attribute Toolbar.

Figure 4.7
Using the Transform Tool allows you to size text visually without losing its status as a text object.

Even after you've transformed the text, you can still edit it as described above under "Creating Type."

CAUTION

If you resize text using the Transform Tool, you won't be able to deform the text afterward, such as using Horizontal Deform or Vertical Deform under the Mode option on the Text Tool's Attribute Toolbar.

Style

Text Style options appear in both places: the Attribute Toolbar and the Text Entry Box. In the Attribute Toolbar, you'll find a Style menu that contains a variety of options in several categories. Here you can change the typographic style of text, as well as its alignment, but you can also make much more fundamental changes to the way type appears. These changes include such things as the preset collections of appearance attributes found in the three Type Galleries. The Text Entry Box has some of the same controls as the Style menu, along with some extras that are accessible only here (see Figure 4.8).

Figure 4.8
You can hide or display the Text Entry Box's text formatting options by clicking the button at the upper right corner of the dialog box.

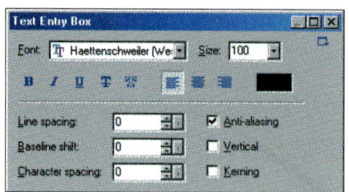

Galleries

Three of the EasyPalette Galleries meant for text objects that are included with PhotoImpact are accessible via the Style menu on the Text Tool's Attribute Toolbar:

▶ **Material**—This Gallery contains surface textures that can be applied to PhotoImpact objects, including type. The categories include Metallic, Plastic, and Realistic textures (such as Wood, Paper, and Fabric). Most of these surfaces won't really show up on a 2D object, such as plain type. To make the most of them, use one of the 3D modes (see "Mode" further on in this chapter). To apply any Material setting, double-click on its thumbnail image.

▶ **Deform**—The Deform Gallery contains presets for deforming type in various shapes. There are two sets of Deform presets—those for horizontal type and those for vertical type. By default, all type is horizontal, but Vertical is one of the options in the Style menu; see "Typeface Styles" below for more information. To apply any Deform setting, double-click on its thumbnail image; double-click on the first thumbnail, labeled "Reset," to return your type to its normal appearance. If you want to deform type manually, see "Deform" in the "Mode" section ahead.

▶ **Wrap**—Here you'll see options for wrapping text around other objects (or itself) in various ways. You can experiment with the different wraps and waves. To apply any Wrap setting, double-click on its thumbnail image, and you can always return your type to its normal appearance by double-clicking on the first thumbnail, labeled "Reset."

TIP

You can also wrap text—or any other object—by clicking to select the text, then right-clicking to display a contextual menu and choosing an option from the Wrap submenu. This is the same as the Wrap submenu in the Object menu on the Text toolbar, which you'll see if you've selected a text object with the Pick Tool instead of the Text Tool.

Typeface Styles

The second set of options on the Attribute Toolbar's Style menu, denoted by separators, contains the basic text formatting style choices that are available in most page layout or word processing programs. These styles also appear in the Text Entry Box in the form of buttons, as follows:

▶ **Normal**—This is the default text style. Choosing this option in the Style menu removes any other style options you've applied. There's no button for Normal in the Text Entry Box—you'll just have to click the individual buttons for style options to turn them off.

▶ **Bold**—If the typeface designer has included a bold version of a typeface in the font installed on your computer, then this choice will change the text to the bold version. It has no effect if the font doesn't include a bold version.

▶ **Italic**—This option works regardless of whether the typeface designer has included a true italic version of the typeface in the font. If an italic version isn't included, PhotoImpact just slants the type a bit to create obliqued ("fake" italic) text.

▶ **Underline**—To place an underscore below the text, choose this option.

▶ **Strikethrough**—This style puts a line through the middle of each letter.

▶ **Outline**—Using the outline style creates a hollow version of the text, with the outside outlined in the selected color and the interior transparent.

You can mix these styles by applying more than one. To remove any style, choose that option again from the Style menu or click on the button again in the Text Entry Box. To remove all styles, choose Style > Normal.

Orientation

By default, all text in PhotoImpact is created horizontally, the way this book is set. You can change the orientation of text to vertical by choosing Style > Vertical in the Text Tool's Attribute Toolbar or by clicking the Vertical checkbox in the Text Entry Box (see Figure 4.9).

Figure 4.9
A checkbox in the Text Entry Box allows you to run type vertically rather than horizontally.

Alignment

The default alignment setting in PhotoImpact is left-aligned, which means that the text you create will start where you click the Text tool in the image window and proceed to the right from that point. The other options are Right and Center. To change alignment in the Attribute Toolbar's Style menu, choose any option; to change alignment in the Text Entry box, click any of the three buttons.

Shadow

Giving text a shadow is an attractive way to make it stand out from a background. If the Text Tool is active, you can apply a shadow to a text object by clicking on it and then choosing Style > Shadow in the Attribute Toolbar. When you're using the Pick Tool, you can click on a text object and choose Object > Shadow, just as you would for any item in PhotoImpact. This is also discussed in Chapter 3, "Objects and Selections: Built for Speed."

The Shadow dialog box looks the same whether you're applying a shadow to a text object or to any image object (see Figure 4.10). The first thing you need to do to create a shadow is to click in the Shadow checkbox at the top of the dialog box. The rest of the controls are as follows:

Figure 4.10
The available controls in the Shadow dialog box vary depending on the type of shadow you're creating.

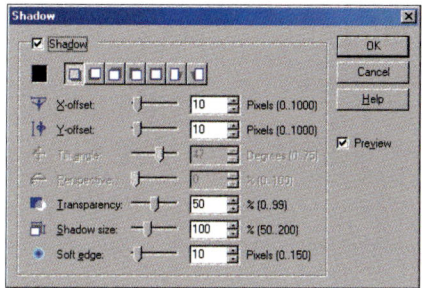

▶ **Color**—The first control in the Shadow dialog box is a color swatch; click on it to display the Color Picker and choose a new color for the shadow.

▶ **Type**—Next to the color swatch are seven buttons for various types of shadow. The first five give you drop shadows, each with the shadow offset at a different angle from the text—below and to the right, below and to the left, above and to the right, above and to the left, or directly behind the text. This kind of shadow makes the text appear as though it's floating above the page. The sixth and seventh buttons produce cast shadows, which make the text look as though its base is planted on the page and the rest of it is extending upward from the page. See Figure 4.11 for examples of the different shadow types.

Figure 4.11
A drop shadow (top) makes the shadowed object appear to be floating above the page, while a cast shadow (bottom) makes the object look as though its base is standing on the page.

▶ **X-offset**—This setting determines the horizontal distance in pixels between the shadow and the text that's casting the shadow. It can range from 0 to 1000, and it's available only when you're creating a drop shadow, because cast shadows always start at the base of the type.

▶ **Y-offset**—This setting determines the vertical distance in pixels between the shadow and the text that's casting the shadow. It can range from 0 to 1000 and, like X-offset, is available only when you're creating a drop shadow.

▶ **Tilt angle**—You can set the Tilt angle only when you're creating a cast shadow, because drop shadows lie flat against the image rather than tilting. The higher the setting, the farther off to the opposite side the invisible light source casting the shadow appears to be. You can set the angle anywhere between 0 and 75 degrees.

▶ **Perspective**—Like Tilt angle, the Perspective setting is available only when you're creating a cast shadow. It determines the height of the light source casting the shadow. At the highest setting, the light source appears to be level with the base of the text. The Perspective value is a percentage and can range from 0 to 100 percent.

▶ **Transparency**—This setting allows other objects to show through a shadow. At 99 percent, the shadow almost completely disappears, while at 0 percent it's completely opaque. The default setting is 50 percent. You can't set the Transparency to 100 percent.

▶ **Shadow size**—You can set the size of a shadow with respect to the size of the text casting the shadow. The default value is 100 percent, which gives you a shadow the same size as the text. You can make the shadow as small as half the size of the text (50 percent) or as large as twice the size of the text (200 percent). This setting comes in handy most often when you're creating a drop shadow directly behind the text, because the shadow must be larger than the text if you want it to show up well.

▶ **Soft edge**—The Soft edge of a shadow is what makes it look like a shadow rather than any other object. This setting is expressed in pixels, with a range from 0 to 150, so the value you'll want to use depends on the resolution of the image you're working in. For lower resolutions, use lower Soft edge values to make the same size shadow.

NOTE
The fifth button for shadow type gives you a shadow that's placed directly behind the text. You can get the same effect by setting both the X-offset and Y-offset to 0 when using any of the other four drop shadow types.

Click the Preview checkbox in the Shadow dialog box to see the results of your changes as you make them. When you're done, click OK to apply the shadow to the text. Once you've applied a shadow to text, it will move with the text, and it will reform itself as you reshape the text in any way, such as by wrapping it or transforming it. (For more information about wrapping text, see "Wrapping Type" later in this chapter.)

If you want to separate a shadow from its text, click on the text with either the Text Tool or the Pick Tool. If you're using the Text Tool, choose Style > Split Shadow on the Attribute Toolbar; if you're using the Pick Tool, choose Object > Split Shadow. Once you do this, you can't change the shadow's settings, so make sure you've got it just the way you want it before splitting it off from its object.

Anti-aliasing

The final option in the Style menu is Anti-aliasing, which is a default setting that you'll probably never find a good reason to turn off. (The one exception is that, at small font sizes—below 8 points—this can increase clarity.) Anti-aliasing blurs the edges of each letter slightly so that they appear smooth on-screen; without it, the edges of the letters would appear jagged (see Figure 4.12). You can also control whether text is anti-aliased by clicking the Anti-aliasing checkbox in the Text Entry Box.

Figure 4.12
The left-hand letter appears jagged, while the right-hand one appears smooth due to anti-aliasing.

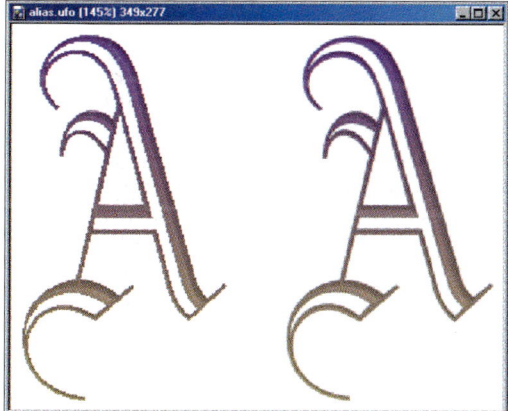

Color

Although the text you enter in the Text Entry Box is always black (so it will be easy to read), you can make text within an image any color or texture you want, using the same color controls that you'd use to change the color or texture of any object within PhotoImpact. The color of text can be set in either the Text Entry Box or using the Attribute Toolbar's

Color option when the Text Tool is active. In each case, you change the color by clicking on the color swatch and choosing a color selection method from these options:

▶ **Ulead Color Picker**—This is the color picker created specifically for PhotoImpact.

▶ **Windows Color Picker**—This color picker is the one that comes with Windows. Figure 4.13 shows the Ulead and Windows color pickers side by side.

Figure 4.13
The Ulead Color Picker (left) and the Windows Color Picker (right) accomplish the same thing—use whichever one you're more comfortable with.

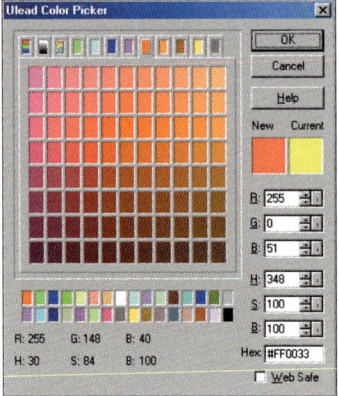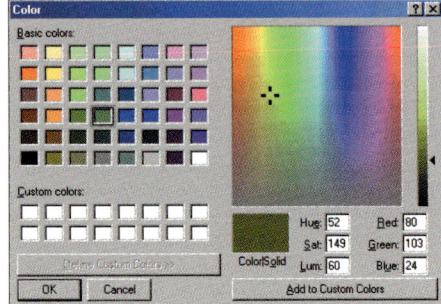

▶ **Eyedropper**—The Eyedropper dialog box shows the image in a window so that you can click on a color from the current image.

▶ **Color on Screen**—After choosing this option, your cursor will change to an eyedropper. Click anywhere on the screen, within the PhotoImpact window or anywhere else, to choose a color.

▶ **Foreground Color**—This sets your text color to the current foreground color.

▶ **Background Color**—This sets the text color to the current background color.

▶ **Quick Pick Squares**—Here you'll see two sections of color swatches, one reflecting the current set of colors active on the Color Palette and one with the thirty-two most popular colors as determined by Ulead, the makers of PhotoImpact.

▶ **Gradient Fill**—The Gradient Fill option leads to the Gradient Fill dialog box, which allows you to determine the direction and colors used in a gradient fill.

▶ **Magic Texture Fill**—PhotoImpact comes with a set of textures that you can apply to any object, including text. This option opens the Texture Library to the Magic Texture set, consisting of abstract patterns; to apply any texture, double-click on its thumbnail image (see Figure 4.14).

Figure 4.14
Magic Texture Fills
and Natural Texture
Fills are both part of
the Texture Library and
work the same way—
double-click to apply
any of these textures.

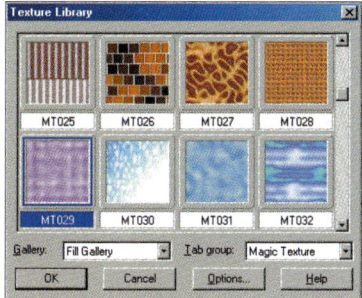

▶ **Natural Texture Fill**—These textures work the same way the Magic
Textures do, except that they're patterns from nature, such as a field
of flowers or a pile of chili peppers. Apply a texture by double-
clicking on its thumbnail image.

▶ **Fadeout**—This color option allows you to create gradient in which
one "color" is transparent. You can determine the angle and the
transparency level (see Figure 4.15).

Figure 4.15
The Fadeout option
allows you to create a
gradient that goes from
color to transparency
to color.

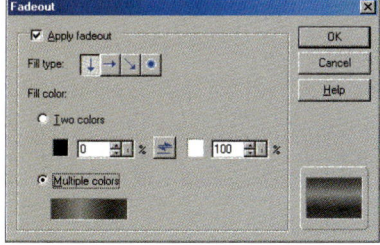

TIP

When you're working in the Fadeout dialog box to create a partially
transparent gradient, remember that the effect uses the color, pattern, or
gradient that's already been applied to the text object. The black swatch in the
Fadeout dialog box represents the current color of the text, whatever that may
be, while the white swatch represents the transparent area.

Text Spacing

The Text Entry Box contains several options that aren't available
anywhere else. Each of these controls determines some aspect of how
part or all of the text is spaced, as follows (see Figure 4.16):

Figure 4.16
The Text Entry Box is
the only place you'll
find these text spacing
controls.

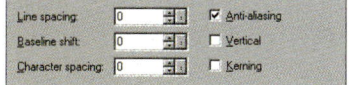

▶ **Line spacing**—This determines the spacing between successive lines of text, as measured from the baseline of one line down to the baseline of the next line. In the design world, this measurement is usually called leading, a reference to the strips of lead inserted between lines of metal type to increase the space between them. Like type size, line spacing is measured in points. This setting applies to all the text in the Text Entry Box. You can't use different line spacing values for each line of text unless you create each line as a separate text object.

— **Baseline shift**—If you want one or more letters to sit above or below the baseline, you can select those letters and enter a Baseline shift value in this field. The value is measured in points, like line spacing, and it can range from 2184 to -2184. To place a letter below the baseline, enter a positive number, and enter a negative number to move the letter above the baseline. This setting applies only to the letters that are selected when you change this value.

— **Character spacing**—To add additional space between letter pairs, either because the text is hard to read or for a special design effect, select the letters you want to space out and enter a number between -2184 and 2184. This setting applies only to the letters that are selected when you change this value.

— **Kerning**—This is an on/off toggle switch—check the box to enable kerning, or uncheck it to turn kerning off. Kerning refers to spacing between specific letter pairs, designed to fit them together more neatly and give the appearance of even spacing—if there actually were the same amount of space between each pair of letters, they would look unevenly spaced because of their different shapes. In general, there's no reason to turn kerning off, since text looks much better when it's properly kerned. This setting applies only to the letters that are selected when you change this value.

NOTE

A confusing aspect of using type is that 72-point type isn't really 72 points tall—and if you use 72-point line spacing, the letters in the lines won't touch each other, because there will be some space between them. This probably seems strange, but there's actually a reason for it. It's left over from the days when text was set with metal type. Each letter was formed in relief on a block of metal. The point size of the letter was determined by the size of the metal block, which was a bit larger all around than the letter itself. As such, a 72-point letter might measure 66 points tall. Line spacing, on the other hand, *is* measured exactly, so if you use 72-point line spacing, the distance between the lines will be exactly 72 points, which equals one inch.

CHAPTER 4

Mode

The Attribute Toolbar's Mode menu contains four basic modes for text: 2D, which gives you flat text and is the default; 3D, which allows you to make text look as though it's fully three-dimensional; Deform, which allows you to reshape text in a variety of ways; and Selection, which allows you to convert text to a selection.

2D

The Text Tool's default for the Mode option is 2D Object, but each time you use the Text Tool, it copies the settings from the last text object you worked with, including the mode. If you want to make 3D text two-dimensional again, choose Mode > 2D Object.

3D

3D text comes in several varieties, each of which is intended to make text look as though it's a three-dimensional object rather than part of a flat image (see Figure 4.17). The 3D options in the Mode menu are as follows:

▶ **3D Round**—This option gives text a raised appearance with smoothly rounded edges.

▶ **3D Chisel**—Chisel provides a sharply beveled raised surface.

▶ **3D Trim**—A very subtle effect, Trim chisels the very top and very bottom of the text object horizontally, making it look just slightly three dimensional.

▶ **3D Pipe**—This option outlines the edges of each letter in the text with round "pipes."

▶ **3D Custom**—The Custom option uses one of five different custom bevel designs that raise and lower different areas of the text object's surface. The options are available through the Bevel tab of the Material dialog box (see "Bevel" in the "Material" section of this chapter for more information).

Figure 4.17
3D type comes in multiple styles.

Once you've made a text object 3D, you can customize its appearance by changing the width of the border or bevel, the depth of the raised surface, the light source, and the surface material. All these settings are located in the Attribute Toolbar.

Each 3D effect consists of a raised surface with a border area around the edges of the letter that makes the transition between the level of the page and the level of the raised surface. You can control the width of this border by changing the setting in the Attribute Toolbar's Border field. The lowest possible setting is 1 pixel, and the highest setting varies according to the size of the type you're working on, because the border can't be wider than the type itself.

A separate setting, Depth, controls how high above the surface of the page the surface of a letter appears to be. PhotoImpact represents this depth primarily by shadowing the sides of the letter, so a greater depth results in darker shadows. The Depth can range from 1 to 30 pixels.

The light used to cast that shadow can also be controlled—you can create more light sources, position them, and change their type. By default, 3D text is created with a single light source. To move it around, click the Light button on the Attribute Toolbar and then click and drag in the image. You won't see the light source, but you can follow its position by observing its changed effect on the text you're creating. If you want to add more light sources, or change their type, click on the drop-down menu button to the immediate right of the Light button and scroll down to the Options choice. This opens the Material dialog box to the Light tab (see "Light" in the "Material" section of this chapter for more information).

Deform

The two Deform options in the Mode menu allow you to reshape text so that it's no longer confined to that boring straight left-to-right (or top-to-bottom) orientation. Deformed text can curve, curl, wave, and in general take on any shape you like—the only restriction is that you can curve only the sides or only the top and bottom, not all at once. Here's how it works:

1. Switch to the Text Tool.

2. Select the text object you want to deform.

3. If you want to curve the top and bottom of the text, choose Mode > Horizontal Deform. To curve the sides, choose Mode > Vertical Deform.

4. Click on any of the four corner handles and drag it to change the shape of the text (see Figure 4.18).

If you chose Horizontal Deform, you'll notice that the sides can slant only as you move the corners around, but the top and bottom can curve. If you chose Vertical Deform, the opposite is true: The sides curve as you move the corner handles, but the top and bottom of the text stay straight.

Figure 4.18
When deforming text, you can shift the positions of the corners and adjust the curvature of the sides (Vertical Deform) or the top and bottom (Horizontal Deform).

5. Once you've positioned the corners where you want them, click on the end of the curve handles—the long levers extending from the corner handles—and drag them to change the shape of the curved top and bottom.

6. When you're done reshaping the text, switch to a mode other than a Deform mode, like 2D Object, and see the results of your changes (see Figure 4.19). You can also switch to another tool, like the Pick Tool, to get out of a Deform mode, but you'll have to go back to the Text Tool to make any further modifications.

Figure 4.19
The "deformed" result.

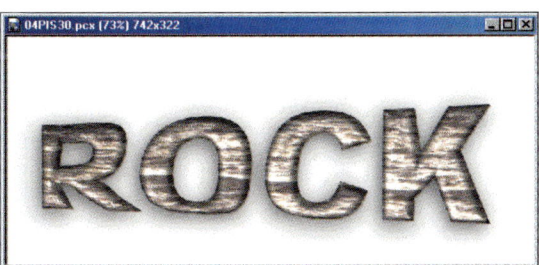

TIP

You'll probably find that the best results with Deform are obtained with text set in all capital letters. This allows the shape of the deformed text block to show better, rather than the ragged effect you get when you have a mix of upper- and lower-case letters.

Selection

The final Mode menu option allows you to convert text into a selection that you can use in the same ways you would use any selection. For example, you might paste an image into the selection using Edit > Paste > Into Selection, or you might place the selection over an image and apply a special effect, such as Format > Invert (see Figure 4.20).

Figure 4.20
Once you've turned the text title for this book cover into a selection, you can fill it or apply special effects within it to define the letters.

For more information on creating and using selections, see Chapter 3.

CAUTION

Once you've converted text into a selection and then dropped the selection, the text is gone for good. If you want to preserve the text for future use either as text or to create another selection, be sure to copy it and then change the copy to a selection.

Material

The Material dialog box, with its nine tabs, contains the most options for changing the appearance of text of any dialog box within PhotoImpact. Some of the controls duplicate those you'll find elsewhere in the program, such as in the Attribute Toolbar, and others aren't available anywhere else. You can also jump to other dialog boxes from the Material dialog box, such as the Shadow dialog. The Material dialog box is the same when you're working with text objects as it is for other objects.

The following sections describe the controls you'll find in each tab of the Material dialog box, some of which are available only if you're working with a 3D object.

Color/Texture

Crammed into one tab of the Material dialog box are all the controls you'll ever need for changing the color of a text object (see Figure 4.21). Click on One color and then on the color swatch to use a single color fill; click on Gradient color and then on the color swatch to fill the text with a gradient between two or more colors. For a texture fill, click on Texture and then on the color swatch; choose between Magic Texture and Natural Texture and then choose a texture from the Texture Library. Finally, you can fill type with an image by clicking File and choosing an image file.

Figure 4.21
The Color/Texture tab of the Material dialog box.

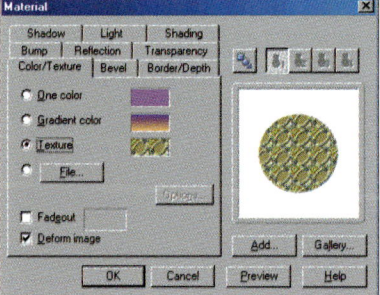

Two other options in the Color/Texture tab allow you to create a transparent gradient by clicking Fadeout and then clicking the swatch to open the Fadeout dialog box or to force the texture, image, or gradient fill you've just chosen to follow the contours of the type as it's deformed. To learn how to deform type, see "Deform" in the "Mode" section.

Bevel

In the Bevel tab, you can change the mode of a text object from 2D to any of the 3D modes and back again (see Figure 4.22). This is also where you can choose options for the 3D Custom mode. Five different buttons show the different edge treatments that you can use for the border of a 3D text object—think of these options as picture frame moldings. You can also choose from two different Bevel joint options, miter and round, which will affect how the "moldings" are joined at the corners of the letters in the text object.

Figure 4.22
The Bevel tab of the Material dialog box.

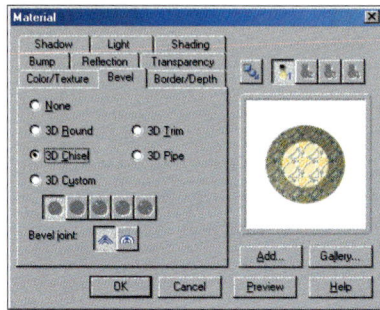

Border/Depth

The Border and Depth fields in this tab duplicate the ones in the Attribute toolbar (see Figure 4.23). Here you can also adjust the Maximum border width up to 99 pixels, and you can set the border to appear inside the shape of the letters (the default), outside them, or both (which can result in some pretty bizarre-looking text). Clicking Smooth spine can smooth out the surfaces of irregularly shaped letters.

Figure 4.23
The Border/Depth tab of the Material dialog box.

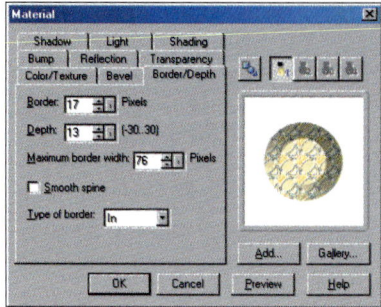

Shadow

Here you can apply a shadow by clicking in the Shadow checkbox. You can also jump to the Shadow dialog box to change the shadow's attributes by clicking Options, and then determine how light is reflected from a transparent object to create the shadow by clicking Render backface (see Figure 4.24). If the text object is transparent, turning on Render backface reflects light from the back surface of it, clarifying and intensifying the appearance of both the text and its shadow.

Figure 4.24
The Shadow tab of the
Material dialog box.

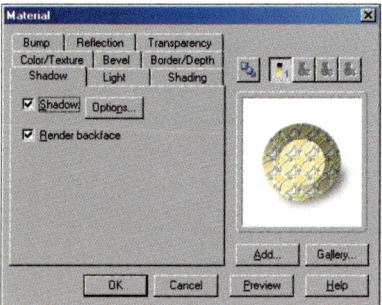

Light

Here you can control the type, number, and position of the imaginary light sources that are used to create 3D effects (see Figure 4.25). The Lights field allows you to choose the number of lights (between one and four), and the individual Light menus allow you to determine whether each light is a Direct light or a Spot light, which is more focused and intense. By dragging the Ambient slider, you can control how much light appears to come from all around the text object—the higher the Ambient light level, the less intense the other lighting effects appear. These options are all grayed out if you're working with a 2D text object.

Figure 4.25
The Light tab of the
Material dialog box.

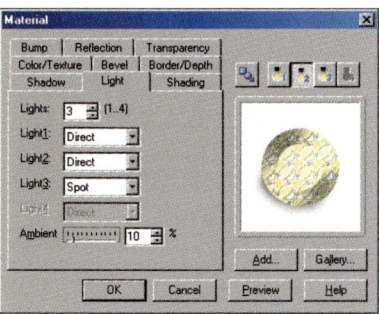

Shading

The name of this tab is a bit misleading, because it might seem that these settings would affect shadows on a text object (see Figure 4.26). They do, but indirectly: Shading refers to how the surface of a 3D object is colored in. The Phong option results in a shiny object, while the Metallic option gives you a matte finish. Within these categories, you can drag the Shininess slider to increase or decrease the shine on the surface, and you can do the same with the Strength slider to determine how bright the highlights are on the surface.

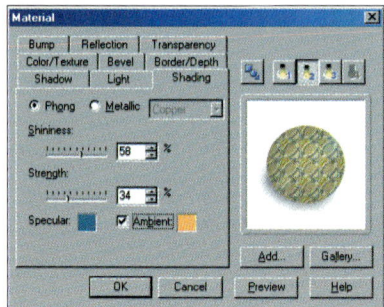

Figure 4.26
The Shading tab of the Material dialog box.

Because 3D effects are created by duplicating the effects of light on a surface, you can get different results by changing the color of the light itself. Click on the Specular color swatch to change the color of the light sources (see "Light," earlier in this chapter, to change the number, position, or type of lights being used), and click on the Ambient swatch to change the color of the light that surrounds the object.

All of these options are grayed out if you're working with a 2D text object.

Bump

The Bump tab allows you to apply a texture to a text object's surface that's based on an image (see Figure 4.27). Click on Bump map, and then click the File button to choose the image file. Once you've selected a file, the other options become available:

▶ **Density**—Drag the Density slider to determine the intensity of the bump effect—at 100, it's at its strongest, and at 0 you won't see it at all.

▶ **Use bump map as reflection**—When checked, this option forces the bump image to follow the contours of the text object's 3D surface. This gives you a more realistic effect.

▶ **Invert bump map**—This option uses an inverted version of the selected image to create the bump map.

Figure 4.27
The Bump tab of the
Material dialog box.

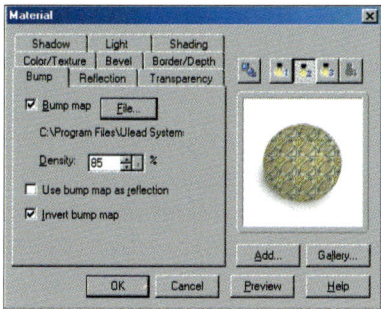

All the options on the Bump tab are grayed out if you're working with a
2D text object.

Reflection

You can add a realistic reflection to a 3D text object by clicking Reflection
map and then clicking File to choose the image that will be reflected (see
Figure 4.28). The Density slider allows you to determine how visible the
reflection is; at 0, it doesn't show up at all, and at 100 percent, it's as dark
as possible.

Figure 4.28
The Reflection tab of
the Material dialog box.

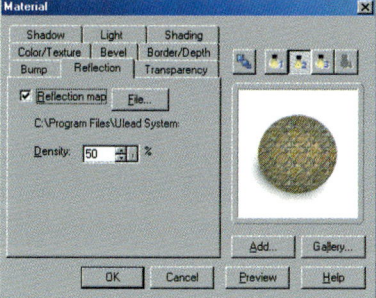

TIP

Unless the text is set at a fairly large size, the reflection won't be particularly
recognizable. For smaller text with more letters, you may want to stick to
images of repeated patterns, such as clouds or foliage.

The Reflection tab's options are all grayed out if you're working with a
2D text object.

Transparency

The final Material tab allows you to make text objects transparent (see Figure 4.29). Click on Transparency to make the object transparent, then choose a percentage. At 100 percent, the object will be completely transparent. Like a clear glass object, though, you'll still be able to see it because of the light reflecting from its surface—and at 0, it will be completely opaque. These options are all grayed out if you're working with a 2D text object.

Figure 4.29
The Transparency tab of the Material dialog box.

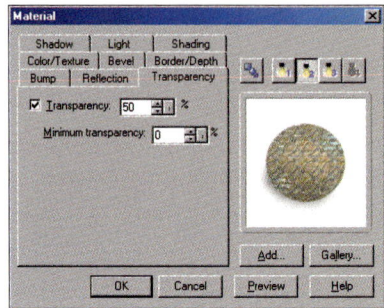

Creating Special Type Effects

PhotoImpact has a selection of built-in special effects designed specifically for use with type. You'll find these in two places: the Creative submenu of the Effect menu, and the EasyPalette's Type Gallery. In addition to giving these presets a good workout, you should feel free to experiment with PhotoImpact's other filters and effects (some of which will convert a type object to an image object).

Creative Type Effects

One of the last options in PhotoImpact's Effect menu is Creative > Type Effect, which brings up a dialog box containing twenty different preset effects you can apply to type, along with controls for customizing those effects (see Figure 4.30). You can also add your own combinations of settings created here to the Type Gallery in the EasyPalette—see "Type Gallery" ahead—by clicking Add and choosing Add Image, then giving the effect a name and choosing which Gallery and which Tab group it should appear in.

Figure 4.30
The Type Effect dialog box allows you to customize your type to the extreme.

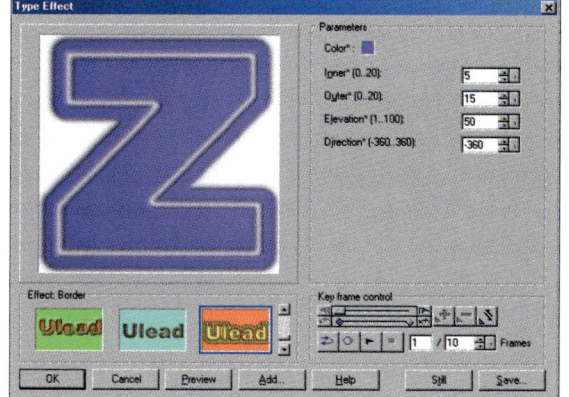

CHAPTER 4

Here's a rundown on the nineteen effects that you'll find in the Type Effects dialog box:

Hole

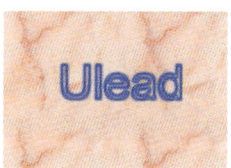

Glass

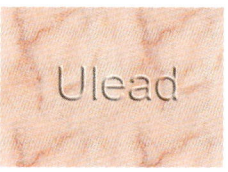

Emboss

▶ **Gradient**—With this effect, you can create an instant two-color gradient in three shapes: linear, rectangular, and circular. You can determine the angle of the gradient and the second color; the first color is the original color of the text.

▶ **Hole**—This effect punches holes through the text in any of more than a hundred shapes. You can choose the size of the holes and determine whether they vary in size or are all the same. You can also choose a color to show through the holes, or click Invert to change the text to the specified color and have the original text color show through.

▶ **Glass**—The Glass effect turns the letters transparent, with colored light shining off the shapes to define the corners. You can specify how reflective the glass is, set the fuzziness of the highlights, and choose a color.

▶ **Metal**—Similar to the Glass effect, the Metal effect turns the text into a metallic framework with a hollow interior; you can choose the reflectiveness of the metal and the fuzziness of its highlights.

▶ **Emboss**—Embossing makes the letters look as though they're part of the background image, stamped into the surface with an embossing die. You can set the thickness of the letters, the amount of height the letters have, and the direction of the light that shows the embossing. There are also three different shapes: Smooth, Plateau (with a flat top), and Steep (extra tall).

Emboss Outline

Sand

Fire

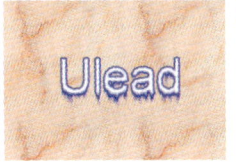

Snow

Seal

▶ **Emboss—Outline**—This effect works just like the Emboss effect, except that it embosses the outline of the letters. The Thickness, Amount, and Direction controls are the same as for Emboss.

▶ **Emboss—Texture**—The Emboss—Texture effect uses a specified file to create the embossing effect in the shape of the selected text object. You can specify the size of the texture image, its transparency, and the amount of embossing applied.

▶ **Concrete**—Parameters for the Concrete effect include a Roughness slider with a range of 1 to 20 and a Direction slider for the lighting. You can also specify the color of the light. You end up with text that has the texture of concrete.

▶ **Sand**—A similar effect, Sand results in text that looks as though it's been drawn on a wet, sandy beach. The parameters are the same as for Concrete, except that you can't choose a color for the light.

▶ **Lighting**—Resulting in a shiny 3D effect, Lighting allows you to choose colors for both the text and the light, as well as specify a bump map image if you desire. You can also set the elevation of the letters' surface and the direction of the light.

▶ **Fire**—For flaming text with just a few mouse-clicks, this is the effect you want. You can choose three colors for the flames—inside, middle, and outside—with the defaults being yellow, orange, and red. You can also set the height of the flames by adjusting the Strength slider between 10 and 100.

▶ **Snow**—This effect isn't nearly as realistic as the Fire effect; it results in a fuzzy white coating on the letters. Actually, you can choose the three colors for the inside, middle, and outside of the letters, so your snow could be pink if you prefer, or any other color. As with the Fire effect, Snow can vary in intensity from 10 to 100.

▶ **Neon**—If you want to make your text glow like neon, here's your chance. The parameters include the neon color as well as the width of the glow and whether it shows inside the letters, outside them, or in both directions. This is strictly a glow—there are no neon tubes.

▶ **Seal**—The Seal effect gives the impression that the text has been stamped into the image with colored ink or wax; you can choose the color of the wax as well as the pressure used to make the impression.

Imprint

Reverse Emboss

Chisel

Double

Gradient-Light

▶ **Imprint**—This effect is what's sometimes called pillow embossing; it gives you smoothly embossed letters with a crease along their outside edges where the image is slightly depressed. The embossed letters are filled with a color of your choice. You can set the softness of the embossing effect, the thickness of the 3D border, the amount of embossing, and the direction of the light source.

▶ **Reverse Emboss**—The idea behind this effect is to make the text look as though it's printed on a U.S. car license plate, and it's a pretty good representation of that kind of type. You can choose a fill color for the type, and the other parameters are softness, inner depth (a higher value depresses the interior of the letters), direction, and amount.

▶ **Chisel**—A hand-carved look, this effect adds texture to the interior of the letters and places a bit of a glow around them, as well as extruding them from the image's surface. Among the parameters are the fill color, the amount of variation in the interior texture, and the height of the letters from the surface.

▶ **Border**—This effect gives the letters a 3D border, losing a lot of detail in the interior of the letters. You'll want to stick with large, blocky type for this effect, which allows you to choose the fill color, the distance of the border's inner and outer edges, the elevation of the border, and the direction of the light source.

▶ **Double**—This effect creates an offset duplicate of the type before applying a smooth, metallic surface to it. You can control the vertical and horizontal coordinates of the offset version, as well as the elevation, direction, and softness for the 3D effect.

▶ **Gradient—Light**—Finally, this variation on the Gradient effect applies a multi-color gradient that's lighter at the bottom and top. You can set the thickness of the 3D effect, as well as the amount of contrast between the gradient colors. The Hue and Saturation sliders allow you to choose a color—increase the saturation for a more intense color.

Other PhotoImpact Effects

The PhotoImpact Effects menu contains dozens of filters that can be used to jazz up type even more. You should know, however, that most of the effects are applicable to image objects rather than to text objects, so the only way these will have an effect on text is by converting it to an image object. After that, you won't be able to edit the type or apply any of the special type effects described in this chapter. You'll want to make sure these effects are the last thing you do to a text object, after you're certain it says the right thing and is set in the right font.

Type Gallery

The Type Gallery in the EasyPalette (choose View > Toolbars & Panels > EasyPalette) lists the same prefab special effects that you'll find in the Type Effects dialog box (see "Creative Type Effects"). There are a couple of differences, however. First, the Type Gallery contains several variations on each theme; for example, there are five different versions of the Concrete effect. The preview icons use a letter "A" to show the effects, and you can apply them to the selected text object by double-clicking on a thumbnail.

CAUTION

Once you've applied an effect from the Type Gallery to a text object, it becomes an image object. That means you won't be able to edit the type or apply any of the Mode settings discussed previously in this chapter. So be sure that the effect is the one you like and that the text says what you want it to say before using the Type Gallery effects.

5

Working with Shapes: The Path Tools

Paths are the outlines of objects. You can create paths in standardized shapes using PhotoImpact's library of shapes, or you can create paths in any shape you like, using special drawing tools. Text can also be converted into paths so that you can reshape it, or you can trace objects to create paths. Once you've created paths, you can resize them, edit them to modify their shapes, combine them into more complex shapes, and convert them into image objects or selections.

In this chapter, you'll learn how to create paths, how to resize and reshape them, and how to apply fills and 3D attributes to them.

Creating New Paths

There are several ways to create paths. The Path Drawing Tool creates filled paths; the Outline Drawing Tool creates unfilled paths with borders; and the Line and Arrow Tool creates lines and curves, with or without arrowheads. You can also convert text into paths, which is a great technique for customizing logos. Paths created in other programs can be imported so that you can edit them in PhotoImpact; or you can trace PhotoImpact objects to create paths that follow their outlines. And you can create selections from paths, which is one of the best ways to select complicated areas of an image. For example, you can draw a path around the central object in an image so that you can delete the background—a technique called *silhouetting*.

All paths are composed of anchor points and straight or curved lines connecting the points. For example, a square has four anchor points, one at each corner, with straight lines connecting them, while a circle also has four points with curved lines connecting them. To draw a path, regardless of its type, the first action you'll take is to click to place the first point.

The Path Tools are located in a fly-out menu in the fourth position on the Tool Panel. The main tool (the one that's showing if you've just started up PhotoImpact) is the Path Drawing Tool (see Figure 5.1).

Figure 5.1
Three of the path tools are used for creating paths, while the fourth is used for editing them.

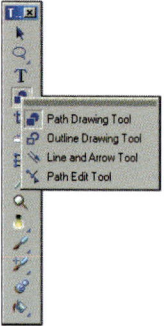

Drawing with the Path Drawing Tool

The basic path tool is the Path Drawing Tool, which allows you to create several different varieties of standardized shapes, choose shapes from PhotoImpact's Shape Library, or draw freeform shapes. All of these options are available in the Shape menu in the Path Drawing Tool's Attribute Toolbar. Any of these categories of paths can be edited once they are drawn; the idea is to choose the shape that's closest to what you want to end up with and then edit it if you need to.

All shapes drawn with the Path Drawing Tool are filled using the currently selected color in the Attribute Toolbar. If the Attribute Toolbar isn't visible, choose View > Toolbars & Panels > Attribute Toolbar.

To draw using the standard shapes:

1. Switch to the Path Drawing Tool.

2. In the Attribute Toolbar, click on Shape and choose one of the first six options:

    ▶ Rectangle

    ▶ Square

    ▶ Ellipse

    ▶ Circle

    ▶ Rounded rectangle

    ▶ Diamond

3. Click the Color swatch in the Attribute Toolbar to choose a fill for the shape.

4.   Click and drag in the image window to draw the shape (see Figure 5.2).

Figure 5.2
PhotoImpact uses the
currently selected color
and Material options to
fill in the newly created
path shape.

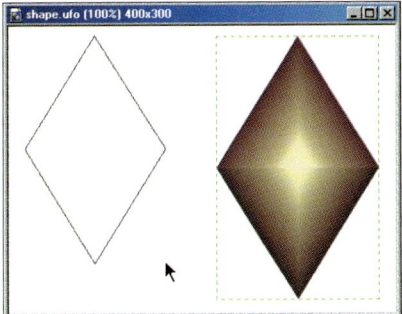

PhotoImpact offers many more choices than the six shapes shown in the
menu, however. You can access a collection of custom shapes by clicking
Custom Shape at the bottom of the Shape menu. This opens the Custom
Shape Library (see Figure 5.3) to display dozens of shapes ranging from a
heart to a leaf to the universal "No" symbol—a circle with a diagonal line
across it. Double-click any of the shape thumbnails to set the Path
Drawing Tool to use that shape. Choose a color, then click and drag in the
image to draw a custom shape of any size.

Figure 5.3
These are just a few
of the Custom Shape
options available.

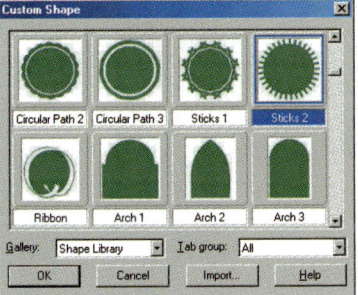

If these shapes aren't what you're looking for, you can draw freeform
shapes in either of two styles: Spline and Bezier/Polygon. Although you
can create the same shapes using either method, the Spline option is
easier to use; PhotoImpact helps you along by creating smooth curves for
you as you place points. Drawing Bezier curves is a bit more complicated,
but they offer you more control over the shapes as you create them. And
the Polygon aspect of the Bezier/Polygon option allows you to build
shapes with straight sides.

CHAPTER 5

To create freeform Spline shapes:

1.   Switch to the Path Drawing Tool.

2.   In the Attribute Toolbar, click on Shape and choose the seventh option, Spline.

3.   Click the Color swatch in the Attribute Toolbar to choose a fill for the shape.

4.   Click in the image window to place the first point.

5.   Click to place the next point. As you move the mouse away from this second point, PhotoImpact changes the straight line between the two points into a smooth curve (see Figure 5.4).

Figure 5.4

The first two points are connected by a path segment, and the next segment "follows" the cursor as you position it for the next anchor point.

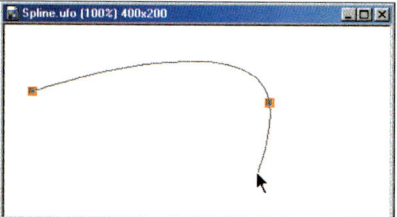

6.   Click to place each successive point. PhotoImpact displays the curve that will be created as you move the mouse around the image window.

7.   Double-click to place the final point. PhotoImpact automatically connects the curve to the first point (see Figure 5.5).

Figure 5.5

The completed path consists of anchor points and smooth path segments between them.

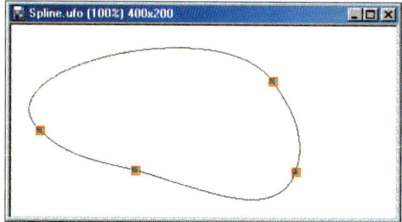

When you use the Spline shape, PhotoImpact creates the curves between pairs of points, so they may not be shaped exactly the way you want them. Concentrate on placing the points where you want them, and when you're done you can go back and reshape the curves (see "Editing Paths," below).

For more control over the shape as you're creating it, you can use the Bezier/Polygon option in the Shape menu. To draw Bezier shapes:

1.   Switch to the Path Drawing Tool.

2.   In the Attribute Toolbar, click on Shape and choose the eighth option, Bezier/Polygon.

3. Click the Color swatch in the Attribute Toolbar to choose a fill for the shape.

4. Click in the image window to place the first point. Without releasing the mouse button, drag away from the point to extend a curve handle in the direction of your next planned point (see Figure 5.6).

Figure 5.6
Bezier curves are shaped by the positions of their curve handles.

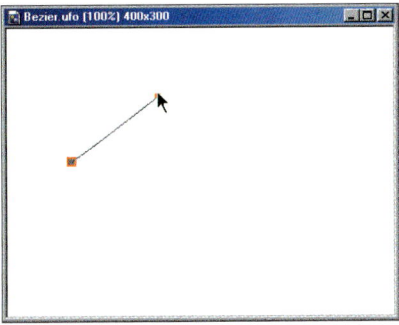

5. Click and drag to place the next point. This extends a curve handle from this point that you can manipulate to reshape the curve before placing the next point.

6. Click and drag to place each successive point. PhotoImpact displays the curve that will be created as you move the mouse around the image window.

7. Move the cursor so that it's over the first point you created—it turns into cross hairs (see Figure 5.7).

Figure 5.7
The cross hairs indicate that the cursor is positioned to close the shape.

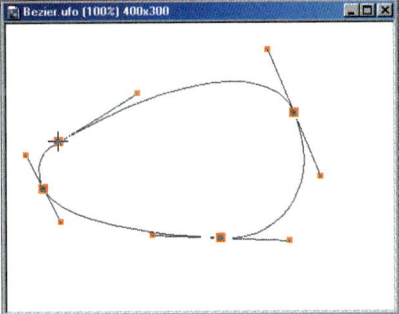

CHAPTER 5

8. Double-click to place the final point. PhotoImpact automatically connects the curve to the first point.

Either the Spline option or the Bezier option is great for creating curved paths, but why would you want to create a shape that has all straight sides? That's where the Polygon aspect of the Bezier/Polygon Shape option comes in. To draw straight paths:

1. Switch to the Path Drawing Tool.

2. In the Attribute Toolbar, click on Shape and choose the eighth option, Bezier/Polygon.

3. Click the Color swatch in the Attribute Toolbar to choose a fill for the shape.

4. Click in the image window to place the first point.

5. Click to place each successive point. PhotoImpact displays the line that will be created as you move the mouse around the image window (see Figure 5.8).

Figure 5.8
Creating straight-sided shapes is just a question of clicking to place the anchor points.

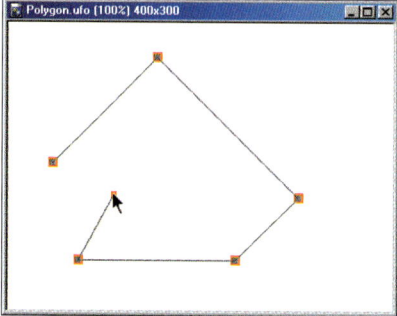

6. Double-click to place the final point; PhotoImpact automatically connects the curve to the first point.

TIP

To restrict the angle of the page segments to 45-degree increments, hold down SHIFT as you click to place anchor points.

You can combine the Polygon and Bezier methods of drawing to create shapes in which some segments are curved and others are straight. Click and drag to draw a curved segment, or just click to draw a straight segment. PhotoImpact also allows you to change the character of segments after a path is created, from a curve to a line and vice versa. For more information on changing the shape of existing paths, see "Editing Paths" further on in this chapter.

NOTE

For PhotoImpact to automatically close a path when you double-click, the path must have at least two points *before* you double-click, so that the double-click creates a third point. A closed path has to have at least three points to exist, or it would just be a line and there would be no need to close it.

Drawing with the Outline Drawing Tool

Like the Path Drawing Tool, the Outline Drawing Tool allows you to draw standard path shapes, shapes from the Outline Library, or freeform shapes. It works the same way as the Path Drawing Tool, with a few added options in the Attribute Toolbar:

▶ **Border**—The width of the outline border can range from 1 to 99, and you can set that value by entering a number in the Border field or by dragging the slider.

▶ **Style**—PhotoImpact offers eight line style options, including solid and seven variations on dotted and dashed lines. Choose any of these options from the Style menu.

▶ **Width**—This menu duplicates the functions of the other controls on the Attribute Toolbar: It offers a choice of nine border widths for the outline (from 1 to 9 pixels), along with a More option that leads to the Color & Line dialog box. Here you can change the outline's color, its width, and its style. This dialog box also includes controls for arrowheads. For more information on creating lines with arrowheads, see "Drawing with the Line and Arrow Tool."

NOTE

When you first create an outline path, the Border values available via the Attribute Toolbar are sometimes restricted to 1 and 2. To get a wider border, choose More from the Width menu and make the setting there; after that, you'll be able to set the outline's width to anything between 1 and 99 using the Border field.

NOTE

PhotoImpact handles dotted and dashed lines neatly by adjusting their spacing so that the line never contains a partial dash or piece of a dot. This means that blank spaces in a dashed or dotted line may coincide with a path's corners; if you see this phenomenon and don't like it, the only solution is to adjust the size of the path a bit so that the corner falls at a dot or dash.

Drawing with the Line and Arrow Tool

The Line and Arrow tool is used—as you might suspect—for drawing straight lines that may or may not have arrowheads at one or both ends. There are two ways of using it, so you can choose whichever you're more comfortable with.

To draw straight lines:

1. Switch to the Line and Arrow Tool.

2. Click the Color swatch in the Attribute Toolbar to choose a fill for the shape.

3. Choose a line style from the Style menu in the Attribute Toolbar. These are the same options available for the Outline Drawing Tool.

4. Choose an arrowhead style from the Arrow menu in the Attribute Toolbar (see Figure 5.9).

Figure 5.9
Some of the arrowhead styles aren't actually arrowheads.

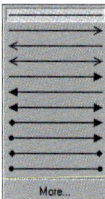

5. Click in the image window to place the first point.

6. Either drag to draw the rest of the line, releasing the mouse button when you're done, or click to place the second point. The line is drawn as soon as you release the mouse button (see Figure 5.10).

Figure 5.10
The line is selected as soon as it's created.

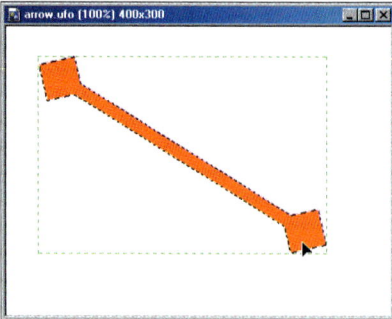

If you want more arrowhead options than you see in the Arrow menu, click More to open the Color & Line dialog box. This is the same one that's accessible via the Width menu when you're working with the Outline Drawing Tool. If you open it when the Line and Arrow Tool is active, the arrow options become available (see Figure 5.11). Here you can set the size and style independently for the arrowheads on either end of the line. The ends are designated as "Begin," the first point you created, and "End," the second point. To change the style of either end, choose an option from the appropriate Style menu. To change the size, choose from the three options in the Size menu for that end; it shows small, medium, and large versions of whichever arrow style is selected.

Figure 5.11
The arrow options are available only when you're using the Line and Arrow tool.

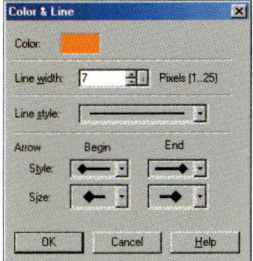

Tracing Objects and Images

If you want to create a path whose shape is based on part of an image, or on an image object, the answer is to trace the image or object. PhotoImpact offers two tracing methods, one that requires you to make a selection first and one that looks at the image and draws a path based on the image's contrasting colors.

The former method is best for image or text objects and for areas within images that don't stand out from their backgrounds strongly. To create a path from a selection:

1. Create the selection using any method (see Chapter 3, "Objects and Selections: Built for Speed"). For objects, just click on them to select them.

2. Choose Edit > Trace > Selection Marquee to display the Trace dialog box.

3. Adjust the settings using the right-hand preview window as a guide—this preview shows the path you're creating (see Figure 5.12).

   — **Tolerance**—The lower this value is, the more accurately the path follows the selection. Lower settings, however, mean more points, so keep the Tolerance setting as high as possible without losing accuracy. The range is from 0 to 1000.

— **Jump point**—A lower value for Jump point results in smoother curves, while a higher value makes the path simpler by using more straight line segments. The range is from 1 to 100.

— **Threshold**—Adjust this slider to fine-tune which pixels are included within the path based on their brightness values. The range is from 0 to 255.

Figure 5.12
The preview shows you the shape of the path you're creating.

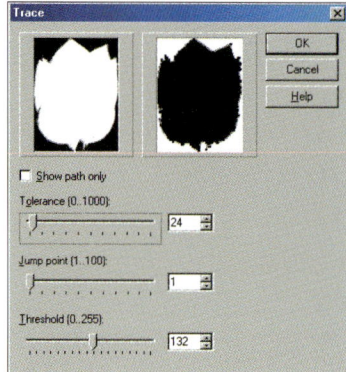

4. Click OK to create the path on top of the object you're tracing. PhotoImpact automatically switches to the Path tool so you can begin working with the path (see Figure 5.13).

Figure 5.13
Once it's created, you can edit the traced path for accuracy.

If you want to trace an image that contrasts sharply with its background, you can skip the selection step and use the second tracing method, as follows:

1. Choose Edit > Trace > Image to open the Trace dialog box.

2. Adjust the settings in the same way you would if you were tracing based on a selection. In this situation, however, the Threshold setting is much more important (see Figure 5.14).

    — **Tolerance**—Lower this value to make the path follow the object's outlines more accurately.

    — **Jump point**—Lower this value for smooth curves; raise it for straight segments.

    — **Threshold**—Lower this value to exclude darker pixels from the selection; raise it to include darker pixels.

Figure 5.14
The Trace controls are the same whether you're working from a selection or from the image brightness.

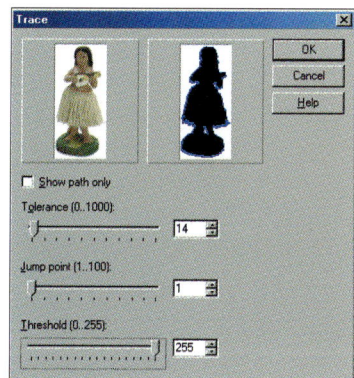

4. Click OK to create the path on top of the object you're tracing. PhotoImpact automatically switches to the Path tool so you can begin working with the path (see Figure 5.15).

Figure 5.15
The Trace command works well on images that stand out sharply from their backgrounds.

Creating Paths from Text

There are a lot of things you can do with text, but there are even more that you can do with text that's been converted to paths. For one thing, you can separate the individual letters and rearrange them, overlapping them and stacking them in any pattern you wish. You can apply different fills and effects to the different letters. And, best of all, you can reshape the letters at will.

To convert text into paths, the first thing to do is create the text. Complete instructions for creating and editing text are in Chapter 4, "Working with Words: The Text Tool," but here's a capsule description of the process to get you started:

1. Switch to the Text Tool.

2. Click anywhere in the image window to bring up the Text Entry Box (see Figure 5.16).

Figure 5.16
You can do almost all your text formatting and appearance customization in the Text Entry Box.

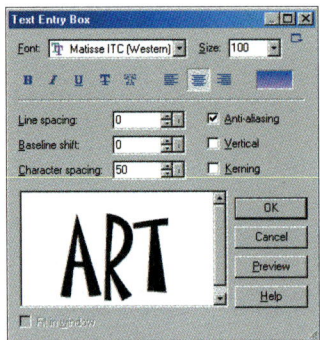

3. Type in the text you want to create.

4. To see a preview of the text in the image window as you type, click the Preview button.

5. When you're done, click OK.

Before you convert the text to paths, make sure it says what you want it to say and that you apply any text formatting and special text effects first. Once the text object has been changed into paths, it can't be turned back into text, so if you want to edit it, you'll have to recreate it.

Once you have the text the way you want it, click to select it with the Text Tool—the cursor will have a small T inside the arrow when it's over the text. Then choose Object > Convert Object Type > From Text to Path. The text object is converted to paths, with all the letters selected. Of course, it doesn't look any different, because the Text tool is still active. To see the paths, switch to the Path Edit Tool and click the Toggle button at the left end of the Attribute Toolbar (see Figure 5.17).

Figure 5.17
Because text is created from outline information stored in Windows font files, the paths PhotoImpact creates from text are very accurate.

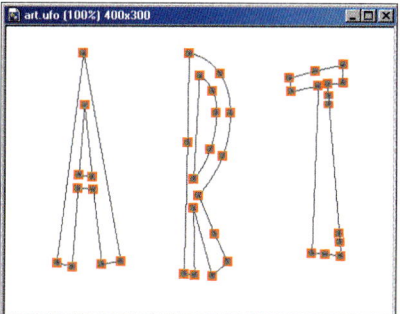

Each letter is now composed of at least one path. You can move them around and edit them at will (see "Editing Paths" later in this chapter), but be aware that some letters are made up of multiple paths. For example, an upper-case "B" has three paths—one for the outside of the letter and one for each of the two counters, or holes, in the letter. If you want to keep these parts together, be careful to select all of them by clicking above the letter and dragging down to select the entire letter.

Importing Paths

If you have artwork created in another program, such as CorelDRAW or Adobe Illustrator, and it's been saved in Adobe Illustrator format (with a filename extension of .AI), then you can import it into PhotoImpact and work with it there. The process is a bit convoluted, but it's not difficult. Here's how:

1. Switch to the Path Drawing Tool.
2. In the Attribute Toolbar, click on Shape and choose Custom Shape.
3. In the Custom Shape dialog box, click Import.
4. Locate the Illustrator-format file in the Input AI File dialog box, then click Open.

CHAPTER 5

5. Back in the Custom Shape dialog box, click on the new shape—it's named with the original filename—and click OK (see Figure 5.18).

Figure 5.18
The Custom Shape dialog shows a preview of the imported path.

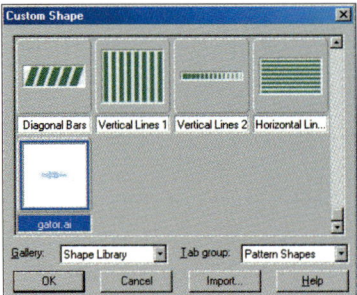

6. Click the Color swatch in the Attribute Toolbar to choose a fill for the shape.

7. Click and drag in the image window to create the shape. Regardless of the original size of the shape, you can draw it at any size you want (see Figure 5.19).

Figure 5.19
Once it's imported, you can use the shape like any other custom shape.

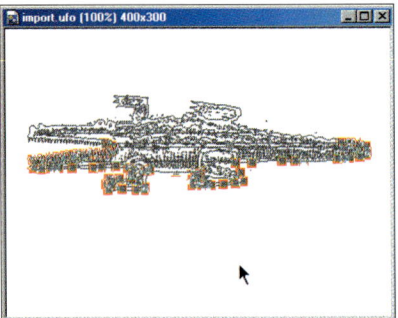

Once you've drawn the shape, it can be treated just like any custom shape—apply colors to it, reshape it, move it around, and even convert it to an object if you like.

Creating Selections from Paths

If you're handy with the path tools and you need to select irregular areas of an image, you'll love the Bezier Curve Selection Tool. This selection tool—it's not technically a path tool—is designed for creating paths that you convert to selections when you're done editing them.

To create a path that you can convert to a selection:

1. Switch to the Bezier Curve Selection Tool—it's the fourth option in the Selection Tools.

2. In the Attribute Toolbar, choose an option from the Shape menu: Rectangle, Square, Ellipse, Circle, or Free Path.

3. For any of the first four Shape options, click and drag in the image window to create the path.

4. For Free Path, draw the shape the same way you would if you were using the Path Drawing Tool with the Bezier/Polygon option: Click and drag to form a curved segment, or just click to form a straight segment.

5. To finish a free path, place the cursor over the first point you created and double-click.

6. If you want to edit the path, click Edit existing path in the Attribute Toolbar, then edit the path the same way you would edit any other path (see "Editing Paths").

7. When you're done editing the path, click the Toggle button at the left-hand end of the Attribute Toolbar to change the path into a selection.

If you decide that you want to edit the path before you use it as a selection, you can click the Toggle button again to return to Path mode. If you happen to lose the path in Selection mode, use the Pick Tool to select it again. You can then switch back to the Bezier Curve Tool for further editing.

TIP

An alternative method of creating paths that are destined to be selections is to use any of the path tools, then select the path and choose Mode > Selection in the Attribute Toolbar. This allows you to use any of PhotoImpact's custom shapes or those you've imported from other programs (see "Importing Paths").

Editing Paths

There are a couple of reasons you might want to edit a path:

▶ You want to use a custom shape for the path, but you want to further customize it yourself.

▶ You created a freeform path, but it's not quite right and it needs tweaking.

The following sections look at each aspect of editing paths: selecting and moving them, working with their anchor points, working with curve handles to reshape path segments, and combining paths.

Selecting and Moving Paths

Before you can edit a path, you need to select it. Although you can select a path with the tool that you used to create it, the best way to select a path for editing is to switch to the Path Edit Tool. This allows you to select multiple paths that have been created using different path tools, and it allows you to edit the paths without having to click the Editing button at the right end of the Attribute Toolbar.

If you want to select more than one path, make sure the Path Edit Tool is active. Select the first path, and then hold down either CTRL or SHIFT on your keyboard as you click on the other paths. The handles become visible as each path is selected. You can then move the paths by clicking on any line segment and dragging the paths around the image window.

Grouping paths allows you to select multiple paths by clicking on any path within the group. You can move grouped paths as a block, and you can transform or warp them as a single unit. The grouping stays in place as long as you stay in Path mode. If you click the Toggle button at the left-hand end of the Attribute Toolbar to view the paths in Object mode, the paths will no longer be grouped when you toggle back to Path mode. To group paths, select them and right-click, then choose Group Paths from the contextual menu. You can't edit grouped paths; if you want to edit the paths, or if you need to ungroup them for any other reason, select the group by clicking on any of the paths it contains, then right-click and choose Ungroup Path from the contextual menu.

Reshaping Paths

The idea behind paths is that you can manipulate them to create any shape you can imagine. This entails moving their anchor points around, as well as adjusting the curved and straight line segments between anchor points. It's helpful to know a little bit about how paths work before you start editing them.

The shape of each line segment that makes up a path is determined by the position of the anchor point and by whether that anchor point has curve handles. A straight segment doesn't require curve handles on the anchor points at either end of it, while a curved segment does require curve handles. The position of the end of each of an anchor point's two curve handles determines the shape of the curve—so you can adjust the curve by moving the curve handles. It may seem odd not to just click on the curve and drag it directly, but the fact is that this method, which is based on a mathematical concept called Bezier curves, actually allows you to shape curves more precisely and efficiently.

To reshape a path:

1. Switch to the Path Edit Tool.
2. Click on the path to select it.
3. If you can't see the path's anchor points, click the Toggle button at the left-hand end of the Attribute Toolbar to switch to Path mode.
4. Click and drag any anchor point to move it (see Figure 5.20).

Figure 5.20
Any anchor point can be moved independently of the others.

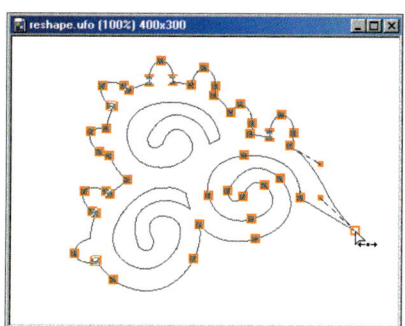

5. To reshape a curved segment, click on the anchor point at one end to reveal the curve handles.
6. Click on the curve handle that extends toward the segment you're editing and drag it to a new position. Concentrate on getting that end of the segment the way you want it and don't worry too much about the other end (see Figure 5.21).

Figure 5.21
Moving a curve handle affects the entire length of the curved segment, not just the end to which the curve handle is attached.

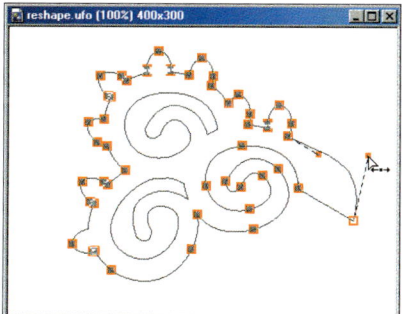

7. Repeat steps 5 and 6 with the anchor point at the other end of the segment, and continue editing each segment around the path.

http://www.muskalipman.com

CHAPTER 5

TIP

The longer a curve handle is, the more a change to its position will affect the entire curved segment. To make changes to one end of a segment without affecting the other end as much, drag the curve handle toward its anchor point to shorten it.

To change a path segment from a curve to a straight line, or vice versa, you can click one of the Convert line buttons on the Attribute toolbar. Click on the path segment first to select it—it turns red to signal that it's the active selection. The change won't affect the adjacent segments, and you can change the segment back if you like by clicking the other button. If you change a curved segment to a straight segment and then back to a curve, it won't have the same shape. Instead, it will be a symmetrical convex curve (one that extends outward from the center of the path).

As you reshape a curve by moving a curve handle, you'll notice that the opposite curve handle moves with it, staying at 180 degrees from the curve handle you're moving. This is intended to make sure that curves stay smooth, with no sharp corners at anchor points. If, however, you *want* sharp corners, you can change the Edit mode in the Attribute Toolbar:

▶ **Non-free edit mode**—If this button is clicked, curve handles stay stuck at 180 degrees from each other. This is the default mode.

▶ **Free edit mode**—If this button is clicked, curve handles can move independently from each other. This keeps changes to one segment from affecting the adjacent segment, and it allows you to create corners at anchor points (see Figure 5.22).

Figure 5.22
Free edit mode allows you to create corner points.

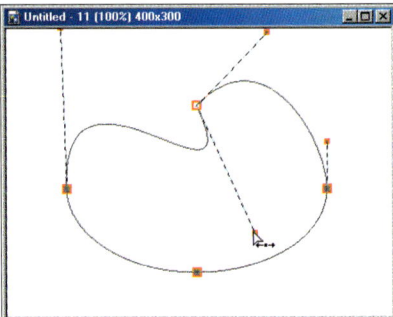

Adding and Deleting Path Points

The fewer anchor points a path has—in other words, the simpler it is—the better. Simpler paths take up less space in your images (resulting in smaller file sizes) and are more likely to print without clogging the printer's memory and causing an error. So the ideal is to have anchor points only where they're needed, eliminating extraneous anchor points.

The Path Edit tool has three modes that allow you to select, add, and delete anchor points. To switch modes, click one of the Edit point buttons on the Attribute toolbar, as follows (see Figure 5.23):

Figure 5.23
You can access the different Edit point modes on the Attribute Toolbar.

- ▶ **Pick point**—This is the default setting for the Path Edit Tool. It allows you to select anchor points, move them, and move their curve handles.

- ▶ **Add point**—If you click this button, the cursor changes to an arrowhead with a plus sign any time you place it over a path. Clicking creates a new anchor point—with curve handles if you click on a curved segment and without curve handles if you click on a straight segment.

- ▶ **Delete point**—Clicking this button allows you to delete anchor points by clicking on them, joining the adjacent segments into one. If both adjacent segments are straight, the new segment will be straight; if one of the adjacent segments is curved, the new segment will be curved.

Creating Complex Shapes from Paths

Sometimes it's quicker and easier to build a complex shape out of several individual shapes rather than try to create it from one complex path. PhotoImpact allows you to combine multiple paths as you draw; the overlapping paths can all have the same fill or the overlapping areas can be transparent. To create a composite path:

1. Draw a path using the Path Drawing Tool or select an existing path that was created with the Path Drawing Tool.

2. Choose Mode > Continue Draw from the Attribute Toolbar.

3. Draw another path (see Figure 5.24).

CHAPTER 5

Figure 5.24
You can create as many paths as necessary to build the object you have in mind.

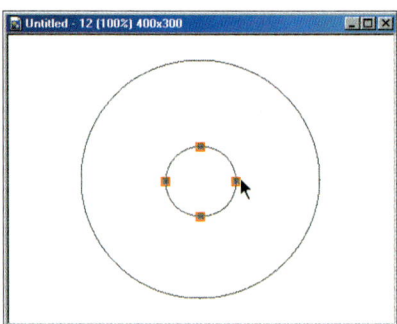

4. When you're done drawing paths, switch to any tool except the Zoom tool to see the results. Alternatively, you can also switch to a different mode, like Mode > 2D Object.

5. To determine whether overlapping areas are transparent or filled, select the composite path with the Path Drawing Tool and choose Options > Even-Odd Fill in the Attribute Toolbar (see Figure 5.25).

Figure 5.25
The Even-Odd fill option makes the hole in this "doughnut."

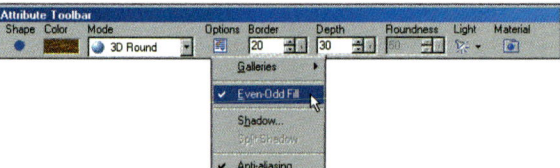

If Even-Odd fill is turned on, making overlapping areas transparent, these areas are treated as hollow when you apply any 3D effect. Gradients, images, and patterns applied to the surface of a composite path extend across the entire surface as though it were a single object.

Customizing Paths

Like text, paths can be either 2D objects or 3D objects, and you can fill them with any color, pattern, or texture, and even apply shadows to them. In fact, paths all by themselves aren't particularly exciting—but if you think of them as key to creating any object you can imagine within PhotoImpact, they get a lot more interesting. Here's a look at some of the ways you can customize the appearance of paths within PhotoImpact, using the Material dialog box.

The Material dialog box has nine different tabs, each allowing you to control a different aspect of a path's appearance. Here's a quick run-down on what's available (for more information, see "Material" in Chapter 4, "Working with Words: The Text Tool"):

▶ **Color/Texture**—In this tab, you can apply a single color fill, a gradient fill, or a texture fill, or you can fill the selected path with an image by clicking File and choosing an image file (see Figure 5.26). The Fadeout option allows you to create a transparent gradient using the selected fill option, while the Deform image checkbox forces an image fill to follow the contours of a 3D path.

Figure 5.26
The Color/Texture tab of the Material dialog box.

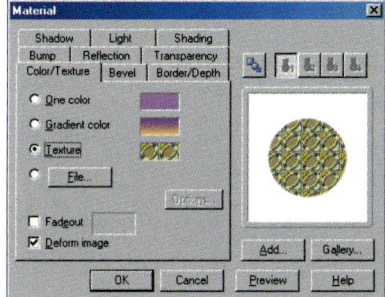

▶ **Bevel**—These controls determine whether a path is 2D or 3D, in Round, Chisel, Trim, or Pipe flavors, along with Custom (see Figure 5.27). The five buttons under the Custom option show the different edge treatments that you can use for the path's border of a 3D text object.

Figure 5.27
The Bevel tab of the Material dialog box.

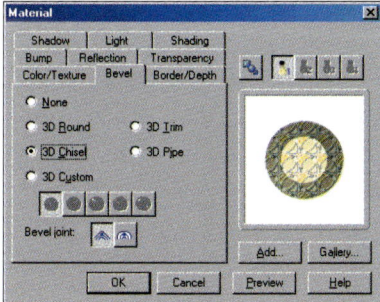

▶ **Border/Depth**—If you've applied a 3D effect to a path, either in the Bevel tab or by choosing one of the 3D options from the Mode menu on the Attribute Toolbar, you can use these Border and Depth fields to control the height of the object and the width of the "sides" (see Figure 5.28). The Type of border menu determines whether the border appears inside the path, outside it, or both.

CHAPTER 5

Figure 5.28
The Border/Depth
tab of the Material
dialog box.

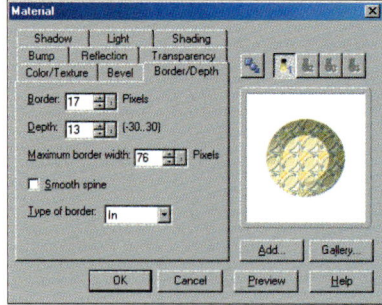

▶ **Shadow**—Click on Shadow to add a shadow to the selected path,
and click Options to set the shadow's attributes (see Figure 5.29).
For more information on shadows, see "Object Effects" in Chapter 3,
"Objects and Selections: Built for Speed."

Figure 5.29
The Shadow tab of the
Material dialog box.

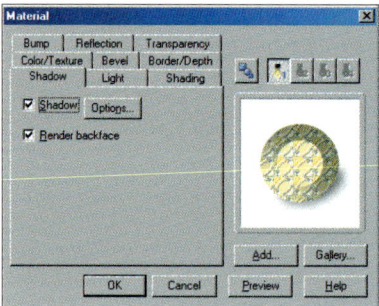

▶ **Light**—3D effects are created using highlights and shadows generated
by imaginary light sources. In this tab, you can set the number and
type of light sources, as well as the amount of ambient light
surrounding the path (see Figure 5.30).

Figure 5.30
The Light tab of the
Material dialog box.

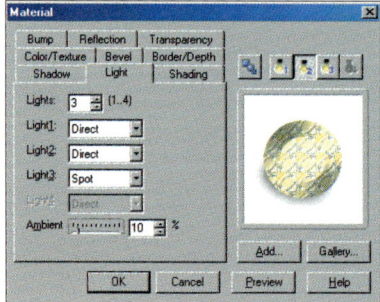

▶ **Shading**—These settings control the reflectivity of the path's surface. You can choose Phong for shiny objects or Metallic for matte objects, as well as setting the Shininess of the surface and the Strength of its highlights (see Figure 5.31). The Specular and Ambient color swatches allow you to control the color of the ambient light and that of the light that's creating the highlights.

Figure 5.31
The Shading tab of the Material dialog box.

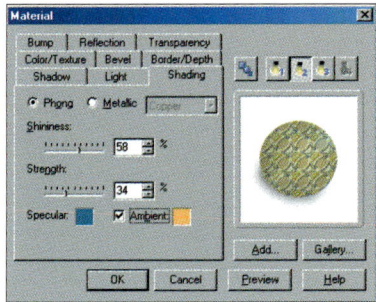

▶ **Bump**—In this tab, you can choose an image to be mapped to the surface of a 3D path as a texture based on its various brightness levels (see Figure 5.32). The Density setting determines the intensity of the bump effect.

Figure 5.32
The Bump tab of the Material dialog box.

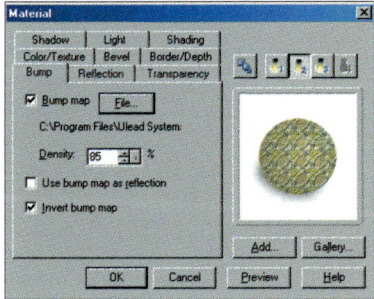

CHAPTER 5

▶ **Reflection**—The surface of a 3D path can show a reflection of any image file, with the Density slider determining the visibility of the reflection (see Figure 5.33).

Figure 5.33
The Reflection tab of the Material dialog box.

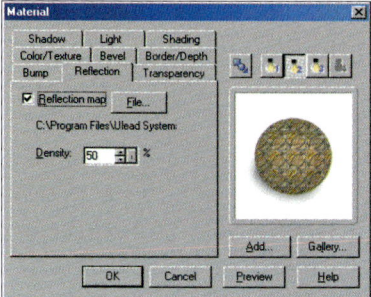

▶ **Transparency**—3D paths can be transparent, with a percentage slider determining *how* transparent the object is (see Figure 5.34).

Figure 5.34
The Transparency tab of the Material dialog box

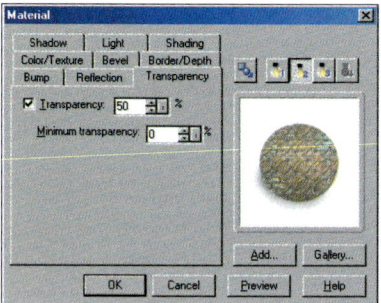

Placing Text and Graphics along a Path

PhotoImpact's Wrap command allows you to place text or path objects along a path that you can then reshape. The EasyPalette's Wrap Gallery contains four different tabs of preset wrap options for you to apply and then customize. Wraps are based on a path along which the text or multiple copies of the object are placed, so you can customize the shape of the wrapped text or paths by editing that wrap path.

To set text along a path:

1. Switch to the Text Tool.

2. Click anywhere in the image window to open the Text Entry Box.

3. Enter your text, choose formatting options and a fill, and click OK.

4. Choose Style > Galleries > Wrap from the Attribute Toolbar to open the EasyPalette Wrap Gallery.

5. If necessary, click on the plus sign to the left of the Wrap Gallery title to show the four different tabs available, then click on Text Wrap if your text has a single line; click on Multi-Text Wrap if your text has more than one line (see Figure 5.35).

Figure 5.35
The Text Wrap options are designed for text set on one line.

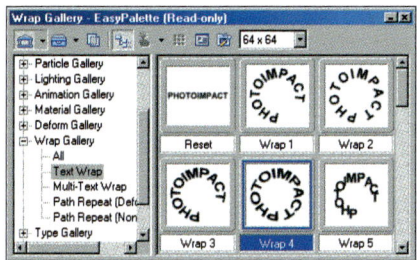

6. Apply a wrap option by double-clicking any of the thumbnails on the right-hand side of the dialog box.

7. To modify the wrap path, switch to the Path Edit Tool and click the Toggle button to switch from Object mode to Path mode (see Figure 5.36). The wrap path is selected, and you can edit it as you would any other path (see "Editing Paths").

Figure 5.36
Wrap paths can be edited to take any shape.

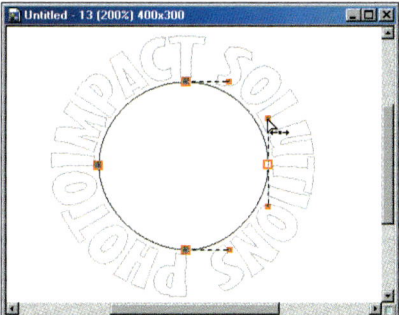

TIP
Text on a path usually looks better the longer your text is; with only a few letters, it's hard to see the shape that the path is supposed to be taking because of the space between the letters.

CHAPTER 5

To place path objects along a path:

1. Create a path using the Path Drawing Tool.

2. Choose Options > Galleries > Wrap from the Attribute Toolbar to open the EasyPalette Wrap Gallery.

3. If necessary, click on the plus sign to the left of the Wrap Gallery title to show the four different tabs available, then click on Path Repeat (Deform) to allow the copies of the object to be reshaped as they follow the wrap path; click on Path Repeat (Non-Deform) if you want the copies of the object to retain their current shape (see Figure 5.37).

Figure 5.37
The Path Repeat (Non-Deform) options make certain that the objects along the path won't be reshaped to follow the curves of the path.

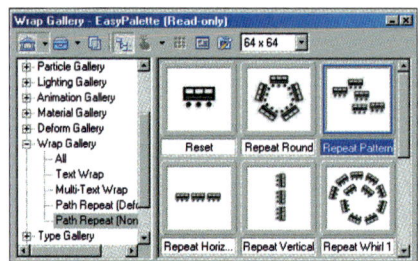

4. Apply a wrap option by double-clicking any of the thumbnails on the right-hand side of the dialog box.

5. To modify the wrap path, switch to the Path Edit Tool and click the Toggle button to switch from Object mode to Path mode (see Figure 5.38). The wrap path is selected, and you can edit it as you would any other path (see "Editing Paths").

Figure 5.38
Once you've used a standard wrap, you can make its shape whatever you want it to be.

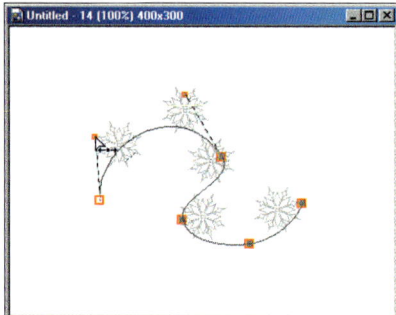

6

EasyPalette:
Your New Best Friend

Creating artwork in PhotoImpact is a complex process: You integrate photos and other images with text, path objects, and effects to create something entirely new. Keeping track of what you're doing so that you can reproduce the process for other images can be difficult. Fortunately, PhotoImpact has one feature that offers a solution to both of those problems: the EasyPalette.

What Is the EasyPalette?

The EasyPalette is one of the keys to using PhotoImpact. With it, you can:

▶ Apply hundreds of varied visual effects to objects or images.

▶ Store and retrieve objects and images from libraries.

▶ Manage and manipulate the various objects in a document.

The EasyPalette's effects are categorized in Galleries, while objects, images, and shapes are stored in Object Libraries. You can create your own Galleries and Libraries, add elements to them, and export them as separate files that you can exchange with other users or save as backup files.

To view the EasyPalette, click the EasyPalette button on the Attribute Toolbar, or use CTRL+F1 on your keyboard. In the EasyPalette, you'll see a list of the available Galleries or Libraries on the left, in an outline tree form. On the right, you see thumbnail examples of the selected Gallery's effects or the selected Library's contents. Or, if you're using the Layer Manager function of the EasyPalette, you see a thumbnail and the name of each object or image.

CHAPTER 6

A built-in toolbar at the top of the palette allows you to control how the EasyPalette looks and works (see Figure 6.1).

Figure 6.1
The EasyPalette contains its own integrated toolbar controls.

The first three buttons in the toolbar allow you to switch back and forth among the EasyPalette's functions: Galleries, Object Libraries, and Layer Manager. The Galleries and Object Libraries buttons have drop-down menu buttons next to them so that you can switch Galleries or Libraries if the outline tree isn't visible. The other buttons across the top of the EasyPalette control the appearance of the palette. For more information on using these options, see "Tweaking EasyPalette Options" later in this chapter.

The Galleries

The special effects in the EasyPalette are created using a variety of tools and processes, most of which you can access elsewhere in the program. EasyPalette saves you time and effort, though, by gathering their results together in one place, so that you can apply them in (almost!) less time than it takes to think about it. The settings used to produce these prefab effects are "generic" settings—they may not work well for the particular image you're working on. If that's the case, you can use the original dialog box, or you can stick with the EasyPalette and modify the settings. See "Modifying an Effect Before Applying" in the "Applying Gallery Effects" section of this chapter.

These effects are categorized into a selection of Galleries based on their nature, and each Gallery has several tabs. Here's a rundown on the Galleries available in the EasyPalette.

Fill Gallery

The effects in the Fill Gallery include gradients and textures. Some of them are also available via the Color menu such as the Magic Texture Fills and the Natural Texture Fills, while others are found in the Background Designer (see Figure 6.2). The Texture Mixtures and Artist Textures have built-in Painting Effects applied to them.

Figure 6.2
The Fill Gallery.

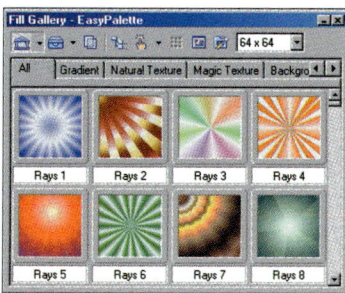

Applying some of the options in the Fill Gallery will turn a path or text object into an image object, so you'll no longer be able to edit it as you would a path or text object. (See Chapter 5, "Working with Shapes: The Path Tools," and Chapter 4, "Working with Words: The Text Tool," respectively.) The fills that have this effect are Gradient, Background Texture, Shells, and Artist Texture.

Gradient

▶ **Gradient**—These complex gradients are created using settings in the Magic Gradient dialog box (choose Effect > Magic > Magic Gradient on the text toolbar). Each one has built-in variations that you can access by right-clicking on the thumbnail and choosing Variations from the contextual menu. The variations are slight changes in scale or the angle of rotation.

Natural Texture

▶ **Natural Texture**—If you choose Natural Texture Fill from the Color menu, you'll see the same textures you see here. They originate in image files that come with PhotoImpact. You can create your own by choosing Texture in the Material dialog box's Color/Texture tab and locating one of your own image files to use as a fill.

▶ **Magic Texture**—These textures are similar to the ones in the Natural Texture tab, but they are more abstract and less realistic. They're the same textures you'll see if you choose Magic Texture Fill in the Color menu.

Background Texture

▶ **Background Texture**—Created using the Background Designer (choose Web > Background Designer), these textures are suited for backgrounds. To make them the background of your image, click in the image away from any text or objects and then choose a Background Texture option from the EasyPalette.

CHAPTER 6

Artist Texture

▶ **Texture Mixtures**—The Texture Mixtures tab contains a selection of "combo" textures, which have been modified using the Painting dialog box (choose Effect > Creative > Painting).

▶ **Artist Texture**—These textures are combinations, too, but they're made by mixing textures with gradients, yielding some very cool results. You can access the settings used to create these presets by choosing Effect > Creative > Artist Texture.

Filter Gallery

These effects are based on the filters you'll find in the Effects menu, along with some of the Format menu's options (see Figure 6.3). Like the Fill Gallery, the Filter Gallery contains effects that can't be applied to path or text objects. If you do apply these effects to those objects, they'll be turned into image objects. This is the case for all the options in the Filter Gallery.

Figure 6.3
The Filter Gallery.

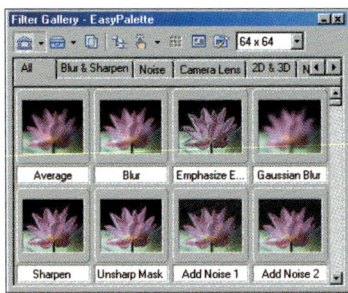

Some of the effects in this Gallery can be combined—for example, you can apply the Tile filter and then the Emboss filter, and you'll get embossed tiles. Other effects cancel out any filter that's been applied previously.

Blur & Sharpen

▶ **Blur & Sharpen**—These effects are the same as the matching commands in Effect > Blur & Sharpen. The thumbnails give you a good idea of the results of applying each effect.

▶ **Noise**—The two options here add the same amount of noise, but Add Noise 1 uses Uniform Distribution and Add Noise 2 uses Varied Distribution—the latter option giving you a more natural effect.

▶ **Camera Lens**—The Camera Lens filters apply similar effects to those produced by specialty lenses used with 35mm cameras: four different color filters, one for motion blurs, and four that apply "funhouse mirror" effects such as making objects in the image look fat.

2D & 3D

Custom

Kaleidoscope

Light

Creative Warp

▶ **2D & 3D**—Similar to what are called "distortion" filters in Photoshop, these eight effects do things like rippling and "pinching" the image.

▶ **Natural Painting**—Created with the four Natural Painting effects filters, the Natural Painting tab effects include multiple versions (with different settings) of Watercolor, Charcoal, Colored Pen, and Oil Paint.

▶ **Special**—The effects located in the Special tab are created using Effects filters in the Special submenu; this is the jumble sale tab of the Filter Gallery, with such unrelated effects as Emboss, Puzzle, Tile, and Wind.

▶ **Custom**—Here you'll find inspiration to experiment with the Custom Filter and Custom Effect commands in the Effect menu. The filters shown are created with those commands and display the wide range of effects you can achieve with them.

▶ **Kaleidoscope**—These filters cut an image into small pieces and reassemble them in one of a variety of patterns, just as a real kaleidoscope does. The effects are achieved using the Kaleidoscope filter in the Magic submenu of the Effect menu.

▶ **Light**—Originated using the Light filter in the Magic submenu of the Effect menu, these effects apply different lighting colors and angles to an image.

▶ **Turnpage**—If you want to flip a corner of your image down to show what's behind it, here you'll find a variety of shapes and degrees of corner flips. This tab contains seventy-two different applications of the Magic filter Turnpage, eighteen each for the four corners of the image.

▶ **Creative Warp**—Similar to the Kaleidoscope filters, but more complex, the Creative Warp effects were created using the Creative Warp filter in the Creative submenu of the Effect menu. Their intricate patterns are reminiscent of those in Oriental rugs.

▶ **Brightness & Contrast**—If you don't like fiddling with the Brightness & Contrast dialog box in the Format menu, you can simply apply one of these effects. They have settings for Brightness, Contrast, Gamma, and Thumbnail variation.

▶ **Hue & Saturation**—Five thumbnails offer five different combinations of the settings in the Format menu's Hue & Saturation dialog box: Hue, Saturation, and Lightness.

CHAPTER 6

▶ **Color Balance**—Again, this tab offers five different variations on the settings in the Color Balance dialog box from the Format menu. This command allows you to change one color within the image without affecting the rest of the image, while the presets in this tab may be useful for removing specific color casts, in which the entire image tends too much toward one color or another.

▶ **Two Color**—New to PhotoImpact 6, the final tab in the Filter gallery allows you to create what's called in the printing industry "duotones" —images made from only two colors.

Style Gallery

The effects presets in the Style Gallery are designed to operate on specific tones within an image that are characteristic of objects commonly photographed (see Figure 6.4). For instance, the Sky effects make changes to sky-blue areas within an image, while the Face effects look for "flesh" tones and work only on those. You can use these effects on images that don't match the tab category, such as using Face filters on an image of a peach-colored vase, but for the most part you'll get the best results by using them as intended.

Figure 6.4
The Style Gallery.

Building

▶ **Fading**—These effects will make an image look as though it's an aging color photograph by fading and yellowing it.

▶ **Face**—The thumbnails in this tab give you a pretty good idea of what its effects are for: compensating for off-color faces in photos. You can darken or lighten the "flesh" tones in an image (they seem designed to work with light-skinned faces), apply a tan or a sunburn, or make someone pale or blonde.

▶ **Building**—Operating on light stone and masonry colors, the Building effects can modify the tones in a building, making it more golden, more red, more vibrant, or whiter.

Flower

Light

Dawn

Season

Filter

▶ **Flower**—Using split thumbnails like those in the Face tab, these effects look for a specified color and swap it with another specified color, such as changing red flowers to white or pink ones to yellow.

▶ **Leaf**—Working specifically on green tones in an image, these effects are designed to change the colors of foliage and groundcover. The names give a good idea of each effect's results. The Withered Leaves effect, for example, browns the leaves on trees and bushes.

▶ **Light**—These effects give the impression of various colors and intensities of light being applied to an image. The default thumbnails give you a good idea of what kind of image each effect is intended to be used with. If the thumbnail is a beach scene, then use that effect on landscapes; on the other hand, if the thumbnail is a statue, then use that effect on object photos.

▶ **Dawn**—You can create the impression of a sunrise or sunset using these three presets: Late Sunrise, Early Sunrise, and Sunset. They don't add a rising or setting sun to the image, but rather change the color of its light.

▶ **Sculpture**—These presets apply a color cast to an image based on various metals; they're intended to be applied to grayscale or low-saturation images of objects against neutral background, such as sculptures.

▶ **Nature**—Designed to be applied to the landscape types indicated by their names, these presets amplify the colors of water, earth, or snowy rocks.

▶ **Season**—You can change the apparent season of a landscape image by applying one of these presets: Spring, Summer, Autumn, or Winter. They change the light color in an image to give the impression of a different time of the year.

▶ **Sky**—Obviously, these presets are designed to be applied to images containing a lot of sky, and their names indicate their effects, such as Sunrise to Daylight.

▶ **Filter**—If you'd like to apply a specific color cast to an image, rather than rely on a preset, choose one of these options. They're named according to the color they use, as well as its percentage, such as Cyan 20 percent.

▶ **Other**—This is the catch-all category of Style effects, with four thumbnails: Colorful, Sunglasses, Early Twilight, and Sulphur. Each changes the lighting in the image in the way implied by the title.

CHAPTER 6

Painting Gallery

Using the Creative Painting command (choose Effect > Creative > Painting to create similar effects from scratch), these effects include dozens of "fine-art" techniques such as stippling (see Figure 6.5). They combine 3D, color, and texture effects to reproduce real-world artists' techniques such as decoupage and finger painting. There's only one tab in the Painting Gallery: The Painting Effects tab.

If you like the looks of one of the effects but want to modify it slightly for use on your own image, see "Modifying an Effect Before Applying" in the "Applying Gallery Effects" section of this chapter.

Figure 6.5
The Painting Gallery.

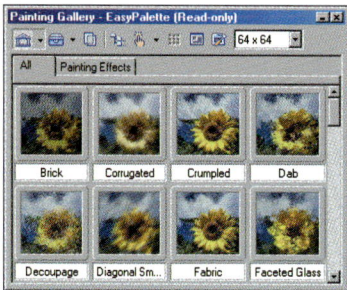

Brush Gallery

The effects in the Brush Gallery are a bit different from those in the first four Galleries (see Figure 6.6). First of all, they work with the Paintbrush tool, not on an existing image. Second, they're intended to be invoked before the tool is used rather than after, as with the other Galleries.

Figure 6.6
The Brush Gallery.

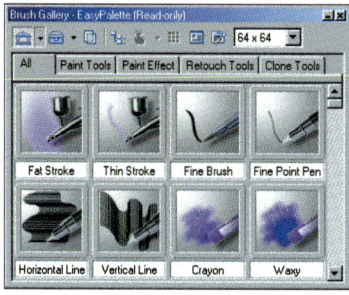

▶ **Paint Tools**—The effects in this tab allow the Paintbrush tool to assume the identity of other artists' tools, such as pencils, ink pens, and chalk. Each preset lends painted strokes a different texture and shape.

▶ **Paint Effect**—These effects, on the other hand, are like nothing in real life; they're special effects that you apply with the Paintbrush, such as "fireflies" that you can paint into an image with a single stroke of the brush.

▶ **Retouch Tools**—Intended for use by both serious retouchers and those who want to do things like give portrait subjects chipmunk cheeks, these presets allow you to adjust images a little or a lot. They include the ability to remove red-eye effects and scratches as well as highlight or darken an image.

▶ **Clone Tools**—You can combine these presets with the Clone tool to create artistic versions of existing images; just choose a preset, click in the image you're copying, open a new, blank image window, and start painting. The original image will be cloned using the style of the preset you choose.

▶ **Object Clone**—This is another fun tool. Use it to sprinkle small objects around an image, either to jazz it up or to create a background.

Particle Gallery

Unlike the Painting Galleries, these effects don't require you to paint them into the image; rather, they insert objects (particles) into the image at a preset position and size (see Figure 6.7). They're remarkably realistic—one of the quickest ways to completely change the character of an image without changing its original contents at all. To create your own Particle effects, choose Effect > Creative > Particle.

Figure 6.7
The Particle Gallery.

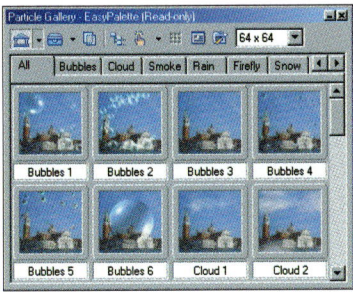

CHAPTER 6

Bubbles

Rain

Stars

▶ **Bubbles**—This tab includes six different presets for inserting transparent bubbles into an image. Naturally, the bubbles all have appropriate reflections of the image.

▶ **Cloud**—The eight presets here insert a variety of clouds into an image, ranging from small white cirrus clouds up to heavy thunderclouds and even fog.

▶ **Smoke**—To add a smoky effect to an image, choose one of these presets. If you want to restrict the smoke to one part of the image, select that area before applying the effect.

▶ **Rain**—You can apply three different varieties of rain to an image, from a quick shower to a steady downpour.

▶ **Firefly**—If fireflies came in assorted magical pastel colors, this effect would be more realistic. As it is, it looks like something you'd see on the opening credits of the *Wonderful World of Disney*—a pretty effect, if not a realistic one.

▶ **Snow**—Another way you can change the weather is to add snow, in three levels from "flurries" to "blizzard."

▶ **Stars**—Again, these are not realistic stars; they could be considered surrealistic. To make sure they don't get applied in front of buildings and other earthbound elements in an image, use the Magic Wand tool to select only the sky before using these presets.

▶ **Fire**—Set the world on fire with these three presets, ranging from campfire to inferno.

Lighting Gallery

The effects in this Gallery allow you to apply just about any kind of light you can think of to an image. Most of the variations you'll see in each tab are in color, position, and intensity (see Figure 6.8). You can layer these effects on top of each other for some *really* intense lighting effects, and they can be applied to objects and text as well as images (just remember that doing so will convert a path or text object to an image object whose shape can't be edited).

Figure 6.8
The Lighting Gallery.

Fireworks

Lens Flare

▶ **Lightning**—This tab contains presets for lightning in different shapes and colors and levels of "forkiness."

▶ **Fireworks**—From a few sparks to the grand finale, you can insert fireworks into any image. Note that they'll usually look best in an image with a dark sky—while they show up fine in a daytime image, they don't look particularly realistic.

▶ **Light Bulb**—Rather than looking like actual light bulbs, these lighting presets look like stylized suns, rising or setting, high in the sky, or hovering just above the horizon. You could combine these with some of the Style presets to create a faux sunrise or sunset.

▶ **Lens Flare**—These presets add lens flares—such as the bright highlights one sees on chrome or glass objects in the sunlight—in various colors and configurations.

▶ **Halo**—Want to add a magical, colored halo around an object—maybe an aura? This tab contains five different variations on that look.

Flashlight

▶ **Spotlight**—These effects make an image look as though it's lit up like the stage of a rock concert, with various colored spotlights at different angles.

▶ **Flashlight**—Similar to the spotlight effects, these presets use a smaller light source and the same color throughout, because most flashlights don't have colored lens covers.

▶ **Meteor**—If you're looking to create the effect of a meteor (or maybe a UFO) crashing to earth within your image, this is the tab you'll want. The six presets offer numbers and colors of meteors.

▶ **Comet**—Here's another set of effects that look best with a black or dark background; these night effects look less like comets across the sky than colored spotlights.

Laser

▶ **Laser**—These effects add colored swirls of intense light to an image, giving the effect of a laser light show.

Animation Gallery

You can use the effects in the Animation Gallery in one of two ways—as animations or as still images (see Figure 6.9). If you want to add an animation to an image or an object, be sure you're done editing it in other ways, because the only way to include an animation in the file is to save the image out in the GIF format. On the other hand, you can use the animation *keyframes* to add a still effect to an image or object that's a variation on the original effect.

CHAPTER 6

Figure 6.9
The Animation Gallery.

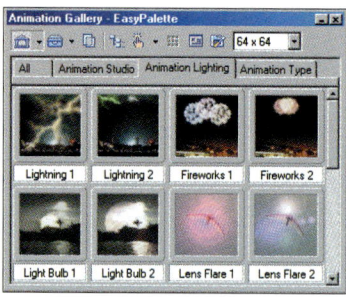

Double-clicking on any of these effects opens a dialog box in which you
can preview the effect and change its settings (see Figure 6.10). Once
you've got it the way you want it, you have two choices:

Figure 6.10
When you apply an
effect from the Lighting
tab in the Animation
Gallery, the Lighting
dialog box appears.

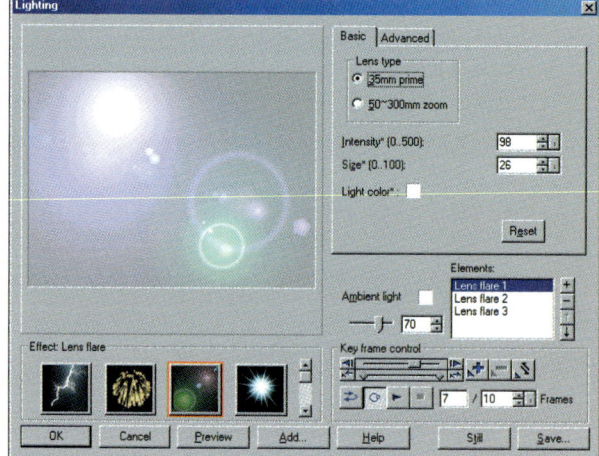

▶ To create an animation, click Save and save the image or object as
    a GIF file. The animation will play when the image is opened in a
    Web browser.

▶ To apply the effect to a still image, click the arrow button at the right
    end of the Key Frame control slider to view each frame in the
    animation. When you see one you like, click OK to apply the effect
    shown in that frame to the image or object.

Here's a rundown on what you'll find in the three Animation Gallery tabs:

▶ **Animation Studio**—These animations are based on filters and effects
    found in the Effects menu, applied to a greater or lesser degree in
    each frame to create the change that gives the impression of motion.
    For example, you can create an image that blurs and then becomes
    sharp again, or one that ripples and then becomes smooth again.

▶ **Animation Lighting**—If you've just come from the Lighting Gallery, these effects will look strikingly familiar. They're based on Lighting presets such as lightning and fireworks, only with an animation added, which can make for some pretty cool Web images and buttons.

▶ **Animation Type**—Intended for use on text or path objects, these presets won't have any effect on image objects—a dialog box warns you that there's no selected object suitable for applying the animation. Each effect shows a standard effect from the Type Gallery, with the animation created by applying the effect in greater or lesser degrees to change the image in each frame.

Material Gallery

Designed for use on objects rather than images, these effects are based on the controls in the Material dialog box. They allow you to change the apparent material from which an object is made, from its color to its texture and beyond (see Figure 6.11). Applying these presets to text doesn't change its status as a text object. The first five tabs relate to specific Material controls, so you can combine these to reproduce effects similar to those in the latter five tabs, which are combinations of the settings in the first five tabs that are designed to look like specific materials.

Figure 6.11
The Material Gallery.

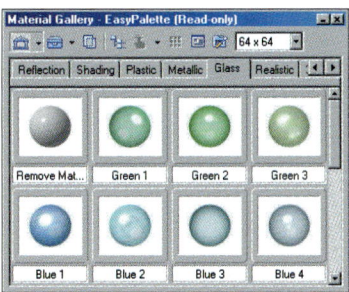

Texture

▶ **Color**—This tab contains more than a hundred different colors and gradients that you can apply to text and objects.

▶ **Texture**—It might be more accurate to call these presets patterns rather than textures, because they aren't 3D textures. They are applied on top of any color or gradient that you've already applied.

▶ **Bump**—These presets are more what one might expect from the Texture dialog box—they change the surface texture of an object by giving it ridges, golf ball dimples, or a fabric weave.

Reflection

Metallic

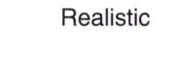

Realistic

3D Collection

▶ **Reflection**—You can increase the realism of an object by adding a reflection of another object or image to its surface. This tab includes a couple of dozen options for reflections.

▶ **Shading**—Most of these presets are named by the metal they mimic, varying the amount of shine and reflectivity they possess.

▶ **Plastic**—Using one of the presets in this tab removes any other Material effects you've applied; these presets offer a variety of shiny plastic surfaces to apply to objects.

▶ **Metallic**—Like the Plastic presets, these options cancel out any other Material effects; these are a selection of metallic surfaces with different color, reflection, and shading settings.

▶ **Glass**—The third in the set of specific material tabs produces objects that are highly reflective and somewhat transparent, just as if they were made of glass.

▶ **Realistic**—These Material settings can make an object look as though it's made of wood, fabric, leather, stone, or paper.

▶ **3D Collection**—In this tab, you'll find a miscellaneous selection of effects, some more realistic than others. There are some glass settings, a Cookie setting that looks more like corrugated cardboard, and more.

Deform Gallery

The Deform presets are designed for use on text, to shape it into funky forms for use in logos and other text treatments (see Figure 6.12). You can apply these to objects, but you'll have to experiment to get just the effect you have in mind.

Figure 6.12
The Deform Gallery.

▶ **Horizontal Text**—These are intended for use with horizontal text. They are the same basic shapes as those you'll find in the Vertical Text tab, but they're created with a horizontal orientation in mind.

▶ **Vertical Text**—These are intended for use with vertical text. To learn how to set vertical text, see "Orientation" in the "Style" section in Chapter 4.

Wrap Gallery

The first two of the Wrap Gallery's four tabs are designed for use with type, while the latter two are designed for use with path objects (see Figure 6.13). Applying a Wrap preset removes any Deform effects you've applied to either text or a path object. However, once you've applied a wrap effect, you can modify its shape by editing the path that controls the positioning of the text or objects. See "Placing Text and Graphics along a Path" in Chapter 5 to learn how to do this.

Figure 6.13
The Wrap Gallery

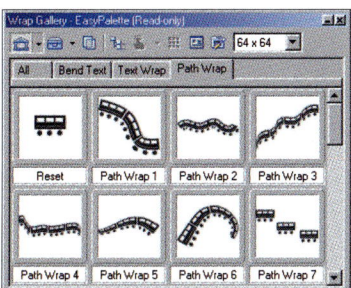

▶ **Text Wrap**—Use these presets to control the shape of single-line text objects; they come in two categories: wraps, which have a circular orientation, and waves, which curve but don't form a circle.

▶ **Multi-Text Wrap**—Try these effects for text that contains more than one line. The shape of each line of text will be modified to accommodate the other lines within the wrap.

▶ **Path Repeat (Deform)**—These options are designed for use with an object. They place copies of the object along a path. The "Deform" label indicates that the repeated objects will be deformed as necessary to conform to the wrap path.

▶ **Path Repeat (Non-Deform)**—If you don't want the shapes along the wrap path to be deformed, use these options. They include simpler path shapes that can accommodate objects that are all shaped and sized the same.

Type Gallery

These effects are designed specifically for use with text (see Figure 6.14). Because they're described in detail under "Creative Type Effects" in Chapter 4, we won't elaborate on them in this section.

Figure 6.14
The Type Gallery.

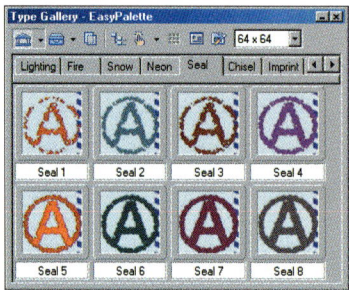

Button Gallery

If you're creating buttons for your Web site, you've come to the right place. These effects are designed specifically to be applied to path objects to create buttons. The first tab contains effects designed for rectangular buttons, while the effects in the second tab work well with buttons of any shape at all (see Figure 6.15). The effects don't affect the shape, color, or pattern of a selected object, just its 3D bevel. Some of the button effects are concave and others are convex. You can make use of both types if you want to create an animated button that pushes in when clicked.

Figure 6.15
The Button Gallery.

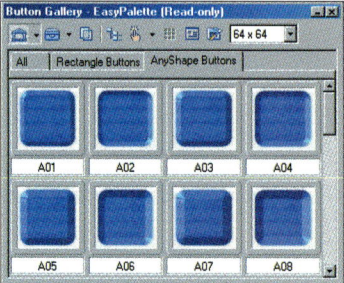

► **Rectangle Buttons**—There are twenty-one of these effects; some with borders of a different color. If you want to see why these effects are recommended for use on rectangular objects, try applying one of those to a circular object.

► **AnyShape Buttons**—With thirty different options, there's room for both concave and convex button shapes.

Frame Gallery

There are two basic types of frame contained in this Gallery: ones that look like physical picture frames, and ones that apply what's often called edge effects (see Figure 6.16). The former group of presets can actually enlarge the image's canvas size so that the frame doesn't cover part of the image. If you want to create your own frames from scratch, choose Format > Frame & Shadow.

Figure 6.16
The Frame Gallery.

Edge

Classic

▶ **2D&3D**—There are sixty different 3D frames in this tab, with a variety of shapes—some rectangular, others circular, or even star-shaped. PhotoImpact enlarges the canvas size of an image to make room for these frames.

▶ **Edge**—The presets shown in this tab produce edge effects, applying a texture to the edge of the image itself so that it looks as though its edges are ripped paper, or a paint stroke, or cut with those special scissors people use for scrapbooks. These settings don't enlarge the image.

▶ **Magic**—These frames look like a cross between the 2D&3D frames and those in the Edge tab. They're not realistic—in fact, they don't look much like real-life frames at all. These effects look like something you'd create with felt-tip markers in wild colors.

▶ **Classic**—The Classic frames are the ones that look most like actual picture frames. There's a variety of styles and colors, but they all look like something you might buy at a department store.

My Gallery

Here's where you can store your very own effects or modified versions of the effects in the other galleries. For more information on storing custom effects, see "Adding Effects to the EasyPalette" ahead in this chapter.

Applying Gallery Effects

Using Gallery Effects is designed to be simple. The process is at its simplest if you want to use the unmodified version shown in the EasyPalette. If you want to make changes to a preset before applying it, you need to invest a bit more effort—but still not very much.

Applying an Effect

Any effect can be applied in two ways: by double-clicking or by dragging and dropping it into the image window. Regardless of where you drop the effect, it will be applied to the selected object or area of the image, so there's really no advantage to using drag-and-drop. Effects that have centers, such as pattern fills, will always be centered on the object to which you apply them, and effects are applied separately to individual objects even if they're grouped.

Modifying an Effect Before Applying

One of the best parts about using the EasyPalette is that it can function as a starting point for your own experimentation with effects. Most of the effects included in the EasyPalette can be edited before you apply them to your image or object, and once you've created a version you like, you can save it back to the EasyPalette with its own name.

To edit an effect before applying it, right-click on its thumbnail and choose Modify Properties and Apply from the contextual menu. Or, if you prefer, click on the Thumbnail menu commands button at the top of the EasyPalette—the one that looks like a tiny dialog box—and choose Modify Properties and Apply from that menu. This opens up one of several dialog boxes. What you see depends on the filter or command used to create the effect in the first place (most of these are mentioned in the Gallery descriptions above in "The Galleries"). For example, if you modify the properties of the Blur thumbnail in the Blur & Sharpen tab of the Filter Gallery, you'll see the Blur dialog box (see Figure 6.17).

Figure 6.17
You can modify the properties of an EasyPalette effect within the original dialog box used to create the effect.

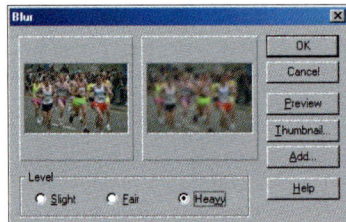

As you make changes in the dialog box, click Preview to see their effects on the image. Along with temporarily applying your settings to the image, this shrinks the dialog box so it doesn't block your view (see Figure 6.18). When you're in this mini dialog box, click OK to apply the effect or Cancel to change your mind. If you want to remove the effect from the preview so you can see the contrast, click Undo and then Redo. To go back to the larger effect dialog box, click Continue.

Figure 6.18
This mini Preview dialog box is small enough to let you see the image you're previewing.

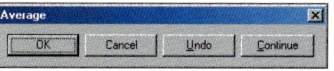

When you reach them through the EasyPalette, all the dialog boxes have a few buttons in common in addition to Preview. Click OK to apply the effect or Cancel to change your mind. To change the size or shape of the thumbnail image displayed in the EasyPalette, click the Thumbnail button's drop-down menu button and choose Use Image as Thumbnails. In the Thumbnail dialog box, choose one of three modes: Click the first radio button to use the entire image, click the second button to drag a box around the image and select part of it, or click the third button to drag a marquee in the image to select part of it. When you're done, click OK.

Finally, there's an Add button that you can click to add modified effects to the EasyPalette; see the next section for more information.

Adding Effects to the EasyPalette

The EasyPalette contains a lot of effects, but by no means does it contain all the effects you can achieve using the tools and commands in PhotoImpact. Fortunately, the means to achieve this is simple: Add your own effects to the EasyPalette. There are two ways of accomplishing this. First, you can modify the settings for effects that are already in the EasyPalette, then add your modified version to the palette. Your second choice is to build an effect from scratch, using the controls in the Material dialog box and elsewhere, and then add it to the palette. In either case, you can choose where the effect is placed—which Gallery and tab—and give it a name that will help you remember what it is.

To modify the settings for an existing effect:

1. Click the effect's thumbnail in the EasyPalette.
2. Right-click to display a contextual menu, or click on the Thumbnail menu commands button at the top of the palette, and choose Modify Properties and Apply from either menu.

3. In the resulting dialog box, make the desired changes. The dialog box will vary depending on which effect you're modifying: It may be the Material dialog, or belong to one of the filters from the Effects menu, or be something else entirely.

4. When you're done making changes, click Add to open the Add to EasyPalette dialog box (see Figure 6.19).

Figure 6.19
You can choose a name and location for any effect you add to the EasyPalette.

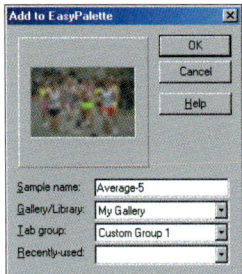

5. Enter a name for the effect and choose a Gallery and a tab group, then click OK.

6. You can also modify the settings for an existing effect without creating a new thumbnail; this procedure is similar to that above, but it makes the changes directly to the original thumbnail. To do this, choose Properties instead of Modify Properties and Apply. Then, when you're done making changes in the resulting dialog box, click OK. In the Update EasyPalette dialog box, change the thumbnail's name if you wish, and then click OK. The thumbnail changes to reflect the modifications you've made.

The second method of adding effects to the EasyPalette allows you to save the properties of objects that you've modified in the EasyPalette. To use this method:

1. Create an object and modify its appearance using the Material dialog box and any effects or filters.

2. When you've made the final change, but before you click OK, click Add to open the Add to EasyPalette dialog box (in an effect or filter dialog box, you may have to click Options before you see the Add button).

3. Enter a name for the effect and choose a Gallery and a tab group, then click OK.

Once you start creating your own EasyPalette thumbnails, you'll realize that you need to get organized by creating your own Galleries and tabs. To create a Gallery, click on the drop-down menu button to the right of the EasyPalette's Gallery button to display the Gallery menu, then choose Create from the Gallery Manager submenu. In the Create Gallery dialog box, give the Gallery a name, choose folder on your computer in which to save it, and click the Add/Remove button to create tabs within the Gallery.

Using the Object Libraries

The Object Libraries differ from the Galleries in a couple of ways. For one thing, you use them to add objects to an image rather than to modify ones that already exist. For another thing, drag-and-drop is worthwhile, because objects dragged out of the Object Libraries and into an image do go where you drop them in the image window. Another technique you can use with the Object Libraries is to double-click an object with no document open; this opens a new, untitled document containing just that object. Several different categories of objects are contained in the Object Libraries, and you can add your own objects to the EasyPalette.

While some of the Galleries are read-only, meaning that you can't add your own effects to them, all of the Object Libraries are available for you to store your own objects. To add an object to the palette, just drag the object into the palette. In the Add to EasyPalette dialog box, give the object a name, choose a Library and a Tab group, and click OK.

The following sections offer a look at what the seven Object Libraries contain.

Image Library

These tabs contain image snippets that you can drop into an image and then resize using the Transform Tool to suit your needs (see Figure 6.20). They're divided into the following fairly self-explanatory categories:

Figure 6.20
The Image Library

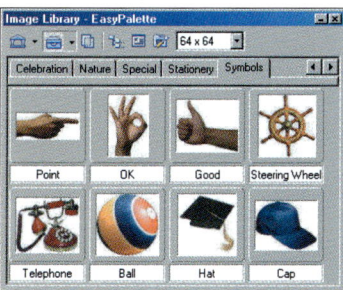

▶ **Buildings**—These are six famous buildings from around the world, including the Eiffel Tower and Big Ben.

▶ **Celebration**—Here you'll find gifts and holiday symbols such as an Easter egg.

▶ **Nature**—Flowers, leaves, fruit, butterflies, and birds make up this category.

▶ **Special**—This tab contains miscellaneous images including sporting equipment, an airplane, and a windmill.

▶ **Stationery**—Media—both traditional and electronic—and office tools are found in this tab.

▶ **Symbols**—These images include three universal hand gestures (but no rude ones), two hats, and a few other assorted images.

Mask Library

The objects in this Library are not intended to be visible in the image; instead, they're used to hide parts of an image (see Figure 6.21). They can be reshaped and resized at will using the Transform Tool, and you can switch in and out of Mask Mode to see their effects and edit them—Switch to Mask Mode (CTRL+K on your keyboard) to see the masking, then switch back to transform the mask. An image can contain only one mask, so if you apply a second one, it deletes the first without applying it to the image. In the Mask preview thumbnails, the white area represents the part of the mask through which the image will show, while the black area represents the mask itself—only the image's background color will show in this area.

Figure 6.21
The Mask Library

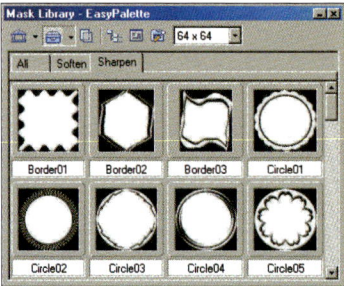

There are two tabs containing a variety of masks:

▶ **Soften**—These masks have soft, blurry edges, great for romantic, old-fashioned images. The effect is what's referred to in traditional photography as a vignette.

▶ **Sharpen**—These masks are hard-edged rather than blurry around the edges.

Shape Library

These are the same shapes found in the Custom Shape dialog box that's used with the Path Drawing Tool (see "Drawing with the Path Drawing Tool" in Chapter 5). Applying them to an image has the same effect as actually drawing one of these custom shapes with the Path Drawing Tool, except that the shape is created in the image at a standard, fairly small size (see Figure 6.22). To make it easy to resize the image; however, as soon as you apply a shape to the image, the newly created shape is selected and the Transform Tool is activated. You now can just drag the shape's corner handles to reshape it.

Figure 6.22
The Shape Library.

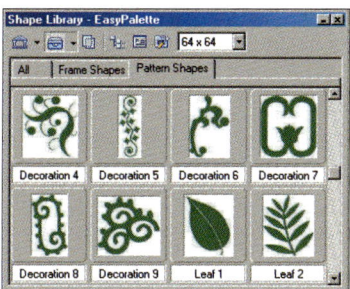

TIP
Hold down the SHIFT key on your keyboard as you drag with the Transform Tool to preserve an object's proportions.

The Shape Library has only two tabs:

▶ **Frame Shapes**—These are larger shapes with lots of room to place other shapes or text in front of them.

▶ **Pattern Shapes**—These are smaller shapes that are perfect for placing along a path as repeating shapes (see "Placing Text and Graphics along a Path" in Chapter 5).

CHAPTER 6

Outline Library

Similar to the Shape Library, the Outline Library contains shapes that have been created with the Outline Drawing Tool (see Figure 6.23). Like the shapes in the Shape Library, these enter your image already selected and ready to be transformed to the size and shape of your choice. There are six tabs full of outline shapes:

Figure 6.23
The Outline Library.

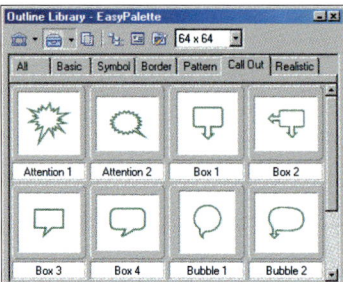

▶ **Basic**—These are basic geometric shapes, including squares, circles, rounded-corner shapes, triangles, and a wide variety of stars.

▶ **Symbol**—These are meaningful shapes such as arrows and a simplified cross, such as is used to signify a hospital.

▶ **Border**—Intended for use as borders with text or objects within them, these shapes are all relatively rectangular with large clear areas within them.

▶ **Pattern**—These are small shapes suitable for repeating along a path (see "Placing Text and Graphics along a Path" in Chapter 5).

▶ **Call Out**—You never realized there could be so many ways to draw comic-strip speech balloons until you see this tab full of them.

▶ **Realistic**—Another name for this tab might be "Objects"; all the shapes here are those of objects you encounter in daily life, such as leaves, a house, and a gear.

Path Library

This Library contains 3D paths, rather than the 2D ones found in the other Object Libraries (see Figure 6.24). Each object is made up of multiple path objects, and you can learn quite a lot about how to create realistic 3D objects in PhotoImpact by just ungrouping one of these objects (choose Object > Ungroup on the menu bar) and separating it into its component shapes. There are two tabs in the Path Library:

Figure 6.24
The Path Library.

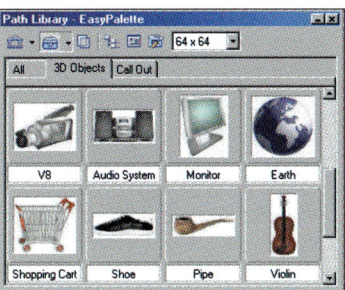

▶ **3D Objects**—These are photorealistic representations of everyday objects, created entirely with PhotoImpact's path objects. Once you've learned how to create such objects by dissecting these, you can add your own to this tab (see "Using the Object Libraries" for directions).

▶ **Call Out**—Like the Call Out tab in the Outline Library, these thumbnails show comic-strip speech balloons; these, however, come in a variety of colors and 3D effects for a much snazzier feel. Once you add these to your image, you can double-click on the text with the Text Tool to change what it says.

Template Library

New to PhotoImpact 6.0 is the Template Library, a collection of templates for the kinds of documents you can create with PhotoImpact (see Figure 6.25). Double-clicking a preview icon for one of the templates always opens a new, untitled document. Each of these templates contains all the elements required for that kind of document, including background images, path objects, and text objects. To use a template, just double-click it to open it in a new document, add your own elements or text where necessary, and save the document with an appropriate name.

Figure 6.25
Card templates in the Template Library.

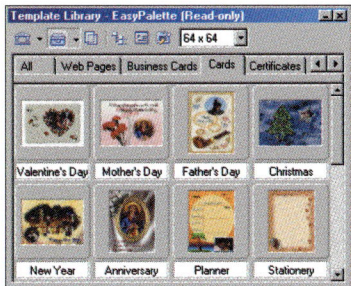

The six tabs in the Template Library are as follows:

▶ **Web Pages**—Ranging from the funky to the professional, these five templates can provide the basis for an entire Web site.

▶ **Business Cards**—These ten designs all include a photo; you can substitute a logo or another graphic if you prefer.

▶ **Cards**—Twenty different card templates include invitations and a variety of generic greeting cards, as well as cards specifically for holidays such as Valentine's Day and Mother's Day.

▶ **Certificates**—Each with a professional, business-like appearance, these five templates can be used to create frameable certificates that you can customize for any person or event.

▶ **Flyers**—Including a couple of "for sale" flyers, a couple of event flyers, and a menu, these templates show off the eye-catching designs you can create in PhotoImpact.

▶ **Labels**—With two CD-ROM labels and a variety of templates in other sizes, these designs can be used for labeling any kind of object or package.

You can add your own templates to the EasyPalette. Because the Template Library is read-only, you can't save them there, but you'll be able to put them in My Library or any new library you create. To add a template, create a new document containing the elements you want to include, then open the EasyPalette. Right-click on the EasyPalette and choose Add Current Document as Thumbnail from the contextual menu. Because you can't save your templates to the Template library, you'll need to let PhotoImpact know how you want to use them: To place a template's objects in the current document, double-click, and to open the template as a new document, right-click on it and choose Copy Object to New Document.

My Library

Although you can add objects to the Shape and Outline Libraries, this one is specifically intended to hold your own custom objects. It's a good holding area for objects you can't quite classify, and until you fill it up, it's easier to find your own objects (such as logos or frequently used graphic elements) here than at the bottom of another tab. If you want to classify your objects in more specific categories, you can also create your own libraries by choosing Object Library Manager > Create from the Object Library's drop-down button menu.

7

Photo Editing Basics: Retouching and Enhancing Your Images

Retouching and enhancing photos is a mixture of art and technology. Graphic design programs have evolved so much in the past few years that you can do almost anything with a digitized photo. Restoring old photos was once an expensive and painstaking process. Similar results can now be achieved with programs like PhotoImpact in a fraction of the time, then printed out via high-resolution printers locally or from Web-based services.

Even in the age of digital cameras and high-resolution scanners, results can still be sub-par. With a few quick tweaks, you'd be surprised at how quickly you can improve any image. PhotoImpact has some superb tools for doing photo retouching; with them, you'll be surprised at how quickly you can accomplish it. In this chapter I'm going to walk you through some of the many options you have for adjusting and fixing problem photos and for tweaking photos for maximum quality. But before we get into that, let's talk about how to get your images into PhotoImpact for editing.

Getting Your Images into PhotoImpact

Before you can start retouching your images, you'll need to get them into PhotoImpact. Beyond the obvious method of File > Open, there are other methods—namely scanners and digital cameras. You can also use screen captures. I won't go into too much detail about scanners and digital cameras here, but PhotoImpact has built-in tools to access your scanner or digital camera images using TWAIN support (**www.twain.org**).

Scanners

You can think of TWAIN as a bridge between your scanner or digital camera and your computer. PhotoImpact has support for TWAIN-compliant scanners. When you click on the scanner icon, it will trigger the scanning software you have loaded on your computer. When the scan is complete, the image will automatically load in PhotoImpact, giving you instant access to it for editing.

Digital Cameras

Similar to the scanner function, this icon triggers the TWAIN bridge to your camera. The way this will function varies greatly from camera to camera, but in most cases it will trigger your digital camera software and show you the images currently on your camera. From there, you can load the images into PhotoImpact.

Screen Captures

Screen captures are useful in a variety of circumstances. As you can see by flipping through this book, screen captures are a critical teaching tool because they show others how to perform actions on the computer. If you're looking at a multimedia presentation and want to grab what you seen on the screen, a screen capture is the way to do it. Many games even support screen captures so players can share images with their friends.

There are a variety of ways to perform screen captures, but they essentially fall into two categories:

▶ **Built-in capture**—By using the Print Screen key within Windows, you can capture a full-screen image to the clipboard. From there you can paste the image into most programs and documents (including PhotoImpact). Some games will dump a screen shot into their respective folders when you press the Print Screen key.

▶ **Screen capture applications**—There are dozens of screen capture utilities on the market, and you may be surprised to know that PhotoImpact 6.0 also includes one. Figure 7.1 shows the setup screen for the screen capture utility—it offers several user options. Because I needed even more options for capturing images of PhotoImpact in action, I chose a third-party program called SnagIt from TechSmith (**www.techsmith.com**). SnagIt is a very versatile program that allows for a variety of screen capture features, including taking stills from video clips. I mapped it to my Print Screen key, and when I press the key it allows me to select which window or part of the screen should be captured.

Figure 7.1
The PhotoImpact
capture setting.

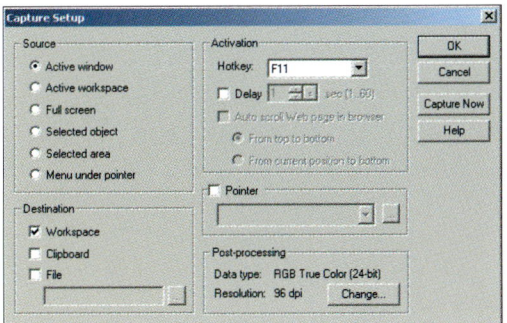

Post-Processing Wizard
for Scanned Images

PhotoImpact has a nice built-in tool for enhancing scanned images—the Post-processing Wizard (found under the Format menu or by pressing F9). It's often difficult for beginners to know where to start because PhotoImpact has so many tools. The Post-processing Wizard rolls seven correction and enhancement tools into a single entity that walks users through the process of fixing up their images. (See Figure 7.2.) Although it says it's for scanned images, this wizard will work on any image, scanned or otherwise.

Figure 7.2
The Post-processing
Wizard for scanned
images.

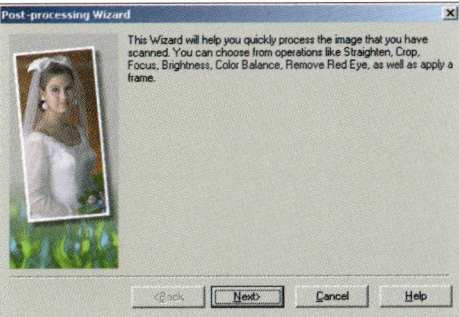

This tool is great for beginners who aren't yet familiar with where to find all the best tools for correcting an image. The wizard walks the user through these tasks:

▶ Straightening the image

▶ Cropping the image

▶ Focusing the image

▶ Adjusting image Brightness

▶ Adjusting image Color Balance

▶ Removing red-eye

▶ Adding a Magic Frame

These correction tools are enough for most basic corrections. Because I'm more of a "hands on" PhotoImpact user, we're going to walk through some of PhotoImpact's most sophisticated tools. These will help you take even the most troublesome photo and turn it into a masterpiece.

Painting

Knowing how to apply a good coat of paint is a skill that is useful in many artistic endeavors. PhotoImpact is no exception. The painting tools in PhotoImpact are very flexible and allow you to create a variety of artistic creations and corrections. The basic concept of digital painting is just like that of the physical world—you pick a brush, you pick a color, and you start painting. Thankfully, the painting options that PhotoImpact gives you are plentiful and less messy!

The Painting Tools

Although I do consider myself a graphic artist, I have no formal art training and drawing by hand isn't one of my strengths. However, if you can draw by hand, PhotoImpact gives you some great tools for it. The painting tools, all found in the toolbar, include Paintbrush, Airbrush, Crayon, Charcoal, Chalk, Pencil, Marker, Oil Paint, Particle, Drop Water, Bristle, and the Color Replacement Pen. When you select the painting tool, the toolbar will load (see Figure 7.3). Each painting tool will have a slightly different toolbar, but most share the same features. From left to right, these are:

Figure 7.3
The Painting toolbar.

▶ **Shape**—This changes the shape of the brush tip that you are painting with (see Figure 7.4): square, circular, and four rectangular shapes at angles. Depending on which you choose, this can have a dramatic effect on the style of your painting. When performing corrections, it's best to use the square brush tip.

Figure 7.4
The Brushes.

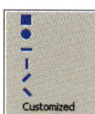

CHAPTER 7

▶ **Size**—This is the size of the paintbrush, measured in pixels. The setting can be from 1 to 100 pixels. The 1-pixel setting is great for making corrections to images (which will be discussed later).

▶ **Color**—Use this tool to pick the color of your paint.

▶ **Trans**—Short for "Transparency," this adjusts the transparency of your brush strokes. The higher the value, the more "ghostly" they'll be. There are some very interesting effects that can be done with semi-transparent paint!

▶ **Soft Edge**—The higher this value is, the more "fuzzy" your paint strokes will appear. When performing corrections, this value should be set to zero.

▶ **Preset**—PhotoImpact includes fourteen painting presets for the regular painting tool alone. Presets like Fat Marker and Ribbon say it all. Each painting tool has its own set of presets, so be sure to explore this menu for each tool.

▶ **Lines**—To assist those of us who are drawing-challenged, Ulead has graciously included the option for lines to be automatically straight or even connected together! This makes drawing custom images much easier.

▶ **Tablet**—This is an option for people with art tablets. A common brand is called Wacom (**www.wacom.com**)—I've owned such an art tablet for a few years now and it's a great tool to have. Art tablets are essentially electronic pieces of paper. A special pen allows you to draw and erase your images, and the mouse cursor moves on the screen in response to the way you move the pen. PhotoImpact supports pressure levels, so the harder you press on the art tablet, the darker the line in your image.

▶ **Texture**—A feature new to version 6.0 is the ability to paint with textures. Your brush takes on the texture selected (see Figure 7.5), and as you paint with whichever color you've selected, the texture you've selected comes out in your painting. Look at the sample image in Figure 7.6. You can also add your own textures.

Figure 7.5
Some of the textures available to you.

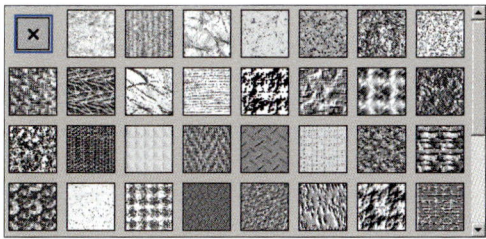

Figure 7.6
Painting with textures.

▶ **Eraser**—This tool does exactly what you'd expect. It functions by removing the effect that was painted on.

▶ **Mode**—This is a very interesting function—when it's toggled, the images that you paint become objects.

▶ **Add**—If you have a brush preset that you find useful and would like to keep, use this to add it to the EasyPalette.

Creative Painting

Whether you're a skilled freehand artist or just someone who doodles, PhotoImpact has some superb creative tools. Although some of this is covered in Chapter 6, "EasyPalette: Your New Best Friend," the most important thing I can tell you is to experiment. There are more than twenty brush settings, and when combined with the nearly infinite colors and textures you have at your disposal, the possibilities are endless. I find that when I'm in a creative mood, the nature of the brushes actually guide my creative process. For instance, Figure 7.7 is just a doodle with the paint tool called "Particle Pen." As I began to play with it, I realized that by drawing two wave shapes that cross over each other, this image closely resembled a multi-colored DNA helix.

Figure 7.8 shows a combination of three elements—the Particle painting tool with the Explode preset chosen, some text using the Astigma font, and a preset from the wrap gallery (Repeat Wave 4). Simple elements combine to form an image with impact. Be creative!

Figure 7.7
Having fun with
the paint tools.

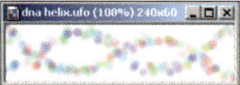

Figure 7.8
The presets in PhotoImpact allow for some wonderful creations.

Corrective Painting

Although less amusing than playing with the particle brush, using the paint tools to correct or alter an image requires an equal amount of creativity. Remember that digital photographs are made up of pixels, so with enough time and patience, even the most minute alterations can be made to look perfect. In the relatively simple example below, I've taken the Adobe Acrobat logo and removed the shadowed edge from it. Figure 7.9 shows the original image, Figure 7.10 shows manipulation with a white brush set at 1 pixel, and Figure 7.11 shows the final result.

Figure 7.9
The PDF file to be edited.

Figure 7.10
Removing the shadow edge.

Figure 7.11
Our final product.

You can also use the Eraser tool to perform similar functions.

Fills

The concept of a fill is simple: Take a selection and place the fill contents into that selection. The reality is that creative use of fills can allow you to do some pretty incredible things! Before going into the fill tools, it's important to understand that the realism of a fill strongly depends on how good the selection is that it's going into. Make sure you've mastered the skill of making a selection from Chapter 3, "Objects and Selections: Built for Speed."

The Fill Tools

Like all the other tools, the Fill function has its own toolbar (see Figure 7.12). The major parts of it are:

Figure 7.12
The fill toolbar.

▶ **Fill Method**—You can choose between two-color or multiple-color fills.

▶ **Fill Colors**—If you want to change the fill color of your single-color image, click once on the color you want to change and you'll be able to select one from the Ulead color picker. If you choose multiple-color, by clicking on the fill color you'll open the Palette Ramp Editor (shown in Figure 7.13). This editor is incredibly flexible in that it offers you more than a hundred preset color ramps, so there's bound to be one nearly perfect for your needs. If not, you can use it to create intricate gradients to meet your exact needs by altering individual color nodes.

Figure 7.13
The Palette Ramp Editor.

▶ **Color Ramp**—This setting determines how the colors change in a gradient fill. The default RGB setting is fine virtually all of the time.

▶ **Transparency**—The higher the transparency value, the more of the original image background will show through. (Compare Figures 7.16 and 7.17 to see how transparency affects the image.)

▶ **Merge**—The Merge setting determines how PhotoImpact merges the fill with the underlying paint colors. In most cases, leave this setting at Always.

▶ **Add**—If you have a particular fill that you'd like to use again, click the Add button to have it added to your EasyPalette gallery.

Figure 7.14 is the sample photo and selection I'm using for the fill examples. The background is a dark color, making it easy to select and fill.

Figure 7.14
The dark background of this image makes it ideal for our experiment.

The fill tool has four different modes:

▶ **Bucket Fill tool**—This tool gives you straight fills, from one color to another. This is useful when you want to replace a background with one of your own devising. The fill color I've chosen for Figure 7.15 makes the match heads stand out very strongly.

▶ **Linear Gradient Fill tool**—This gives you fills that gently transition from one color to another, along a straight line that you define. The fills can be two-color, or multiple-color, allowing a variety of options. Figure 7.16 shows a two-color fill—notice how it's more natural looking than the single-color fill of Figure 7.15. Whenever possible, use a two-color fill, and for a more natural look, choose two colors that are similar. Using the transparency setting can also give it an interesting look. Figure 7.17 has the same color combination, but with a transparency setting of 60 percent.

Figure 7.15
A very strong contrast.

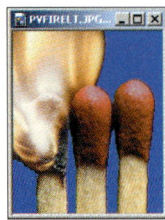

Figure 7.16
A two-color fill.

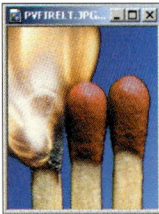

Figure 7.17
A two-color fill with the transparency adjusted to 60 percent.

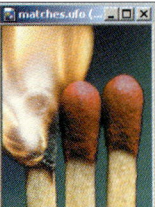

▶ **Rectangular Gradient Fill tool**—This is similar to the Linear Gradient Fill tool; the only difference is that the fills flow in a rectangular pattern. By drawing a rectangle from the center, a gradient is created. Figure 7.18 shows a fill that I created by drawing the fill rectangle near the center.

Figure 7.18
A two-color effect using the rectangular gradient tool.

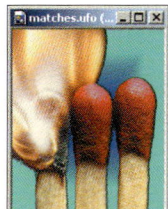

▶ **Elliptical Gradient Fill tool**—This tool is similar to the Linear Gradient Fill tool, only the fills flow in an elliptical pattern. The size and positioning of the ellipse you draw will greatly impact the way your fill looks. Figure 7.19 is the result of a two-color fill drawn with an ellipse in the upper-middle portion of the image, while Figure 7.20 is a multi-color fill with a preset palette ramp chosen.

Figure 7.19
A two-color fill using the Elliptical Gradient Fill tool.

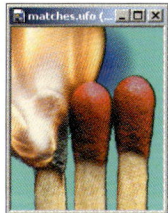

Figure 7.20
A multi-color fill using the Elliptical Gradient Fill tool.

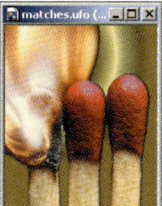

TIP

Observant readers may notice that the file type in Figures 7.17 and 7.18 changed from JPG to UFO. Why? JPG doesn't support the saving of selections, and I took a break while writing this chapter, so I needed to save the selection to use later. When saving your image, always choose UFO unless you're done editing and it's destined for a Web page.

Image & Texture Fills

If the above fill options don't offer you enough variety already, PhotoImpact includes two other incredible fill options: image fills and texture fills. To access these elements of the fill tool, look under the Edit menu and choose Fill, or use the keyboard shortcut: CTRL+F. Figure 7.21 shows the Texture Fill tab of the Fill window. To use a texture fill, simply select one from the list, and click OK.

Figure 7.21
Many textures to choose from.

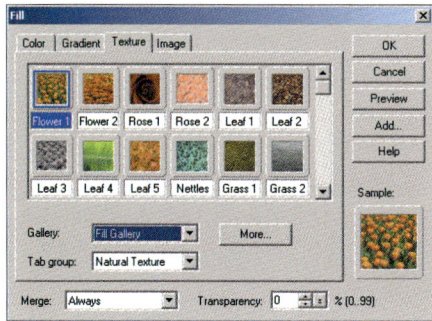

Texture fills, as Figure 7.22 shows, are repeating background patterns that can be used to fill space, usually behind a prominent image. Although this sample image is too small to show the true nature of a texture, if it were larger, the brick pattern would tile seamlessly throughout the background. Options for a texture fill include transparency and merge settings. Figure 7.23 shows the image with an image fill—I selected a sample image of a waterfall for an interesting visual contrast with the flame.

Figure 7.22
Our image with a texture fill.

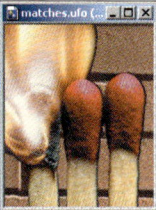

Figure 7.23
An image fill adds an interesting element to our picture.

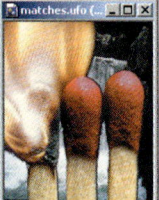

Fixing Problem Photos

No matter how good the photographer, environmental elements will often sabotage what would have otherwise been a beautiful photograph. Bad lighting, bad development in the lab, red-eye on the subject—these are just a few of the things that can go wrong with a photo. In years past, most people would have had to simply accept the fact that a photo was poor. Not any more. PhotoImpact allows you do reclaim all but the most damaged and lifeless of photos. The best way to explain these tools is to show you how they work, so this next section will be a series of step-by-step tutorials. Let's get started!

Out-of-Focus Images

Even with auto-focus cameras, it's a very common photography error to have your subject out of focus; fixing the viewfinder even a little off-center will focus the lens on something other than your subject. PhotoImpact has several tools to correct this, two of which are found under the Effect > Blur & Sharpen menu: Sharpen and Unsharp Mask. The third tool, Focus, is found under the Format menu. Each tool does the same basic thing: It takes a blurry image and brings it into focus. Choosing the right tool depends on your needs. If the image is strictly blurry, choose the Sharpen tool; if the image is both blurry and a little dull from poor lighting, chose the Unsharp Mask tool and adjust the aperture setting to alter the lighting. And if you're looking for a quick, brute-force way to put an image in or out of focus, use the Focus tool.

Figure 7.24 is an image I took with my Kodak DC-265 digital camera, scaled down to 25 percent of its original size. The image is a little blurry because of the scaling, and the coloring is a little dull because the photo was taken on an overcast day. We're going to use the Unsharp Mask to solve both problems at once!

TIP

Remember that most effects can be applied only to a 24-bit color image. You will have to "up-sample" 8-bit and grayscale images to 24-bit before these filters can be used. Chapter 2, "Getting Around in PhotoImpact," has more information on how to change color depth.

Figure 7.24
Our overcast image
needs adjustment.

1. Under the Effect menu, find the Blur & Sharpen group. Inside that you'll find the Unsharp Mask tool. Select it.

2. A series of thumbnails will open. If you're in a rush, you can select the one that looks like the final result you want. But because we're taking our time here, click on Options. This will load the detail settings as Figure 7.25 shows. From this screen we have total control over the Unsharp Mask. The Sharpen factor controls the overall level of sharpening your image will receive. The original image is on the left; the adjusted image is on the right. This makes it easy to see what effect the setting will have on your image. Just like on a 35mm camera, Aperture radius controls the amount of light that is adjusted in an image. A lower value will leave the brightness of your image untouched, and a higher value will brighten up your image.

Figure 7.25
The Sharpen factor and
the Aperture radius
affect the appearance
of the image.

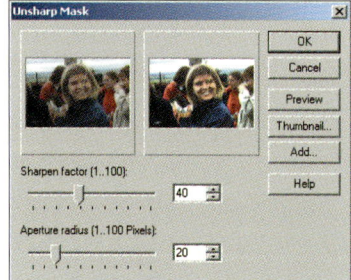

3. This image didn't need very much adjusting. A Sharpen factor of 40 and an Aperture radius of 20 gives me the results shown in Figure 7.26: a brighter, sharper image! I've purposely made the adjustment a little more dramatic than I normally would have to ensure that you can see the differences. It's a good idea to try several settings to find the best one for your image.

Figure 7.26
Our photo after
adjusting—much better!

Removing Red-eye

One common problem that persists, even in the era of digital photography, is the "red-eye" effect. Red-eye occurs when bright light is reflected back to the camera from the blood-rich retina of the eye. Solving red-eye involves having enough direct lighting and choosing the best camera angle. For the sake of this exercise, however, let's assume that you've got a great photo that you want to make even better by removing red-eye. Figure 7.27 shows an image of a baby with the red-eye effect— I've zoomed in a little so you can see it more easily. This problem detracts from an otherwise great picture. Let's fix it!

Figure 7.27
Red-eye detracts from the beauty of this image.

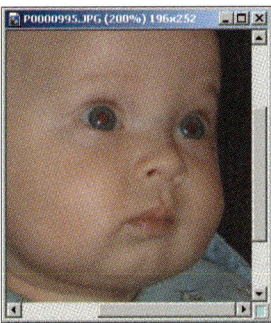

1. Under the Effect menu, choose Camera Lens and then choose Remove Red Eye.

2. The Remove Red Eye settings window will open (Figure 7.28). This is where you control how the red-eye will be removed. First, select the area for filtering (I usually do it one eye at a time for better control). Zoom in on the eye, then adjust the percentage of eye size so that the selection fits the eye closely.

Figure 7.28
The Remove Red Eye settings window.

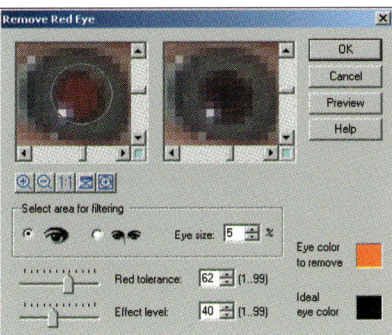

3. Next, adjust the Red tolerance and Effect level. You can see what effect the changes will have by looking in the preview window to the right. Click OK, and you're done!

4. However, if you'd like to get really deep into the tool, click on Eye color to remove, found in the lower right corner of the settings window, and proceed to Step 4.

5. Clicking on the Eye color to remove box will launch the Eyedropper window. Zoom in on the eye and sample the color from the center, then click OK. This will take you back to the Remove Red Eye settings window (Figure 7.29), where you can use the more accurate color to make the correction more effective.

Figure 7.29
Picking the exact shade of red to remove.

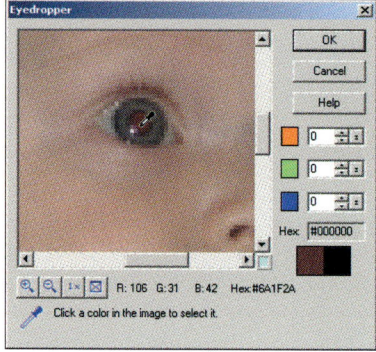

6. We're done! Figure 7.30 shows the correction—now we can see those "baby baby blues" without the distracting red-eye effect.

Figure 7.30
A perfect photo!

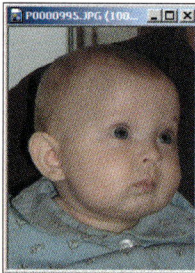

Brightness and Contrast

Poor brightness and poor contrast ruin more photos than any other problem. Lighting is the one of the most critical elements in photography, and when there isn't enough light the image will suffer. Digital cameras are among the worst offenders because they are less able to cope with low-light situations than regular 35mm cameras. Thankfully, PhotoImpact includes some excellent tools for adjusting the brightness and contrast of images. Figure 7.31 is a typical example of this problem: Although the subject is outdoors, there was insufficient lighting. Let's fix it!

Figure 7.31
PhotoImpact can improve the brightness and contrast of the subject in this image.

1. Under the Format menu, select Brightness & Contrast.

2. The Brightness & Contrast settings window will load, as Figure 7.32 shows, and give you a series of previews and presets to choose from. You can click on one to see what effect it will have on your image. I find it useful to position the window next to my image so I can see the changes right away. It's automatic, so you don't need to hit the Preview button for this to happen. For my image, I clicked twice on the preset immediately above the center (original) thumbnail, giving me a brightness of 24, and then manually entered a value of 6 for the contrast.

Figure 7.32
The Brightness & Contrast settings window.

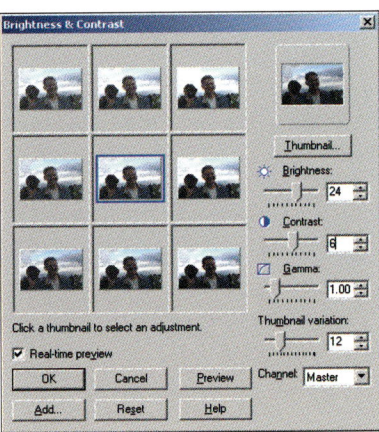

3. Once you have your image adjusted to your liking, click OK and you're done! Figure 7.33 shows my much-improved image. Remember you can press CTRL+Z at any time to undo the effect and try it again. Sometimes it takes a few tries before you arrive at the magical setting. Keep in mind that the more drastic your adjustments, the less realistic the image will look in the end. There's no substitution for a great photo from the start.

Figure 7.33
My image after adjustment is much better!

TIP

Want a fast way to adjust brightness and contrast? Press CTRL+B to open up the settings window, and click once or twice in the preview square directly above the center preview square. I've found that the vast majority of all images can be quickly fixed by these adjustments.

NOTE

You'll quickly find that your equipment, whether a digital camera or a scanner, will have certain predispositions that you'll recognize. My scanner, at its default settings, scans in everything a little too dark. I've learned to recognize this and immediately know the brightness and contrast adjustment I need to fix the image. Get to know your equipment!

Fixing Damaged Photos

Sometimes more than just a brightness adjustment is needed to save a photo. Older photos are especially susceptible to the ravages of time: scratches, tears, and creases. I recently found such a photo, so we're going to take a look at four of the many tools that can be used for repair: Cropping, Remove Scratch, Cloning, and Retouch Sharpen.

Figure 7.34 shows a scan of a photo in need of restoration. The photo has a large scratch in the upper right corner, a piece missing from the lower right, and has a blurry misfocus. Let's get to work!

Figure 7.34
Our damaged photo in need of electronic repair.

Cropping

The first step to fixing Figure 7.34 is to crop it: Why deal with more damaged photo than you have to? By cropping, we're eliminating part of the scratch and the missing piece, so we have less repair work to do. And, like all images, it can use some adjusting of both brightness and contrast. Figure 7.35 looks better already!

Figure 7.35
Our image after cropping.

Remove Scratch

The Remove Scratch tool works quite well. It functions as a sort of smudge tool that samples the coloring of the image and fills in the scratch with the dominant color. To remove a scratch from a photo, follow these steps:

1. Find the Remove Scratch tool under the Retouch Tools area. (Look for the Dodge effect on the tool panel, then click and hold on it to expand the menu.)

2. The Remove Scratch tool will load, giving you the toolbar (see Figure 7.36) with various settings. By now you should be familiar with what these mean. Adjust the shape to fit the size of the scratch, or use a preset. I've chosen the Remove Scratch2 preset.

Figure 7.36
The Remove Scratch tool bar.

3. Remove the scratch by painting over it with the tool. Figure 7.37 shows the tool in action (look in the top right).

Figure 7.37
The image with the scratch being removed.

4. Now here's a little surprise: The scratch tool is also good at removing certain types of elements from a photo. If you look closely to the right of the table, you can see orange text, which is the date stamp from the camera. Using the Scratch tool, on the same setting as before, will eliminate this and give us a better image. Take a look at Figure 7.38 to see what I mean!

Figure 7.38
Our image once the scratch and date have been removed.

Cloning

Cloning is an advanced topic that could take a whole chapter to explore. In essence, digital cloning is defined as taking part of the image and using it to paint over another part. In cloning, you have a source and a target. We're going to use the Cloning tool to eliminate the tear in the bottom right corner of the image by cloning the carpet over the hole.

1. Select the Cloning Paintbrush tool. The Cloning tool panel offers a few different options (see Figure 7.39), but they're identical to those for painting covered earlier in this chapter. The exception is the presets; there are some great presets for "ghost" effects. For our purposes, however, we'll leave everything at default. If your project requires more finesse, adjust the size to be smaller and zoom in to at least 500 percent.

Figure 7.39
The Cloning tool panel.

2. Zoom in on the image and then, holding down the Shift key, click on the area you want to clone. In my case, I want to lift the pixels from the carpet right next to the tear to get the most accurate sample. (See Figure 7.40.) Once the source is selected, you paint over the area you want to clone. This may take some practice, because the clone source doesn't stay still. If you paint downward, your clone source will also move downward. Experiment and you'll see what I mean!

Figure 7.40
Cloning in action.

3. You can reclone areas over and over until you get something that looks realistic. Cloning takes practice (see Figure 7.41).

Figure 7.41
Our image, post-cloning.

Cloning is something that takes skill and practice to do right. I've created a tutorial on the tool that you may want to check out. It can be found at **www.webutilities.com**, just look for "Advanced Photo Retouching."

Retouch Sharpen

The Retouch Sharpen tool is found alongside these other tools, and it differs from the Sharpen filter I talked about earlier in this chapter because the Sharpen effect is painted on. This provides great control over the effect, and lets you adjust parts of the image.

The tool is very simple to use and doesn't require any special steps. Select the Sharpen tool from the Retouch Tool panel. The tool panel (Figure 7.42) has the familiar settings. For this example, I chose a size of 100 so I could make large, sweeping passes at the image.

Figure 7.42
The Retouch Sharpen tool panel.

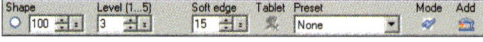

Figure 7.43 shows the final image after all of the adjustments. I chose to paint the Sharpen effect only on the flowers; the background remains a little blurry. The net effect is that your eye is drawn towards the flowers right away, which I'm sure is what the photographer intended!

Figure 7.43
The final image.

Compare Figure 7.43 with Figure 7.34 and you'll see what a difference a few relatively minor adjustments can make.

Hue & Saturation Adjustments

Yet another image problem plaguing photos is hue issues: skin tones that are too red, too yellow, washed out, and so on. In Figure 7.44, the skin tone on the subjects is too red for my liking. A simple three-step procedure using the Hue & Saturation tool will fix this!

Figure 7.44
The flesh tones in this photograph need adjustment.

1. Under the Format menu, choose Hue & Saturation. This will load the settings window (Figure 7.45).

Figure 7.45
The Hue & Saturation settings window.

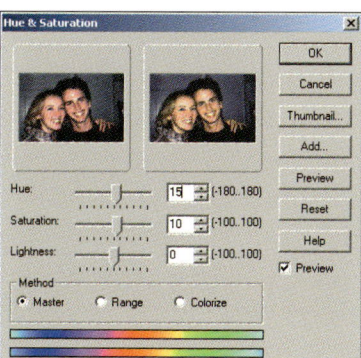

2. Make sure the Preview option in the bottom right is clicked off so you can see the effect of your changes on your large image. This is one of those tools that's great fun to experiment with! We'll use it more creatively in Chapter 8, "Photo Editing: Advanced Special Effects," but for now, a minor adjustment will have a great effect on our image. A Hue setting of 15 magically turns the red skin tones into a more "normal" flesh tone. I bumped the Saturation value up to 10 to make the tones stand out a little more.

3. Click OK, and we're done! Figure 7.46 shows the final image, and comparing the images shows us the final result is a much-improved photo (and, for those that are wondering, there were blue lights in the room, so the bluish tint in the background is normal).

Figure 7.46
Our final image—hue-shifted to perfection!

The Finishing Touch

Almost any image can be restored given enough time and care. I've covered only some of the retouch tools; there are many others that you should explore if you're serious about restoring your photos. Good luck, and remember, that like anything else in life, practice makes perfect!

8

Photo Editing: Advanced Special Effects

Taking a photograph and making a beautiful creation from it is one of my favorite things to do with PhotoImpact. I have no skill at drawing, painting, sketching, or any other form of traditional artwork. PhotoImpact is my canvas. There are many interesting ways to create incredible, exciting, and very strange-looking creations from your photos. Better yet, because PhotoImpact is compatible with most Photoshop plug-ins, you have even more options open to you!

The Art of Digital Special Effects

The key to great digital artwork is to make it look realistic. If you're creating a composite image of your dog walking on the moon, make it look like he's *really there!* Pay attention to every detail, especially the lighting and coloring. It's the small details that make the difference between a digital masterpiece and something that looks faked. Your creations should inspire people to say: *"Is that… real?"*

This chapter happens to be the most enjoyable for me to write. We'll explore these digital tools, discuss samples, and walk through the process together. Roll up your sleeves and get ready to have some fun!

NOTE

In this chapter I won't be showing you many settings screens. Applying effects like these is a highly subjective process and depends greatly on your source image. When you apply an effect, most will give you settings screens similar to the ones you've seen in previous chapters—either a series of thumbnails where you choose the effect you want or a series of slider bars where you can see an instant preview of your image. The best thing you can do is to experiment and have some fun. I'd rather show you where to find the effect, talk about how to use it, and leave the settings up to you!

Built-in Filters for Special Effects

Filters are complicated presets that are applied to your entire image. Some filters require a selection and some do not. Remember, however, that if you want to apply a filter to only part of your image, use a selection. Chapter 3, "Objects and Selections: Built for Speed," is a must-read before you continue with this chapter.

PhotoImpact includes some incredible image effects, and I've spent many hours experimenting with the different tools. There are more than fifty effects built into PhotoImpact, but we can't go through all of them. Let me show you some of my favorites.

Figures 8.1 and 8.2 are the starting images, and you'll be able to compare the enhanced images with these to see how they've changed. For each effect that I'm using, I'll choose one of the starting images to apply it to. I can promise you that some of the effects will be so incredible that you won't need to look back to the original!

CAUTION

Remember to have your Undo settings turned on (File > Preferences > General > Enable Undo) and set to at least twenty levels. I find that when I'm experimenting creatively, it's a good idea to have a lot of Undo levels so I can go back to where I started.

Figure 8.1
Our first starting image.

Figure 8.2
Our second starting image.

Find Edges

The Find Edges filter is found under Effect > Blur & Sharpen > Find Edges on the menu bar. This effect attempts to find the edges of your image and then darkens everything else around it (see Figure 8.3). An effect like this works best with an object selection rather than an entire screen. Prior to applying the Find Edges effect, I used the Lasso Selection tool to draw a selection around the car. The Emphasize Edges effect (found in the same location) performs a similar, albeit less drastic, effect and has more user controls.

Figure 8.3
The Find Edges effect.

TIP

If you want to experiment with different settings but don't want to risk wrecking your original image, press CTRL+D. This command will create a duplicate image onto which you can project your special effects talents.

Background Blur Effect (a.k.a. "Depth-of-Field Effect")

It's a very common practice among 35mm photographers to take a shot where the subject of the image is in focus, but the background is a little blurry. This is sometimes called the "depth-of-field effect." Using a technique like this allows the focus to be completely on the subject. I used this effect constantly when shooting 35mm and greatly missed it when I went digital (it's much more difficult to achieve with a digital camera). Figure 8.14 shows a 35mm photo that used this technique. The good news is that you can create a background blur very easily with PhotoImpact.

Figure 8.4 shows this effect done from a digital camera image. I purposely made the effect a little on the extreme side so it would show up in print, but you can have a lot of control over the effect using different tools.

Figure 8.4
The background blur effect.

There are several blur tools in PhotoImpact. Three standard methods to achieve the effect as seen in the above figure are:

▶ Make a selection around the object, right-click on the selection, and choose Invert. This will create a selection of everything *but* your object. From Effect > Blur & Sharpen on the menu bar, choose either Blur or Gaussian Blur. Each effect has its own fine differences: Blur can be quite subtle, while Gaussian Blur is more extreme.

▶ Use the Blur Retouch Tool from the set of Retouch Tools on the Tool Panel; this allows you to "paint on" the blur effect. This is my preferred method if making a selection is difficult. I simply choose a large brush size and, in smooth motions, paint over the background. Be sure to not "blur" the same section twice, or it will look unnatural. The final effect is fantastic!

▶ An interesting variation on this technique is to use the Motion Blur effect, found under Effect > Camera Lens > Motion Blur on the menu bar. Figure 8.5, using a selection of the background, shows how the Motion Blur can effect your image.

Figure 8.5
The Motion Blur effect.

TIP

Always work with the highest-resolution image that you can if you plan on printing it later (computing power permitting, of course). For instance, if you have a digital camera image that is 1536×1024, don't shrink it down to 640×480 before working on it unless you're *sure* you won't be printing it. The higher the original resolution, the larger and higher quality of a photo print you can get. Remember that if it's a Web image, you can always resize it in the final export step.

Mosaic Effect

The Mosaic effect, found under Effect > Camera Lens > Mosaic on the menu bar, is a simple effect that essentially over-pixelates your image. There are several user-controlled settings, and the effect can be subtle or extreme. Figure 8.6 shows the effect on a relatively mild setting in which the image looks similar to a witness protection effect you'd see on TV. This effect was applied to the entire image, without a selection. Figure 8.7 shows it applied to the background after I inverted the selection of the car. The setting for this figure was quite high, but I think it looks utterly cool!

Figure 8.6
The Mosaic effect applied to an entire image—can anyone say, "Witness Protection Program?"

Figure 8.7
The Mosaic effect applied only to the background.

Natural Painting Effects

PhotoImpact has some beautiful natural painting effects that can make your image look like it was done in watercolor, charcoal, colored pen, or oil pen. These settings are found under Effect > Natural Painting on the menu bar, and each one can be applied to either a selection or an entire image. Of all the effects in PhotoImpact, these are the ones I find among the most powerful. A simple image can be made to look like a hand-drawn sketch, and when printed out by a Web-based, high-resolution photo-printing service, the results are breathtaking (we'll discuss printing services like this in Chapter 13, "Gearing Up: Printing, Sharing and More").

Figure 8.8 shows the Watercolor effect applied to a selection I had around the car, while Figure 8.9 shows the incredible Charcoal effect applied to an entire image (this is one of my favorites). The Charcoal effect is the easiest way to create an impressive-looking image if the original photo was shot properly.

Figure 8.8
The Watercolor effect applied to a selection around the car.

Figure 8.9
The Charcoal effect applied to the entire image.

Figure 8.10 shows the surreal Colored Pen effect. The adjustments on this effect will allow you to create surprisingly different images depending on how you choose your settings. The Oil Paint effect in Figure 8.11 can be beautiful if applied with relatively low settings.

Figure 8.10
The Colored Pen effect applied to the entire image.

Figure 8.11
The Oil Paint effect applied to the entire image.

Each effect has different settings, so be sure to experiment with the various sliders and thumbnail previews to find the setting that's right for your image.

Artistic Hue Shifting

An important element of any image is its color. In the previous chapter, we covered how to use the Hue & Saturation effect to correct color imbalances. What about when you want to get a little creative and have some fun with colors? PhotoImpact offers a few different methods to take a full-color image and turn it into something else.

Hue & Saturation

The first method is the aforementioned Hue & Saturation effect (Format > Hue & Saturation on the menu bar). While small changes result in slight shifts (say, from overly reddish skin tones to more tan-colored tones), larger changes can result in some creative image changes. By using a hue shift value of 130 and a saturation value of 50 on the fellow in Figure 8.12, I was able to get the image shown in Figure 8.13: green skin, purple pants. I just created the Incredible Hulk in one easy step!

Figure 8.12
Our original image.

Figure 8.13
Post hue-shifting.

Remember that just like everything else in PhotoImpact, you can control the way these effects are applied by using a selection. In Figure 8.14 below, I created a selection around the subject's head (covering the face and hair), inverted it (right-click > Invert), and applied the hue shift. Now it looks like he's in a surreal landscape, but not a part of it.

Figure 8.14
Controlled hue-shifting.

Monochrome

Monochrome is a fancy term for "black and white" or "grayscale." You can turn your color photos into monochrome images in a single step by going to Effect > Special > Monochrome on the menu bar. Figure 8.15 shows the original color image, while Figure 8.16 shows the new monochrome image. I'm a huge fan of black-and-white photography, so I often take photos shot with my digital camera and turn them into monochrome images. I've found that many photos will have more visual impact in the monochrome format. In the color image, the multi-colored lights in the top-right tend to draw the eye from the subject (Shaun Verreault from the incredible band *Wide Mouth Mason—* **www.widemouthmason.com**). As a monochrome image, the colored lights are removed from the equation and the focus is on the subject.

Figure 8.15
The original color image—note how the lights are competing with the guitar player for attention.

Figure 8.16
The monochrome version of the image focuses all eyes on the performer.

CHAPTER 8

The Two-Color Effect

The Two-Color effect is similar to the monochrome look discussed above. This feature, however, allows the user to configure which two tones are going to be used. Found under Effects > Special > Two-Color on the menu bar, this tool is true eye candy. You can achieve a myriad of hue effects with it, from the subtle to the surreal. The tool is simple to use. Simply pick the two colors you want to use and watch the preview window to see how the image looks. See Figure 8.17.

Figure 8.17
The two-color version of the image.

The Colorize Pen

The Colorize Pen is a little different than the other effects in this section because it involves actually interacting directly with the image. The concept of this tool is to paint color back into a monochrome image. If you've ever seen the famous black-and-white photographs of a child holding a rose, and the red rose is the only color in the entire image, you've seen this effect in action. The use of this tool is simple, but the execution of it takes practice.

The tool is found under the Retouch Tool Panel, which can be brought up by clicking View > Toolbars & Panels > Retouch Tool Panel (see Figure 8.18). The Colorize Pen icon is also found under the Tool Panel under the same set of Retouch Tools as the Dodge Retouch Tool icon. Using the tool requires you to understand that it will colorize any tone that isn't pure black or pure white. The Colorize Pen will have a greater effect on lighter tones.

Figure 8.18
The Colorize Pen's Attribute Toolbar.

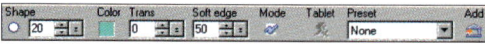

To start, you'll need to take a color image and make it monochrome. Then select this tool (the toolbar shown above is what you'll use). Select the color you want to add to the image, the brush size, and the soft edge (50 is a good setting for this). Start painting! Start with subtle effects at first: Paint something small and see how it looks. Figure 8.19 shows some work I did with this tool. I selected a color I thought would look good in this image and started painting. The final result is a compelling image.

Figure 8.19
A monochrome image that has been recolored.

The Stamp Tool

Paint Shop Pro, another graphics application, had a feature that people really seemed to enjoy: picture tubes. A picture tube was a series of similar images that users would "spray" on to their workspaces, essentially creating a paintbrush of sorts that had images for paint. It was an interesting concept, and one that was frequently requested by PhotoImpact users—so Ulead has given us the Stamp Tool!

Using Stamps

The Stamp Tool has several settings that you'll see when clicking on the Stamp Tool icon. Going from left to right on Figure 8.20, the functions are:

Figure 8.20
The Stamp Tool's Attribute Toolbar.

> **Thumbnail**—The small icon on the far left is the currently selected stamp. To change stamp types, click on it, and a preview window with many stamps will drop down. Select a new stamp with a single click.

> **View**—This function allows you to see the number and type of images inside a stamp preset.

▶ **Trans**—Short for "Transparency," like other functions in PhotoImpact, the higher this value, the more you can see the background through your images

▶ **Scale**—This is the size of the stamp. A value of 100 gives you the image at its original size, but keeping in mind that each stamp will have different sizes, this setting will need some experimentation.

▶ **Spacing**—This value controls the spacing of the images in a stamp. The lower this value is, the more images are placed in a row in any given area.

▶ **Order**—This controls the orientation of your images, giving you the option of Random, Sequential, or Angular.

▶ **Placement**—The placement option gives you a choice of Stamp or Trail. Stamp gives you one image per mouse click, while Trail creates a stream of images.

▶ **Object**—Separate Objects or Single Objects gives you the choice of how your objects will be linked when done stamping. If you're planning on changing an element in all of them (color hue, for example), choose Single Objects. Or, if you're planning on moving each one individually, make sure they're Separate Objects.

▶ **Lines**—These settings help you control how you are allowed to stamp a line of objects. The options are Freehand, Straight Lines and Connected Lines.

▶ **Tablet**—If you have a graphics tablet, you can use its pressure-sensitive features to control the transparency of stamps.

▶ **Add**—You can add a stamp preset to your EasyPalette settings via this button.

The use of the tool is fairly simple, so follow along:

1. Create a new blank image or prepare an image of your own. We're going to create a border of sorts, so the image should have space around the outside with enough room for the stamps. Figure 8.21 shows the image I've created.

Figure 8.21
An image ready for the Stamp Tool.

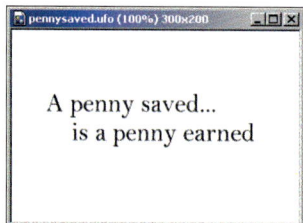

2. Click on the Stamp Tool. The Stamp Tool's Attribute Toolbar will load, giving you access to all the settings you'll need (see Figure 8.20). I'm going to select the coin preset with a transparency of 0, scale of 57, and spacing of 32. I want a constant stream of coins, so the order is set to random and the placement is set to trail. By clicking and holding the left mouse button and dragging the cursor, I can create a stream of pennies as Figure 8.22 shows.

Figure 8.22
Using the Stamp Tool.

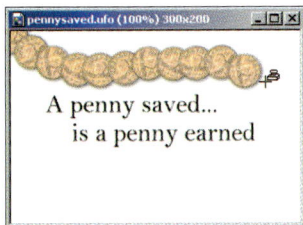

3. When you're done using that stamp, let go of the mouse button, and the stream of images will stop. You can continue to stamp on images as I've done in Figure 8.23 to create a multi-layered effect. Then, you're done!

Figure 8.23
The completed image, created with the Stamp Tool.

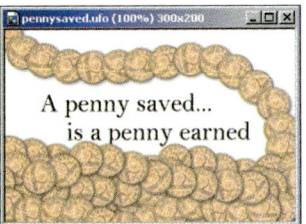

Importing Paint Shop Pro Picture Tubes

Luckily for you and me, there is an entire community of Paint Shop Pro users out there that have been creating picture tubes for years! Ulead recognized this fact and gave us a great import tool that will add the picture tubes into the Stamp Tool. First you'll need to find some picture tubes to download—I've found a few sites for you to download tubes from:

▶ Paint Shop Pro Foundry
(**http://www.digital-foundry.com/paintshop/tubes/library.shtml**)

▶ Anne Gerdes Picture Tubes (**http://gerdesdesign.com/tubes.htm**)

▶ Hood's PSP Downloads
(**http://www.northnet.com.au/~robrow/tubes/downloads.htm**)

CHAPTER 8

Once you've downloaded and unzipped the files (if necessary), you should have .tub files. To import these files, follow these steps:

1.   Click on the Stamp Tool to load the Stamp Tool's Attribute Toolbar.

2.   Click on the small, drop-down arrow next to the image preview. A drop-down menu will appear (see Figure 8.24), and you should select Import Picture Tube.

Figure 8.24
The Import Picture
Tube command.

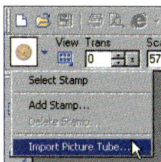

3.   The Open window will appear (Figure 8.25) and you should browse to the location of your .tub files. You'll be able to see a small preview of the picture tube in the lower middle portion of this window. Locate the file, select it, and click Open.

Figure 8.25
The import window.

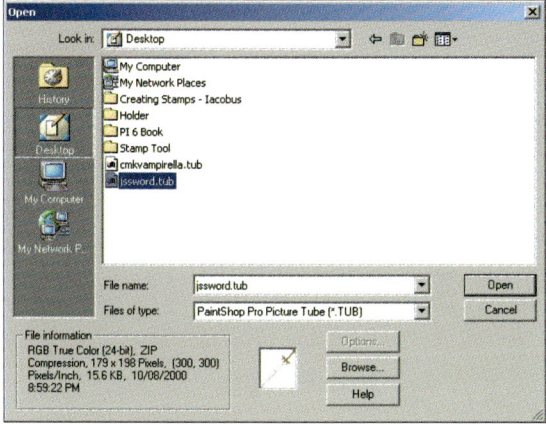

4.   You'll know if the import was successful, because the current selected stamp will be the new import (see Figure 8.26). If this is the case, then you're done!

Figure 8.26
The successfully
imported picture tube
is now a stamp.

Creating Your Own Stamps

Using PhotoImpact to create your own stamps is surprisingly easy. The process is almost identical to importing picture tubes, only you need to make sure your stamp objects are stored as unique file names.

Follow these steps to create your own stamp:

1. In a single file, gather together all of your objects. Each stamp item needs to be a separate object; so, if you're creating a stamp from a dingbat font, make sure that each item is a unique text item. You can import items from the Hemera Photo-Objects collection or you can even draw your own. The key is to have all objects be separate. By using the paint tool in Paint as Object Mode, I created a series of quick doodles shown in Figure 8.27.

Figure 8.27
My objects are ready to become a stamp.

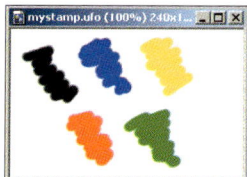

2. I saved this creation of objects as a UFO file, so the objects are intact.
3. Under the Stamp options, select Add Stamp (see Figure 8.24).
4. Browse to your UFO file and click Open.
5. Your objects are now a stamp. If you were successful, the stamp appears in the preview window (see Step 4 of the previous tutorial).

Frames and Edges

PhotoImpact has a massive collection of frames and edges that add a touch of elegance, flair, or creativity to any image. A framed image makes a printed image even better, while adding a drop shadow makes it perfect for Web-based galleries. Figure 8.28 shows a sample image with Classic Frame #32 around it. There are four frame-and-edge groups, all found under EasyPalette's Frame Gallery:

▶ **2D & 3D**—The complex, path-based frames in this section have a bevelled, 3D look.

▶ **Edge**—These simple edge effects add subtle beauty to any image.

▶ **Magic**—These frames are similar to those in Edge but have more complex patterns.

▶ **Classic**—Similar to 2D & 3D, Classic frames are complex and intricate and require much more CPU power and time than the other types. The results, however, are quite impressive.

CHAPTER 8

Figure 8.28
An image with a
Classic frame.

Using Frames and Edges

Applying a frame or edge to your image is simple: Browse through the
EasyPalette, pick the one you want, and double-click on it. That's all!
However, there are some cases where you want to control certain
elements of the frame or edge. Let's take a look at how to do this:

1. Start with an image that would look good with a frame or an edge.
    The image in Figure 8.29 would look best with an edge effect because
    the subject is off-center.

Figure 8.29
The subject in this
image is off-center.

2. When going to the EasyPalette, pick out an edge effect by using the
    thumbnail previews as shown in Figure 8.30. Right-click on the
    thumbnail and choose Modify Properties and Apply.

Figure 8.30
Use this command to
modify edge and frame
properties.

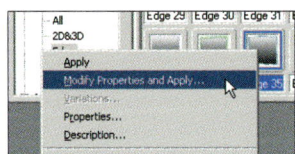

3. A new window will open, giving you access to the various settings for that edge or frame (see Figure 8.31). In our example, I want to change the color of the edge to be a rainbow gradient instead of a single color. To do this, I simply click the box for Gradient color and click the gradient preview to select a new gradient.

Figure 8.31
Frame & Shadow
properties window.

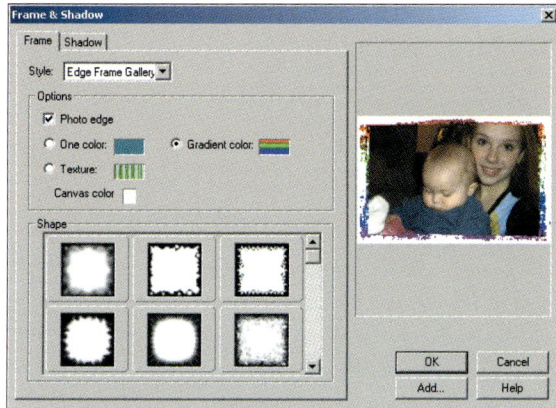

4. If you don't want to apply a shadow to this image, click OK and you're done! In my example, however, I think a drop shadow behind the image would look great. The second tab in Figure 8.31 is for Shadow settings, so once clicked, a window like that in Figure 8.32 will appear. From this window, you can adjust the many options, but all of them are identical to what was discussed in the shadow section of Chapter 3. In my example I'm going to use a standard shadow (10, 10 offset) but with a Soft edge value of 10.

Figure 8.32
Adding a shadow to
the image.

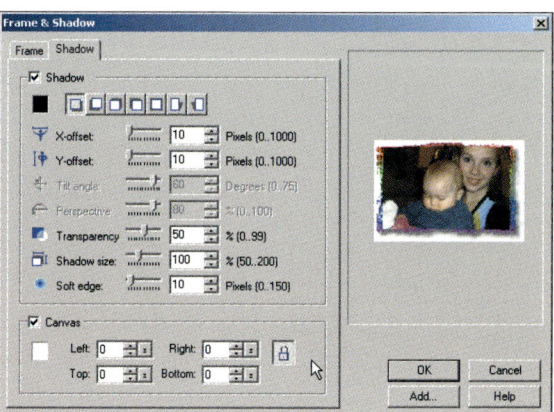

CHAPTER 8

5. The final result of our edge effect and shadow can be seen in Figure 8.33.

Figure 8.33
Our image with an edge effect and shadow.

> **NOTE**
> Most of the frames were created assuming that the subject of your image is in the center. If it's not, you'll find the subject getting trimmed out of the image by the frame. Try using an edge effect or crop your image so that the subject is in the center. It may take a few tries to get right.

Adding New Frames and Edges to the EasyPalette

If you've customized a frame or edge and would like to keep it, it's simple to add your creation to the EasyPalette. I'm creating an online photo gallery with some of my work, but I wanted each image to have exactly the same edge effect, shadow type, and coloring. This was easy once I added the edge effect to the EasyPalette.

To add an edge or frame effect to the EasyPalette, follow these quick steps:

1. Create your edge effect add a shadow if you wish, and then click on the Add button. This button is found in the bottom right corner of the Frame & Shadow settings window (refer back to Figure 8.32).

2. Once you've clicked Add, the Add to EasyPalette window will appear (see Figure 8.34). Give your effect a name, choose the location it should be stored (likely the Frame Gallery or My Gallery), and then click OK. The preset has been stored for future use. It even stores the preview of it on your source image!

Figure 8.34
Adding a frame or edge effect to the EasyPalette.

TIP

Be sure to use a descriptive name when saving your EasyPalette preset so it's easy to find and apply later.

Third-party Plug-ins

As I mentioned in Chapter 2, "Getting Around in PhotoImpact," PhotoImpact has the ability to use Photoshop-compatible plug-ins to create impressive special effects. Plug-ins can be thought of as shortcuts to achieving an effect. While it's always nice to create every effect manually by hand, if your life is hectic like mine, time-saving features are always welcome. Plug-ins install themselves under the Effect menu, so you have quick access to them at all times. There are literally hundreds of free plug-ins found all over the Internet. Here are some of the best places to look:

▶ Plugins.com—**http://www.plugins.com/plugins/photoshop/**

▶ PlugPage—**http://www.plugpage.com/**

▶ Graphic Design Resource Guide—**http://www.graphic-design.com/dtp-resources/photoshop.html**

▶ Ultimate Photoshop—**http://www.ultimate-photoshop.com/filters/**

▶ PC Resources for Photoshop and the Digital Photographer—**http://showcase.netins.net/web/wolf359/plugins.htm**

The best things in life aren't *always* free, so here are three of my all-time favorite commercial plug-in packages: Kai's Power Tools (KPT) and Flaming Pear Software's Blade Pro and Designer Sextet packages.

CHAPTER 8

Kai's Power Tools (KPT)

http://newgraphics.corel.com/products/kpt6.html

Kai Krause is one of the most famous figures in digital design and he was the driving force behind some of the most innovative add-on products created under the Metatools banner. KPT is a collection of plug-ins that function more like miniature programs than simple filters. Figure 8.35 shows the user interface of KPT 6.0, and it's a marvel to behold. You don't even feel like you're using Microsoft Windows anymore! The KPT interface was so well liked that years ago the company even started working on an entire operating system built around it. Sadly, it never came to fruition.

KPT products have been through many versions, and what's interesting is that in most cases, the filters aren't upgrades from previous versions. Each version is totally new. I have both version 3.0 and version 6.0 on my machine, and each offers unique options. See Figure 8.36.

Figure 8.35
The KPT 6.0 interface.

Figure 8.36
Texture Explorer from
version 3.0.

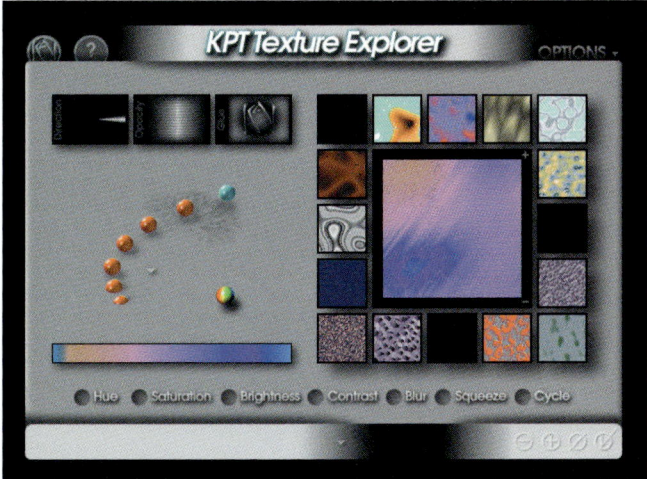

The features for version 6.0 are:

▶ **KPT Goo**—Smear and pull images in unique ways, create animations with this feature.

▶ **KPT Equalizer**—This makes an interesting image adjustment tool. It can be used to sharpen an image or create an artistic, gauzy and dreamlike blur.

▶ **KPT Gel**—Paint over your images with different materials.

▶ **KPT Materializer**—Create dynamic surface textures.

▶ **KPT LensFlare**—You can create powerful lighting options with this one.

▶ **KPT Turbulance**—Words can't really describe this one—2D waves of color can be made into animations.

▶ **KPT Reaction**—Create realistic organic textures.

▶ **KPT SceneBuilder**—Create 3D scenes with this very interesting tool.

CHAPTER 8

▶ **KPT SkyEffects**—This is *the* most powerful tool for creating cloud and sunset effects. Figure 8.37 was created in a matter of seconds.

▶ **KPT Projector**—Although this wasn't listed on the Corel site when I went there, it's included in my KPT 6.0 package. It creates incredible perspective effects (see Figure 8.38).

Figure 8.37
The KPT 6.0 SkyEffects plug-in.

Figure 8.38
My image with the KPT 6.0 Projector plug-in.

The entire KPT line was purchased by Corel in early 2000, so you can purchase this package through them at the link above or from **www.corel.com**. If you're looking for older versions of KPT, try an online auction site such as **www.ebay.com**. Although the current pricing of $149 makes KPT more expensive than PhotoImpact itself, this is a nice package to have if you're interested in creating some incredible effects.

Flaming Pear Software
http://www.flamingpear.com

I think Flaming Pear's products are as unusual as its name. These plug-ins are my most-used third-party tools because they allow me to achieve eye-catching effects in a short period of time. They work with selections or on entire images and are surprisingly affordable, considering their sheer power. There are two plug-in packages I'd like to tell you about: BladePro and the Designer Sextet.

BladePro

Text effects are an essential creative tool for designing Web sites. Used properly, text effects can add style and flair to your site, especially for personal sites where self-expression is key. BladePro, a very popular plug-in with a huge installed user base, is essentially a random text-effect generator that uses textures, reflective surfaces, beveling, and many other effects to creating incredible-looking text. Figure 8.39 shows the user interface for BladePro—you can create random effects, save presets of your own, or use presets that other people have developed. Whether you're looking for text that looks like chocolate or gold, BladePro is a fantastic tool, and relatively inexpensive at $49. You can download a demo from Flaming Pear's Web site.

Figure 8.39
The BladePro user interface.

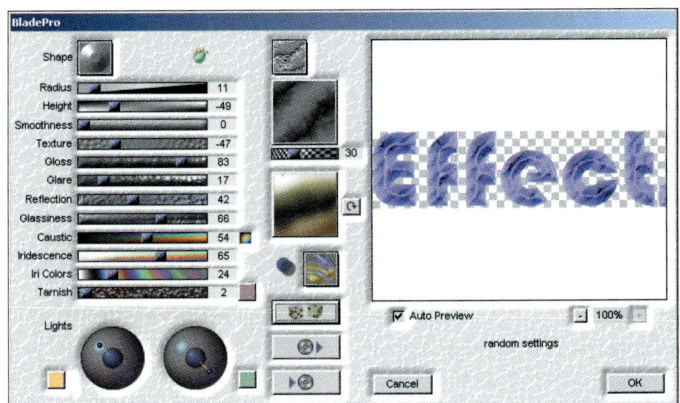

PhotoImpact 6.0 offers some incredible presets for text that BladePro can't match, but the beauty of BladePro is the random effects that can be generated with a few clicks. Figure 8.40 shows the results of a quick application of BladePro's random effect generator and a shadow from PhotoImpact. Remember that like all plug-ins, you can apply this to selections for interesting background effects.

Figure 8.40
A BladePro text effect with a shadow added.

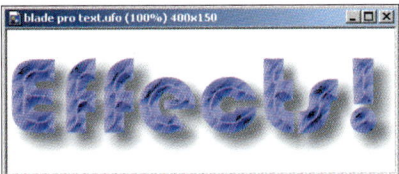

Designer Sextet

In all my years using graphic design programs, I've never encountered effects so beautiful and simple to use as the Designer Sextet filters. This series of six filters consists of:

▶ **Aetherize**—A dreamy, wondrous effect

▶ **Twist**—Churns and smears your image in interesting ways

▶ **Swerve**—Deforms shapes

▶ **Lacquer**—Adds a resin-like effect to images

▶ **Silver**— Silver effects (just as the name implies)

▶ **Glare**—Glorious light effects

My favorite filter in this set is Aetherize. The interface for this tool (Figure 8.41) is very simple to use and, like other Flaming Pear products, clicking on the six-sided die will generate a random effect. The sliders allow you to control every aspect of the effect for tweaking. The effects that this filter generate are gorgeous—a combination of soft focus effects, hue shifting, and gradient fills.

Figure 8.41
The Aetherize plug-in.

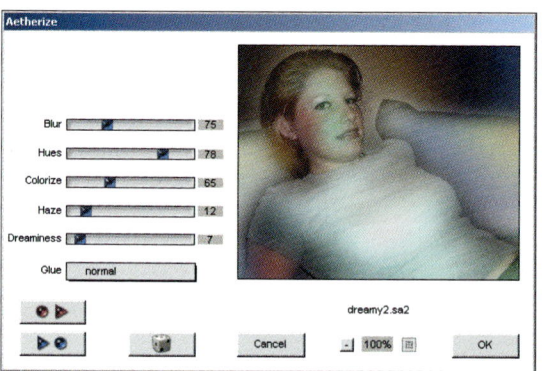

Using these filters involves two steps: click and play. There is no right or wrong way to use them, you just keep clicking and "playing" with the tool until you get the effect you want. You can also save your presets for use later if you've happened upon that "killer" effect. Figure 8.42 is a digital image in its raw form. After applying the Aetherize filter (Figure 8.43), the image takes on a whole new look and will evoke a "Wow!" response from anyone looking at it.

Figure 8.42
Our image before the
Aetherize plug-in...

Figure 8.43
...our image after the
Aetherize plug-in.

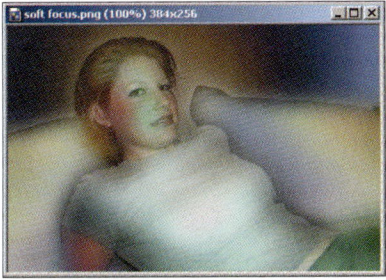

Flaming Pear and PhotoImpact

As you might have guessed by now, PhotoImpact and Flaming Pear
software are two of the best weapons in my graphics arsenal. Keeping in
mind that because Flaming Pear plug-ins can be applied to selections,
you can create some pretty incredible things! Let's look at dramatic before
and after images so you can see what I mean.

Figure 8.44 is a shot I took during a music/drama production. I felt the
image had the potential to be a lot more exciting, so I fired up PhotoImpact
and the Flaming Pear Designer Sextet plug-ins and got to work.

Figure 8.44
Our starting image.

Figure 8.45 is the result of my efforts. I created this image through experimentation. I began by making a selection of the background. This would let me greatly alter the background into an unusual-looking backdrop for the performers. Flaming Pear's Swirl filter did the job perfectly, creating a shiny, metallic, colorfully blended background. You'll notice the selection touched on the darker images in the foreground, so some of the people in the image are also affected by the swirl.

Figure 8.45
After heavy modifications, our image looks quite different.

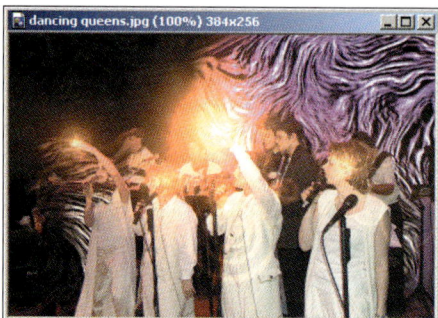

Next, I wanted to add a heavy glowing effect to the singers in the front. Using the Modify Properties and Apply feature of the Lens Flare presets in the EasyPalette, I was able to apply the glow effect exactly where I wanted to and adjust the size and strength of the flair. I also kept the Ambient Light setting quite high so the image wouldn't darken too much.

As you can see, the gold headbands on the singers were perfect points for the glowing effect, so I applied each of them separately. The most powerful glow effect was saved for the centrally positioned performer's hand, giving the viewer a single focal point in this image. After a final tweak of Brightness & Contrast, I was done. This image took roughly fifteen minutes from start to finish, and most of that time was spent positioning the glow in exactly the right spaces. Once you master the basic concepts of selections, you can create some really incredible effects in a surprisingly short amount of time. Enjoy!

9

Graphic Design for the Web: A PhotoImpact Primer

Graphics are an important part of the World Wide Web, and whether you're doing Web graphic design for a business or just for fun, PhotoImpact is the best tool for the job. It offers countless design tools for the Webmaster, both in the form of templates and custom tools for making your own designs. PhotoImpact 6.0 truly is a "Web Studio." This chapter assumes you're familiar with the previous chapters on creating paths, text, and working with objects.

The World Wide Web

The World Wide Web was born in 1989, but it didn't really start to capture the imagination of the mainstream public until the mid-'90s. Early Web sites had few graphics, and with good reason: Modem speeds were a fraction of what they are now. As the Web evolved, it grew from a stomping ground for computer geeks to a massive world-wide network of users who posted Web sites on everything from planting tulips to Tom Jones. The sheer variety of content on the Web never ceases to amaze me, and as someone who has several Web sites, I'm also amazed at how many people will enjoy something that I created on a personal whim. No matter who you are or what you're interested in, sharing with the rest of the world is a wonderful thing! But if you want to do it right, learning to create quality graphics is critical. Content is king on the Web, but presentation of that content is important.

The Basics of Graphic Design for the Web

What is "good" graphic design for the Web? That depends on what your goal is and who your audience is. Are you designing a corporate site, something where clarity is paramount? If so, your design should be subdued, professional, and have simple but powerful navigation. Or is your site a games-and-entertainment portal for tech-savvy hardcore gamers? Then throw in a bit of chaos with creative graphics, visually assault them with interesting colors, and, above all, make your site exciting! The key is to target your audience and design to their tastes or, in the case of a personal site, express your own tastes.

A common mistake beginners make is over-using a certain effect. Flaming text has a nice "wow" factor the first time you see it, but what about the ninth time? Figure 9.1 shows my very first attempt at Web design in December 1995. When I look back on it now, I get quite a good laugh. Like many first-time Web designers, I thought that the incredibly "cool" swirly background was more important than being able to read the words on the page. I was fixated on special effects, at the expense of my content. Learn from my mistake—content should *always* be readable!

Figure 9.1
Learn from my mistakes and don't focus too much on "cool" effects.

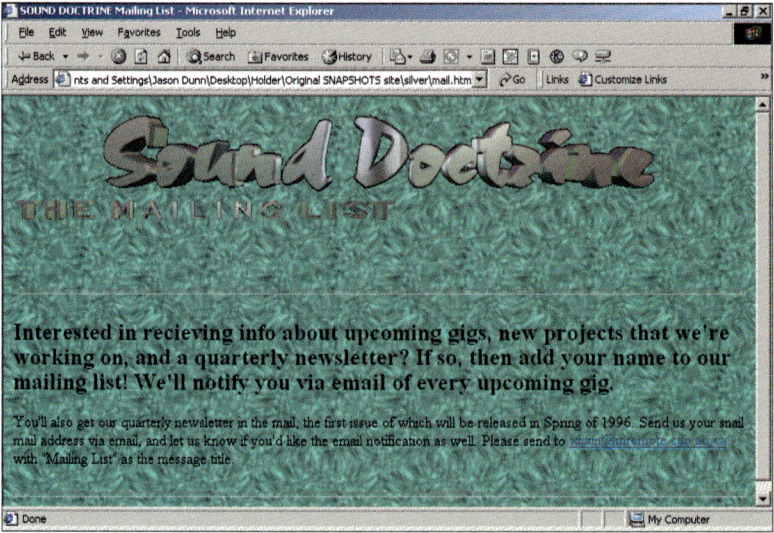

Here are some other things to keep in mind:

▶ **Screen resolution**—Test your design in different screen resolutions and see what it looks like. Don't assume that everyone has the same screen resolution as you do.

▶ **Internet speed**—If you have a cable modem or DSL, try viewing your Web site on a friend's dial-up connection. Do you find it frustrating to surf your own site on a 28.8 modem? If you do, so do others! Most HTML editors also provide a way of indicating how long a particular page will load under a certain type of connection speed. Try to keep it under sixty seconds or less on a 28.8K connection.

▶ **Clarity**—It doesn't matter if you're creating a corporate site or a personal site: Your visitor has to understand what to click to find what they need, or they'll leave the site.

▶ **Get feedback**—Your site may make perfect sense to you, but what about others? Can they find what they're looking for? Ask friends and family to test the site out and give you honest feedback.

▶ **Cool is good…in small amounts**—Don't try too hard to impress your visitors. They can tell!

▶ **The KISS principle**—Some of the best designed sites in the world are surprisingly simple: Keep it simple, sweetie!

▶ **Content**—Having a great-looking site means nothing if you have no content. Strive to put up engaging, interesting, and useful content. Content is king.

▶ **Be inspired by the best**—Take a look at the sites that you like. What is it about them that draws your attention? Combine the best elements of each site into something that is uniquely your own.

The Browser-Safe/ Web-Optimized Color Palette

In many graphics books I've seen, entire chapters are devoted to the "Zen of the Browser-safe Color Palette." What is it? Well, you need to understand that around the early- to mid-'90s, many computers were limited to 256-color (8-bit) displays—sometimes by design, but more often by configuration because users didn't know how to change their color depth settings. Web designers could make images in 16-bit color (64,000 colors) or higher (see Figure 9.2 for the 24-bit color palette), but when an 8-bit color computer tried to render the graphic from 64,000 colors down to 256 colors, it would make guesses about what colors were dropped and what weren't. This often resulted in horrible-looking graphics, which was unacceptable to Web designers.

Figure 9.2
The 24-bit color palette.

CHAPTER 9

Both Netscape Navigator and Microsoft Internet Explorer had special color palettes (collections of color) that they would use to render images (see Figure 9.3). By basing their Web graphics on this limited color palette, the designers could control users' experiences and achieve maximum quality with these limited colors. This didn't always work out nicely, however.

Adding to that fact, forty of those 256 colors show up differently on both Macintosh computers and PCs. Hence, the browser-safe palette contains only 216 possible colors.

Figure 9.3
The browser-safe color palette.

To understand what this looked like in practice, take a look at the source image in Figure 9.4. This is the "original" screenshot of the image in 24-bit color (16.7 million colors). The colors are crisp and defined. Figure 9.5 shows the radical drop in quality that a browser-safe color palette has on an image of this type. As you can see, applying a browser-safe palette to a photo results in a dithered, speckled look that ruins the image.

Figure 9.4
Our image in 24-bit color (16.7 million colors).

Figure 9.5
Our image in the Web-safe color palette (216 colors).

The results are different when you design your graphics (logos, buttons, and so on) from scratch using only colors found in the Web-safe palette, but who wants this limitation? And if you're designing sites for clients, are you going to tell them you can't match their logo colors because they are not in the browser-safe palette?

The reality is that today, the vast majority of users are browsing the Web with 16-bit or higher color depth, at resolutions of 800×600 or higher. TheCounter.com is a Web site counter that Webmasters can install on their sites. It records a variety of anonymous statistics about the user's computer and can be helpful when deciding how to design your Web site. According to the June 2000 sample of 502 million page visits across all the sites that use their counter, the following information was gathered:

► Approximately 93 percent of all visitors were running a version of Microsoft Windows (95, 98, 2000, or NT).

► More than 75 percent of all visitors were using a version of Microsoft Internet Explorer; 16 percent used Netscape.

► About 86 percent of all visitors were running at 800×600 or higher resolution.

► Nine out of ten of visitors were running at 16-bit color (64,000 colors) or higher.

This may seem like a bold statement, but looking at the above statistics, I think it's reasonable to design your Web graphics with the assumption that your users will be using at least 16-bit color and running 800×600 resolution. Leave the browser-safe palette back in the mid-'90s where it belongs, and design your images in thousands of glorious colors!

Creating Web Graphics with PhotoImpact

As you already know, PhotoImpact is one of the best tools for Web graphics on the market, and it's no secret that Ulead has tweaked and tuned its products for the Web. PhotoImpact 6.0, however, goes far beyond previous versions in giving the user many options for designing Web graphics. These options all boil down to making one choice: Do you create your graphics from scratch, or do you use templates?

Graphics from Scratch

Creating Web graphics from scratch is easier than you think. Templates, while great for Webmasters just starting out, don't really cut it on the professional level. Learning to create your own Web graphics from scratch is a skill that you'll find very useful. Creating your own Web graphics combines the topics we've covered in previous chapters: creating shapes with paths, adding text, and using the EasyPalette for special effects and objects. Let's create a header graphic (the kind that sits at the top of the page) for a personal Web page about music.

CHAPTER 9

1. First, create a blank image of the appropriate size. Click the New icon and create an image that is 350 pixels wide by 150 pixels in height, has 24-bit color, and a transparent background. Your image should look like Figure 9.6.

Figure 9.6
Our beginning image.

2. Next, let's create some text. Click on the Text Tool icon on the Tool Panel and create some text (see Figure 9.7). I've created two pieces of text, one with the word "My" and the other with the word "Music"—both in a fancy font. The font I've chosen is Black Chancery; if you do not have this font, choose something similar that expresses the feeling of the graphic you want to create. Pick the color you want as well.

Figure 9.7
Creating text.

3. Arrange the text in an attractive way. In my case, the Black Chancery font has beautiful serifs that allow me to place the text in an overlapping manner, making it look like one object. See Figure 9.8. In fact, that's a good idea—change to the Pick Tool and, while holding down the SHIFT key, click on both pieces of text. You'll see the selection marquee around both pieces of text. Right-click on the object and select Merge as Single Object (see Figure 9.8).

Figure 9.8
Combining the text items into one object.

4. Let's insert something to show the user that this is a music site: In the EasyPalette's Image Library, you'll find an image of a CD. Double-click to insert the CD object. The default size will be quite large (see Figure 9.9), so resize the image to 25 percent of its original size using the Bicubic resize method. Place it under the "My" text (Figure 9.10).

Figure 9.9
Inserting an object that's too big for the image.

Figure 9.10
A more appropriate size for the CD image.

5. Let's get a little fancy here. Make six copies of the CD (using CTRL+C to copy and CTRL+V to paste), and then resize (CTRL+G) each of the six CDs 10 percent smaller than the first. So for the first copy closest to the original image, resize it to 90 percent of the original. For the next, 80 percent, and so on. You should end up with something that looks like Figure 9.11.

Figure 9.11
Our CD objects have been duplicated.

6. Now, using the Order options (found in the left side of the Pick Tool's Attribute Toolbar), arrange the order of the CDs so that, from left to right, each CD is underneath the one to the left of it. Figure 9.12 shows what I mean.

Figure 9.12
Our CD objects arranged.

CHAPTER 9

7. Next, use the Order option Bring To Front to put the "My Music" text on top of the CD objects.

8. Let's adjust the transparency of each CD object. Click on the second CD from the left in the row with the Pick Tool and set the transparency value to 30. Then, for each CD down the row, increase the transparency value by 10. Your last CD should have a transparency value of 80 (see Figure 9.13).

Figure 9.13
Our CDs have been made transparent.

9. Our image is almost done! Let's right-click on the text object and add a simple shadow using an X and Y offset value of 5.

10. Let's add a little flair to the image. Click on the CD in the bottom left and apply the Lens Flare 3 effect from the Lighting Gallery in the EasyPalette.

11. Right-click on the image and select Merge All. Your image should look similar to Figure 9.14. You're done! Another option for export is using the Image Optimizer (explained later in this chapter).

Figure 9.14
The drop shadow lends a nice touch.

TIP

You may notice that in the example I gave the transparent CDs look like they are darker near where they overlap with the other CD objects. This is because when two transparent objects are overlapped, they'll partially show the other object. For perfect multi-object transparency, try to avoid overlapping objects. Remember, you can nudge objects using the direction arrow keys on your keyboard.

TIP

If you had wanted to make the "My Music" text 3D, you need to do so while the text is still a text object. Once we combined the two text objects into one entity, it was no longer a text object and couldn't be edited like regular text.

Template-based Graphics: The Component Designer

If you need a little help getting started, PhotoImpact 6.0 has some great tools for creating Web graphics based on templates. Ulead's Component Designer is a mini-program within PhotoImpact that walks you through every step of creating Web graphics. It can be used to create:

▶ **Banners**—This is perfect for creating a banner if you want to advertise your site on another page.

▶ **Bullets**—Bullets are useful in breaking out points in text or in creative use.

▶ **Buttons**—You can create a variety of buttons that are perfect for building custom site navigation.

▶ **Button Bars**—Button bars are *the* staple of Web site nagivation.

▶ **Icons**—You can make small, cartoon-style graphics on everything from download icons to office supplies.

▶ **Java Rollover Buttons**—These buttons will change when you pass your mouse cursor over them in your Web browser.

▶ **Separator**—Use this tool to break up large amounts of text.

What makes the template such a powerful tool is that you can change any element of the template you want—the text size, font, color, the button color, texture, and dozens of other things. There are literally thousands of potential combinations, so even if you use these template graphics, your Web site can look unique. By now, you know the best way to become familiar with the tools is to use them. Let's get started creating a button bar for Web site navigation!

CHAPTER 9

1. Under the Web menu on the menu bar, select Component Designer.

2. A new window will load. Click on the Button Bar plus sign to expand the view, and select the Rounded collection (see Figure 9.15).

Figure 9.15
Our choices for a Button Bar.

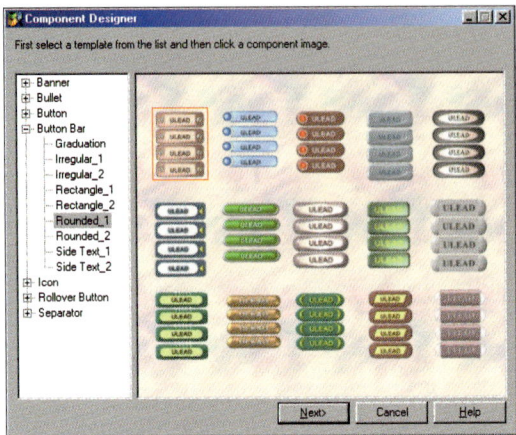

3. Select the third from the left in the bottom row (green with yellow text), then click Next.

4. The next stage of the Component Designer allows you to customize the text, color, spacing, and many other settings for the buttons. Let's start by simply changing the text on the buttons. To do so, click on the text you want to change in the window near the middle (see Figure 9.16), type your own text, and press the Enter key. For the sake of simplicity, we'll assume our HTML work will be done later, so we'll leave the URL, Target, Alt Text, and Status Text empty.

Figure 9.16
Editing the button bar text.

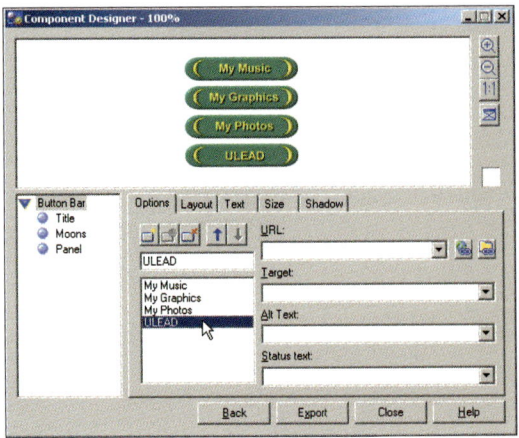

5. Once you've changed the text, let's try changing the panel from green to a texture. On the left side of this window, click on Panel. This loads the color selection tool. The third icon under the word Color is the Textures icon (see Figure 9.17). Select the blue brick texture.

Figure 9.17
Changing the background to a texture.

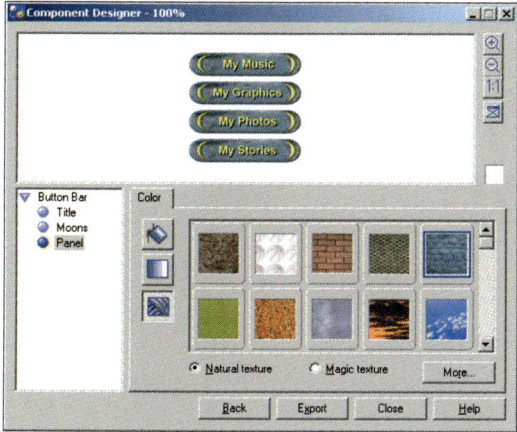

6. We could also change the colors of the moon shapes and text, but the yellow stands out nicely against the blue. We do want to change a few other things, however, so click on the words Button Bar on the left side of the window to put us back into the edit mode.

7. Click on the Layout tab and change the layout of the buttons to be horizontal. Change the button spacing to zero so they're close together (see Figure 9.18).

Figure 9.18
Changing the layout of our button bar.

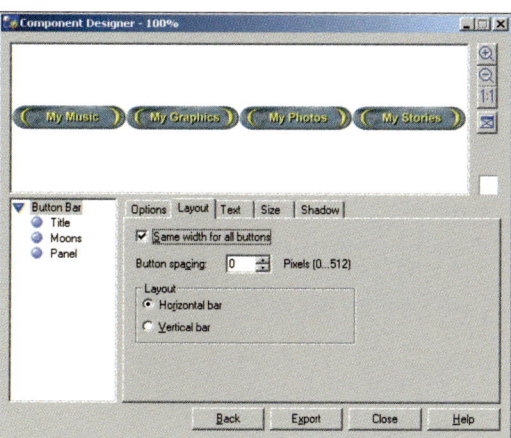

8. Next, the Text tab allows us to change the font on our buttons. The size can't be changed; it automatically sizes the text so that it's as large as it can be without breaking the design. On this screen, in Figure 9.19, select Tahoma as the font and leave it bold.

Figure 9.19
Changing the
button font.

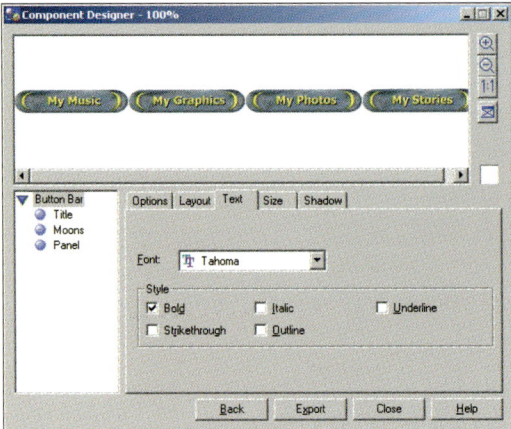

9. Next, click on the Size tab and change the size to 120 percent (see Figure 9.20). This gives us an export size of 576 pixels wide, which is a good size. It's big enough to be seen easily, but not big enough to cause scrolling even on a 640×480-resolution monitor.

Figure 9.20
Changing the size of
our button bar.

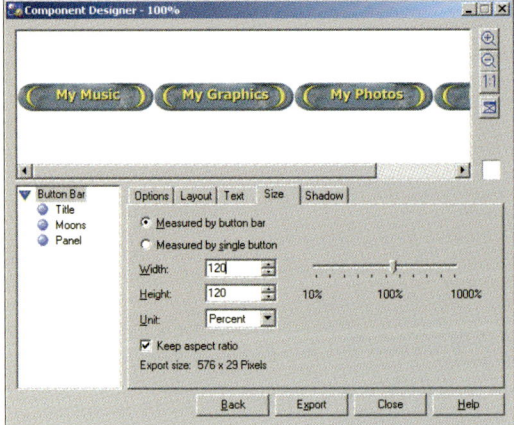

10. The final tab is for adding a Shadow (see Figure 9.21), so click off the box and set an offset value of 5 for both width and height. The other settings are fine at their default values.

Figure 9.21
Adding a shadow.

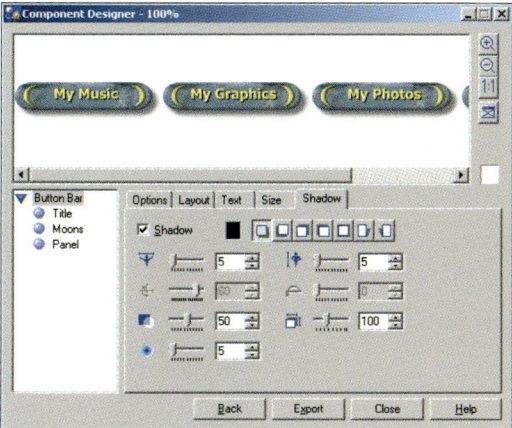

11. Export is the final step. You'll be presented with a list of four choices:

— **HTML**—This allows you to export the project as a series of graphics and HTML code files, complete with a table that matches the size of the pixels between your objects. This code can be easily edited in an HTML tool like Microsoft FrontPage 2000. Figure 9.22 shows the final project assembled in HTML with the inclusion of the header graphic from the previous section.

— **Image Optimizer**—Each button is exported and saved individually as a GIF, JPEG, or PNG file. You also have the option of exporting it as a single graphic (on which you'd use an image map for hyperlinking individual sections).

— **Individual Objects**—Exports each object into PhotoImpact. You have full control over every element, including font sizes. You can then add each button or element into the EasyPalette for use later (see Figure 9.23).

— **Component Object**—Exports the project as a single PhotoImpact object, which can also be added to the EasyPalette.

Figure 9.22
All the pieces put
together in HTML and
viewed in a Web
browser.

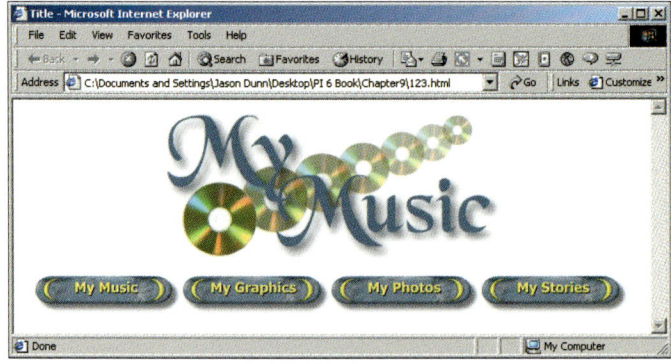

Figure 9.23
Our project exported to
PhotoImpact as objects.

TIP

If you want your buttons to be different sizes depending on the amount of
text they have on them, uncheck the Same width for all buttons box on the
Layout tab.

10

The PhotoImpact Web Design Studio

When I first began using graphics programs for Web design work, I tried several different kinds. I started out with Corel PhotoPAINT, used Paint Shop Pro for a while, and tried PhotoImpact 3.0. I eventually settled on Photoshop 4.0 because there were a lot of resources for it at the time. I enjoyed PhotoImpact 3.0, but as a Web design tool, it was lacking features I needed. When I saw PhotoImpact 4.0 in the stores, I picked it up and was immediately hooked on the great Web features it included. Over the next year I bounced back and forth between Photoshop and PhotoImpact 4.0 but found myself enjoying the speed of PhotoImpact more and more. When PhotoImpact 5.0 came out, it became my primary tool. And, as you might guess, PhotoImpact 6.0 has become my main graphics application. It's a powerhouse program that can do nearly any task I need, and as I wrote this book, I discovered even more about what it can do.

As I explained in earlier chapters, designing Web graphics involves a lot of different elements, but two of the most important things a Web design tool needs are speed and flexibility. Does the tool allow you to create the desired effect in three mouse clicks, or does it take ten? Does the program work the way you do or force you to adapt your methods to its peculiar ways? PhotoImpact is a great application in that there are several ways to do most things, and all of them are fast. And with a fully customizable toolbar and extensive right-click functions, PhotoImpact is one of the most flexible applications around.

Ulead has made this new version a very compelling tool for complete Web site design, from start to finish. It's unlikely this will be the only tool needed for a large site, but the vast majority of people with personal Web sites will find this to be quite a sufficient tool.

This chapter will walk you through the various Web design tools PhotoImpact has, explaining each tool separately. It will then cover the task of creating an actual page with full text and graphics. Let's start with one of the most important tools in this set: the Image Optimizer.

The Image Optimizer

Creating attractive graphics is one thing, but creating attractive graphics that download quickly over any modem is another thing altogether. Broadband Internet connections are rapidly spreading across the world, but those of us lucky to have them are still in the minority. The city in which I live, Calgary, Alberta, Canada, is a test-bed for different broadband technologies, so I was lucky enough to have had a cable modem in 1997. I moved to DSL in late 1999.

With broadband, file sizes are almost irrelevant. Yet even as more and more desktop computers get access to high-speed connections, portable devices are just starting to acquire Internet access—and often at very low speed rates (equivalent to a 14.4 Kbps modem). If I'm browsing a Web site on my iPaq Pocket PC connected to my cell phone, I don't want to wait sixty seconds for a single graphic to download. Waiting that long is both irritating and potentially expensive. Making your graphics lean is a critical step in designing effective Web graphics. The balance between quality and file size is hard to maintain, but you have a great tool to help you out: the Ulead Image Optimizer.

Understanding the Image Optimizer

The Image Optimizer (found under the Web menu on the menu bar) is a powerful tool and should be your final step in prepping your graphics for the Web. The job of the Image Optimizer is to give you, the user, real-time previews of the file formats (GIF, JPEG, PNG) and show you how the image changes as you alter settings. This is invaluable when making your graphics as small as possible, because you can do so without seriously compromising the quality. Let's walk through the various options the Image Optimizer gives you.

In order to activate the Image Optimizer, you first need to have an image open. Then select Image Optimizer from the Web menu. You'll see your image load in a new window as in Figure 10.1: Welcome to the Image Optimizer!

Figure 10.1
The Image Optimizer window.

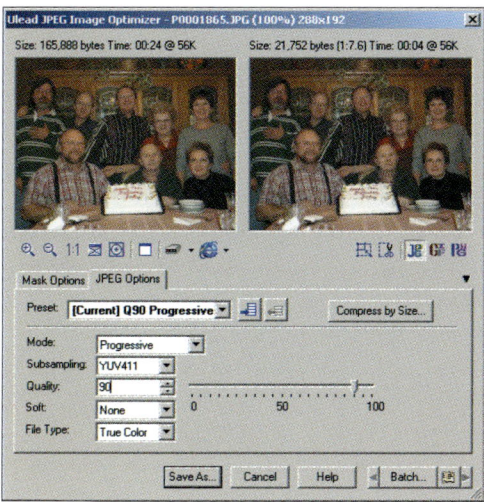

TIP

Looking for a fast way to load the Image Optimizer? Press the F4 key or, if you want to export a single object, right-click on the object and chose Image Optimizer.

There is a wealth of information on this first screen and a lot of icons worth exploring. First, your original image is in the left preview window, while the preview of your changes is in the right window. If you're changing the JPEG quality, the changes will be previewed in the right window. Above each image is the file size, compression ratio, and download time on a 56K modem (this is a default that you can change). Let's look at the icons you'll see on this screen and what they mean.

▶ **Zoom in**—This tool zooms in on the image. It's useful for determining how compression affects an image if you're running in a higher resolution than most of your Web site visitors.

▶ **Zoom out**—This function zooms out from the image and is useful for seeing more of a large image at once.

▶ **Show actual size**—This feature gives you a 100 percent view of the image. This is my preferred mode because you can see the image without reducing the quality, which happens when looking at a zoom level other than 100 percent.

▶ **Fit in window**—This enables you to zoom out on the image until it fits in the preview window.

▶ **Center in window**—You can automatically center the image in the middle of the preview window.

▶ **Display the compressed image**—This function toggles between showing only the compressed image and showing the before and after preview.

▶ **Modem speed menu**—This drop-down menu allows you to select the modem speed at which the estimated download time is based on: 14.4 Kbps modems up to 128 Kbps ISDN. Faster connections (like cable and DSL) aren't listed, likely because they can download images too quickly for this figure to matter. Remember that a 56 Kbps modem tops out around 7 KB per second, and that's under completely ideal conditions!

▶ **Browser preview**—Clicking this shows you your actual image on a temporary Web page, along with a summary of the settings, dimensions, and download time. If you have multiple browsers installed (Netscape and Microsoft Internet Explorer), you can choose which browser you want to use with the drop-down menu as well as add your own, like Opera.

▶ **Resample**—This allows you to make the image larger or smaller, based on a percentage or pixel amount.

▶ **Crop**—This functions much like the regular Crop Tool and other crop methods.

▶ **JPEG Image Optimizer**—This puts the Image Optimizer tool in JPEG mode (see Figure 9.24 in the previous chapter). Options in this mode include applying and saving presets for later use, different modes (Progressive is usually best), different Subsampling modes, the Quality slider, the Soft function (adds a soft-focus blur to your image), and File Type, which is used for creating grayscale images.

NOTE

The acronym JPEG is officially pronounced "jay-peg," not "jay-pee-ee-gee" or "jay-pee-gee."

▶ **GIF Image Optimizer**—This puts the Image Optimizer tool in GIF mode. The options in this mode include using and saving presets; picking the number of colors for your image (see below); what type of palette to use; the Soft function (adds a soft-focus blur); File Type (normal or grayscale); Lossy rating (the higher the number the more pixels are dropped and the resulting file size is smaller—a sort of brute force file size reduction technique); Dither (mixes image colors to make up for lost colors); Interlace (adds to file size slightly but allows progressive downloads—see below for more info); and Transparency (see below). The Weight option allows you to push the palette towards your image colors; if you have an image with a lot of red tones, for example, select the Red option.

NOTE

The acronym GIF is officially pronounced "jiff," not with a hard G. Some people still insist on using a hard G. Let them bask, but Compuserve, which created the format, knows best.

▶ **PNG Image Optimizer**—This puts the Image Optimizer tool in PNG mode, an emerging file format that may eventually replace GIFs, because the format supports high image quality and transparency like GIF but also supports high color quality like JPEG. As with the previous modes, it offers support for presets. The options here are a mix of the JPEG and GIF tools.

NOTE

The acronym PNG is pronounced "ping," not "pee-en-gee."

▶ **Compress by Size**—This function allows you to specify a desired file size or a compression ratio and lets PhotoImpact worry about the actual settings. This is useful for meeting the specific file size limits of certain Web sites (banner ads and so on).

▶ **Batch**—This function allows you to select a specific number of image setting previews, and the Image Optimizer will perform each setting and show you the result (see Figure 10.2). In the example shown, I have ten options, with quality settings from 55 to 100 in five-step increments. This allows me to see what my image would look like at each setting, see the file size for each (from 9K to 54K), and pick the best one for the job.

Figure 10.2
The Batch Results preview window.

▶ **Save As**—When you have the image you want, click Save As, give the image a file name, and choose the location.

NOTE

JPEG has an option for a Progressive mode, and GIF has an option for Interlace. Both of these functions have essentially the same job: When enabled, they allow the user to see a low-resolution version of your image right away, and, as the image downloads, it becomes more clear. In the case of GIF files, this adds about 10 percent to your file size. For JPEG files, it's actually beneficial for file size to leave it on Progressive. The Web design community is divided on the interlaced GIF issue; some people feel it's a gimmick and it's better to focus on making file sizes smaller, while others feel it's a legitimate option designed to reduced the wait time visitors have before they see something. Experiment with this feature and decide for yourself.

TIP

When using JPEG compression, you should experiment with the two different subsamplings modes. YUV411 results in the smallest file size, but if you have red tones in your image, YUV422 will give you much higher quality red tones at the expense of a very slightly larger file size.

JPEG Compression

As explained in Chapter 1, "An Introduction to Imaging Basics," the JPEG file format uses lossy compression. The higher you set the compression, the smaller your file size will be, but the more of your image will be lost. PhotoImpact was one of the first applications to give the user real-time previews of how different JPEG compression settings work. Using compression is simple: the lower the quality value, the more the image is compressed, and the smaller the file size is. As the quality level is dropped, more JPEG artifacts are introduced—artifacts are areas of the image where the data has been lost and will appear "chunky" or distorted. In the following four examples (Figure 10.3 to 10.6), compare the image quality and file size to see how these changes affect the image.

Figure 10.3
This image at 90 percent quality is 20 KB and has no noticeable artifacts.

Figure 10.4
This figure at 70 percent quality is 12 KB and has minor artifacts.

Figure 10.5
This figure at 30 percent quality is 7 KB and has mild artifacts.

Figure 10.6
This figure at 10 percent quality is 4 KB and has heavy artifacts.

As you can see, the file size shrinks a great deal (from 20KB to 4KB) when the quality is pushed down, but the cost is image quality—Figure 10.6 isn't acceptable, and Figure 10.5 is borderline. For my own sites, I use a setting between 70 and 85, depending on the purpose of the site. For general use, a setting of 75 is fine, but when I'm putting up my own photography, I use a setting of 85 to maintain crisp quality. Experiment on your own and find the best setting for your needs. Remember that, with smaller images, someone can browse through your site quickly, but if the image quality is poor, they'll leave even more quickly.

GIF Color Depth

The more colors a GIF has, the bigger the file size. It's a simple rule! Thankfully, Image Optimizer makes it very easy for you to control the exact number of colors your image has. Figure 10.7 shows the GIF interface of the Image Optimizer—changing the number of colors is simply a matter of punching in a number or using the slider. I can't emphasize this enough: Optimizing every GIF on your site can cut down dramatically on the amount of time users have to wait for a download. Be stingy with your file sizes! Try to make them as small as possible.

Figure 10.7
The GIF settings of
Image Optimizer.

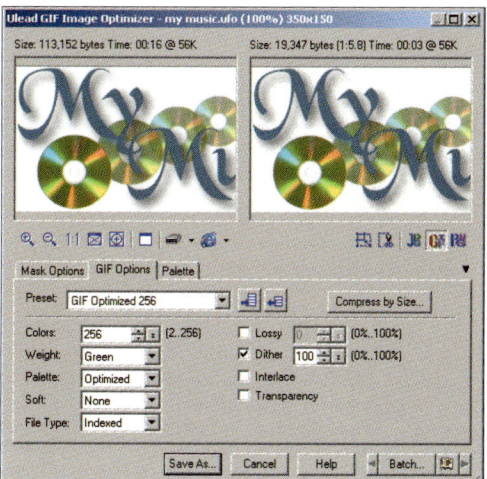

As you drop the number of colors from 256 (the maximum) down to 16 (the minimum), you'll see the file size drop and the image preview on the right change to reflect these new settings. There's no magic setting that's perfect for every image, but here are some things to keep in mind when optimizing your GIF files:

▶ Try your image with Dithering turned off and on. Not all images need dithering, and if the quality is acceptable with it turned off, you'll shave off about 10 percent of the file size.

▶ Experiment with different Palettes. The Detail palette makes the GIF look incredible (nearly like a JPEG file) but the file size will jump between ten and thirty percent. The Optimized palette is a safe tradeoff between quality and file size.

▶ Interlace adds about 10 percent to the file size.

▶ If your image can be made grayscale, select Gray as the file type. Your image will be smaller.

▶ Preview your image at its actual size so you can see the changes (1:1 ratio).

▶ If you're running at 1024×768 or higher, try dropping your resolution down a few notches. GIF quality is hard to benchmark when the image is very small.

▶ Many images can be knocked down to 128 colors and even 64 colors with little loss in quality. Experiment!

TIP
Remember to eliminate as many unnecessary pixels as possible by cropping. The fewer pixels there are in your image, the smaller your overall file size will be.

Transparency

Transparency is a popular Web site effect, but one that can be difficult to achieve on a consistent basis. In the early years of graphic design, applications would let you pick a single color to remove. This was fine if your image was suited to it, but more often than not, single-color transparency resulted in a lot of ugly Web graphics. Modern tools like the Image Optimizer allow multiple-color GIF transparency, and better yet, they make it easy to do. The key to successful transparency is planning ahead. Let's go through a quick example.

1.   Our image in Figure 10.8 needs to "float" on a blue patterned background (see Figure 10.9). While with enough painstaking work we could make a white-backgrounded image float seamlessly on a blue background, there's a faster way: a tuned fill. A tuned fill is simply a background fill that is set to match the color of the eventual background the graphic will need to float over. To get the right color, I first take a sample of the blue tile in Figure 10.9 using the Eyedropper Tool. I chose the most dominant shade of blue in that image.

Figure 10.8
The graphic that needs to be made transparent.

Figure 10.9
The background of the Web page.

2.   Next I'll fill (CTRL+F) the white background with the shade of blue I selected with the Eyedropper Tool. My image now looks like Figure 10.10.

Figure 10.10
A Tuned Fill for our image.

3. Press F4 to launch the Image Optimizer—click the GIF mode icon, check off the Transparency box, and switch to the Mask Options tab. Under the Mask options, use the drop-down menu to select Pick Color, then click on the Add to Mask button as Figure 10.11 shows.

Figure 10.11
The GIF Mask Options.

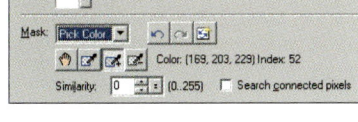

4. The cursor will turn into a small eyedropper—this is the stage where you click on the color you wish to add to the transparency mask. Click on the blue background, and it will disappear (see Figure 10.12).

Figure 10.12
The transparency mask is engaged.

5. Save the image and preview it in the Web browser—Figure 10.13 shows us perfect transparency! It's critical to get the first two steps correct in this process. Figure 10.14 shows an attempt at taking a white-background image and making it transparent without using a tuned fill. You can see the white "halo" around the blue letters; on a Web site, this severely detracts from the overall quality.

Figure 10.13
Perfect transparency.

Figure 10.14
Poorly done transparency.

CHAPTER 10

NOTE
If you're looking for a more in-depth discussion on transparency, check out the two-part series I did for Ulead's WebUtilities Web site: **http://www.webutilities.com/community/tutorials.htm.**

The Background Designer

In the early years of Web design, the biggest way your site could differentiate itself from other sites was with a "neat" background. Tiled backgrounds were difficult to create properly, and many tools and Web sites sprang up to explain the cryptic process. Thankfully, times and tools have changed, and while backgrounds aren't as important as they once were, an attractive background can still add a dash of class to your site.

The Background Designer is found under the Web menu on the menu bar or by pressing SHIFT+B on your keyboard. It has many options (see Figure 10.15), but it's fun and easy to use. Let's start at the top and work our way down. Your first choice is to generate a new file with the background or apply the background to a current image. In most cases, you'll want to create a new file, and 80×80 pixels is fine for most tiling backgrounds. You have the option of selecting from Schema, which are essentially groups of presets. They include everything from random pastel patterns to cloth tartan textures.

Figure 10.15
The Background
Designer.

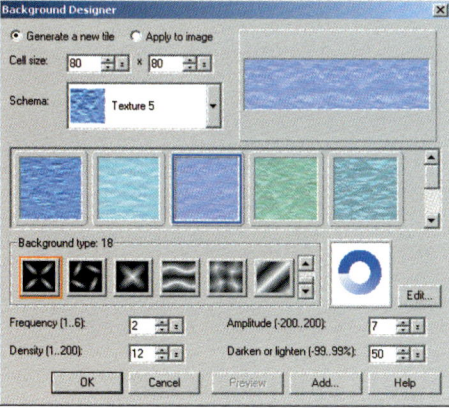

Each Schema contains a group of backgrounds that you can scroll through, and each background has both a Background type and a Palette Ramp that it's based on. There are twenty-three background types to select from, and each one will change the look of your background. Even better, there are 110 Palette Ramps to choose from with vast editing possibilities. And, by changing the Frequency, Density, Amplitude, and Dark/Light factors, you have an unlimited texture generation tool at your disposal.

One word of caution: Backgrounds are good only when used in moderation. They shouldn't obscure your content in any way, nor should they be the focal point of attention. I've found a way to mix textures with content and have them both balance out nicely: HTML tables with single-color backgrounds. Figure 10.16 shows our previous example with some content added. By placing the content in a table with a white background and black bordered edge, I can present the text to the visitor without having my background distract them while still maintaining the look and feel of my site.

Figure 10.16
Texture and content.

TIP
You can also apply your generated background to a selection. So if you want to apply it to some text, select the text using the Pick Tool or Text Tool, create your background with the Apply to Image option selected, and click OK. Instant texture!

Image Maps

An Image Map is a series of X and Y image coordinates that connect with HTML hyperlinks. Image maps are used when designing Web site navigation tools that are more complicated than buttons. Figure 10.17 shows an example of this: I created this graphic using a hand from the EasyPalette Image Library, applied a Natural Painting Charcoal effect to it, created the circles using the path tools and adjusted their transparency, and finally, I added some text. I then combined each text item, and the circles around them, into a single object. And voilà! We have a navigation tool!

Figure 10.17
A complex navigation tool requires an image map.

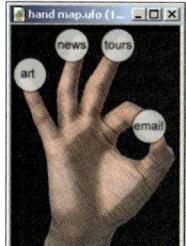

The Image Map function is found under the Web menu on the menu bar or by pressing SHIFT+H on the keyboard. Here's the important part: The Image Map tool will work only on images with separate objects. You can't create an image map from a merged image, so keep your image in its object mode. So, let's create an image map, shall we?

1. Once you've found your way into the tool, you need to set up the map points and hyperlinks (see Figure 10.18). The tool is "smart" in that it detects object groups, and it gives you the option of creating links based on the group or the individual objects within the group. First, select the object you want to be hyperlinked by clicking on it, either in the image at the top or by selecting it from the list on the bottom left.

Figure 10.18
Setting up an
image map.

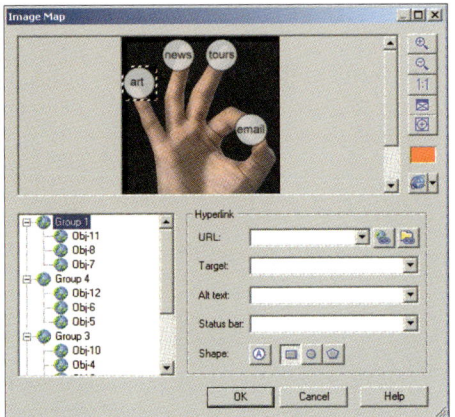

2. Next, select the group you want to hyperlink. In the right side of the
    window you'll find a Hyperlink area. This is where we fill in all the
    hyperlink information. The URL designation is the location of the
    HTML page you want to link to, Target is for specifying a frameset,
    Alt text is what users will see when they hover over the image map
    zone, and Status bar is the text they will see in the bottom status bar
    of their Web browsers. Fill in the appropriate information for each
    section (as I've done in Figure 10.19).

Figure 10.19
Filling in the image
map information.

3. Once you click OK, you'll go back to the main PhotoImpact window.
    The final step is to save your HTML project by looking under the File
    menu on the menu bar and choosing Save for Web > As HTML. The
    results in Figure 10.20 are impressive!

Figure 10.20
Our final image map.

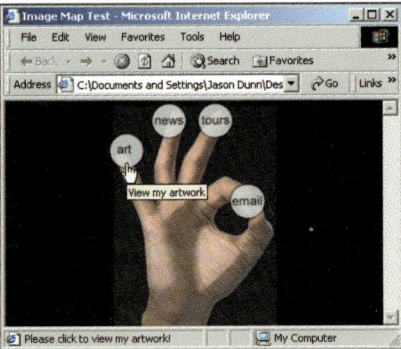

What I found a little surprising is that the UFO file can contain complete HTML information. When you save your image map, and you need to come back later and change the color of one of the graphics, you can do so without altering the map coordinates you've set up previously. You just make the change and export the file again.

> **TIP**
>
> If you're working with a complex image map, it's probably worth your time to name each of the objects so they're easier to work with in the Image Map tool. To do so, right-click on the object, select properties, and change the Name field. This doesn't work with groups—you can't change the name of a group, only the individual objects.

The Button Designer

When I first started using PhotoImpact 4.0, the Button Designer was one of my favorite tools. It's surprisingly fun to create customized little buttons with beveled edges and shiny surfaces! Buttons can be used for a variety of things: navigation, advertising links, triggers for multi-media events, and more. The Button Designer has two modes: Any Shape and Rectangular, each found under Web > Button Designer on the menu bar. The Any Shape mode has presets and more control over lighting, while the Rectangular mode is very basic. Using the Button Designer is a snap. Let's get started by walking through the Any Shape Button Designer.

1. Create a simple shape using the standard Path Drawing Tool on the Tool Panel. I've created an ellipse (Figure 10.21). Make sure the object you've created is selected.

Figure 10.21
Stage one of our button.

2. Under the Web menu on the menu bar, select Button Designer > Any Shape. The Button Designer Any Shape settings window will load (Figure 10.22). There are five tabs that allow for the fine-tuning of your button:

    — **Basic**—This main tab contains the Light angle, Light elevation, Bevel size, Bevel smoothness designations, and more than thirty presets for buttons.

— **Bevel**—This tab controls the Bevel type and assorted bevel controls. If you're looking for some strange bevel effects, this is where to find them.

— **Light**—The Light tab controls the number of lights, the angle and elevation of them, the color, and a few other settings.

— **Shadow**—This feature has all of the controls you know and love for controlling shadows.

— **Warping**—These two controls allow you to alter the Warp level and Smoothness of the warp. Essentially, the Warping feature is an inward distortion on the button.

Figure 10.22
Button Designer (Any Shape) options.

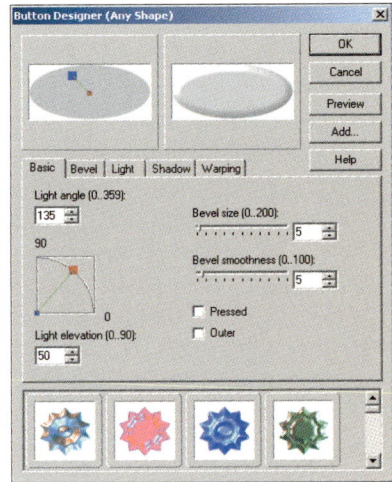

3. On the Basic tab, set the Light angle at 330, the Bevel size at 35, and the Bevel smoothness at 5.

4. On the Shadow tab, add an X offset of 5, a Y offset of 5, shadow with a Soft edge of 10, and a Transparency of 50.

5. Click off the Warping box and enter a Smoothness value of 38 and a Warp level of 60.

6. Figure 10.23 shows our shiny, bumpy button, ready for some text.

Figure 10.23
Our final button.

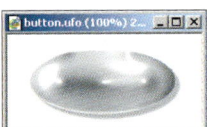

There are a lot of button combinations you can create. Figure 10.24 shows only a few of the possibilities based on the presets.

Figure 10.24
Some of the possibilities with the Button Designer.

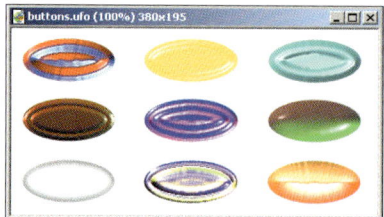

Rollover Effects

Rollover Effects, sometimes called Mouseover Effects or Onmouseovers, are very popular Web site effects that help users figure out what elements they can click on by changing the graphic when they move the cursor over it. Sometimes the rollover graphic will be an inverted color, a glowing effect, or even a new image or text. PhotoImpact supports two- and three-stage rollovers: A two-stage effect changes the graphic when the cursor is moved over it, while a three-stage effect adds a new graphic when the image is clicked on. PhotoImpact 6.0 doesn't allow you to add sound to the rollover, although I hope they add it to future versions. Let's walk though an exercise in using this tool.

1. First we need to create the graphics for the rollover effects. I've used the Path tool to create three simple circular buttons, each a different color, with corresponding text. I created three because I want a three-stage rollover. For rollovers, you need complete objects, not groups. In the case of my graphics, I had to select the blue button, select the text on it, right-click, and choose Merge as Single Object. I then repeated the steps for the yellow and red buttons. See Figure 10.25.

Figure 10.25
Buttons ready for a rollover effect.

2. SHIFT+click on each object to select all three, then look under the Web menu on the menu bar and select Rollover. You can also press SHIFT+R on the keyboard to bring up the window in Figure 10.26. You'll see each of your images previewed. The image on the left is your default image; the one that will load with no cursor over it. The image in the middle is the graphic that will load on the cursor rollover, and the one on the right is the image that loads when you click the graphic. The Preview window provides a live test zone that shows you exactly how your image will look.

Figure 10.26
The Rollover window.

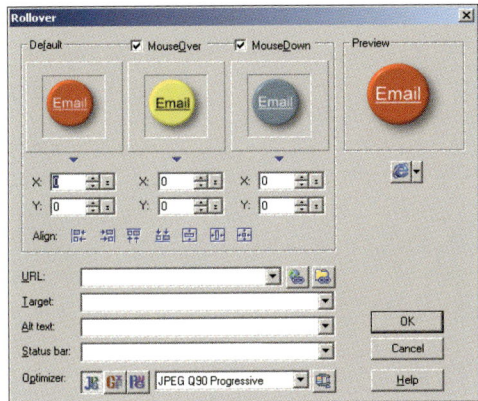

3. Below each image is a small, blue drop-down arrow. When you click the arrow, it drops down a small selection window that allows you to pick which graphic you want in that position (see Figure 10.27). Because I want the blue button to be my default graphic, I'll switch them around. There are options here for X and Y offsets, but unless you're planning on doing something very clever, leave these all at zero. There are also Alignment options you can use if your images are uneven, but I strongly recommend not touching these. Every time I tried to use them, all my images ran together and the rollover effect was ruined. Use them only when one rollover image is bigger or smaller than another.

Figure 10.27
Selecting the appropriate rollover graphic.

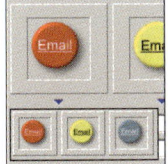

4. The next step is to add in the HTML information for your links (see Figure 10.28). Add in the HTML page URL you want the link to go to, the Target frame (if applicable), the Alt text, and the Status bar text. At this stage you'll also want to optimize your graphics. Click on the graphic mode (JPEG, GIF, or PNG) and use the drop-down menu to select a preset. Alternatively, you can click on the Image Optimizer icon to the right of the drop-down menu and optimize each image on your own.

Figure 10.28
Adding in the HTML information.

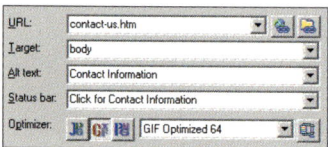

5. Click OK and you'll be returned to your workspace, but your buttons will be merged into one. From the File menu on the menu bar, choose Save for Web > As HTML. You can also use CTRL+ALT+S. Select a file name, and save your HTML file (see Figure 10.29). When you open it up, you should have a fully functioning three-stage rollover!

Figure 10.29
Our final rollover effect.

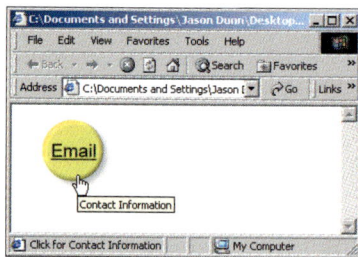

NOTE

If you want to use this rollover in an HTML page that's already in existence, you'll need to copy the code. In most browsers, you can right-click and select View Source to see the code. You'll want to copy everything from <SCRIPT LANGUAGE="JavaScript" TYPE="text/javascript"> to </SCRIPT>. This is part of the JavaScript that makes it all work. The other part of the script is in the code for the image: Look for <A HREF= and copy everything contained within that HTML call. Extracting the HTML code isn't the simplest of tasks, but once you do it, you'll understand a lot more about how HTML and JavaScript work.

TIP

If you want to change an element on one of your buttons, you'll need to break apart the rollover. To do so, right-click on the rollover group, select Web Attributes, then Split Rollover. This returns your buttons to their individual states.

If you make an error on some part of the rollover, you can right-click and choose edit rollover to change any aspect of it. Pressing SHIFT+E also brings up the rollover window.

Small file sizes are absolutely critical when using rollover effects. When the user moves the cursor over the image, the new rollover file needs to download in one or two seconds. If it doesn't, the browser will show the file as a broken image link. What this means in practical terms is that your images need to be extremely small, around 2 Kb or 3 Kb. The exception to this is if you have a preload page where you deliver all the graphics to the user "behind the scenes": When the rollover graphic is requested on subsequent pages, it comes from the cache on the user's hard drive rather than the server.

TIP

If you want to learn to construct your own rollover effects manually in HTML and JavaScript, read an article I wrote on the Ulead WebUtilities site that can assist you: go to **http://www.webutilities.com/community/tutorials.htm** and look for my JavaScript tutorial.

The Slicer

The PhotoImpact Slicer is an often-overlooked tool that has some powerful uses when applied properly. The tool allows you to slice up images in any combination and then export the individual pieces with custom Image Optimizer settings. Some can be GIF, some JPEG, or any combination of the two. The images can also have HTML information for hyperlinks, making it an alternative to the Image Map tool.

Why would you want to slice up an image? There are several reasons:

▶ Small images download faster than larger ones, giving your visitors the impression that the download is happening faster.

▶ If you have images on your Web site that you want to protect, slice them up into six or nine parts. You'll defeat the people who would either link to the image directly from their own site (which steals your site bandwidth) or right-click on the image and use Save As to take it. There are still ways to get around this, but a sliced-up image will deter most image thieves.

▶ If you're exporting an image that needs to have several parts at specific sizes, the Image Slicer gives you exact pixel dimensions. For example, I was creating a new Today screen banner for my Pocket PC and needed to cut the image into two pieces. The top one needed to be exactly 20 pixels high and the bottom one 40 pixels high. I was able to perform this quickly and easily using the Slicer tool.

▶ File sizes can be made smaller if you export the photographic elements in your image as JPEGs and the text elements as GIFs.

Different options include slicing up images evenly (you just punch in the number of rows and columns), manually with horizontal and vertical tools and preview optimization results within the same window. Figure 10.30 shows the tool in action. You can find the tool under Web > Slicer on the menu bar or by pressing SHIFT+S on your keyboard.

Figure 10.30
The Slicer tool with an even 4×4 slice.

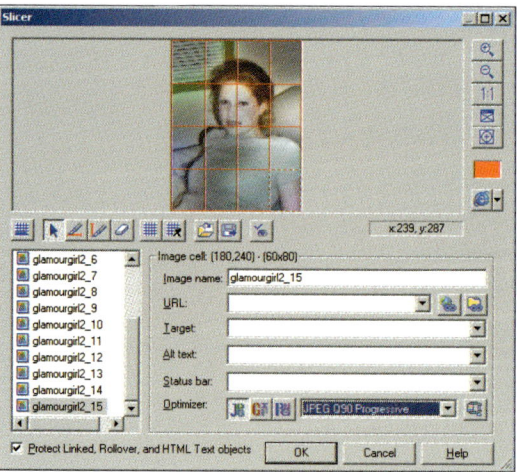

TIP

If you have an image slice that you'll be performing over and over, you can Export the slice table and use it again later by Importing it for the next image.

TIP

For a more detailed look at the subject, read my article entitled "The Benefits of Image Slicing" on the Ulead WebUtilities site: **http://www.webutilities.com/community/tutorials.htm.**

Creating Seamless Tiled Backgrounds

If you don't want to use the Background Designer, or already have an image you want to make into a tiled background, PhotoImpact has a tool you'll find useful: Create Seamless Tile. Found under the Web menu on the menu bar, this tool takes most of the manual work out of creating a seamless tiled background. Let's run through a quick use of this tool:

1. Open the image you want to tile and draw a selection around the part of the image that you want to be the central part of the tile. In Figure 10.31, I have a PowerPoint slide that I think would make an interesting tiled background. Using the Standard Selection Tool, I've drawn a selection around the text in the center. It's important to understand that in order to blur the edges of the image and make it a seamless tile, you need to give the effect room to work. When you draw your selection, do so by drawing 5 percent to 10 percent inside the border of your image.

Figure 10.31
Prepping our image for tiling.

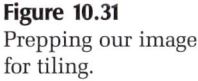
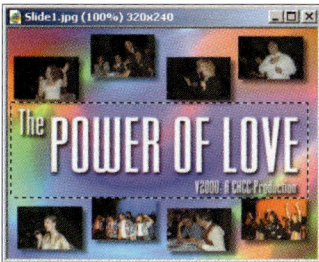

2. Once the selection has been made, go to the Web menu and choose Create Seamless Tile. A small settings window will load (see Figure 10.32). The merge sizes will max different maximum values depending on how much space you had for the selection. Adjusting the Merge Size and Merge Ratio will result in drastically different tiled backgrounds, and you can press the Preview button to see a full screen sample of what your tiled background will look like. Figure 10.33 shows a sample with the Merge size set at 2 and the Merge ratio set at 50, while Figure 10.34 shows a more dramatic blending that occurs when the Merge size is set past 30.

Figure 10.32
Seamless Tile settings window.

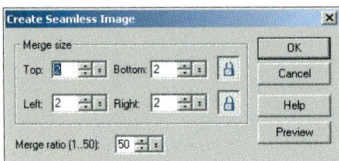

Figure 10.33
A small Merge Size setting produces a subtle effect.

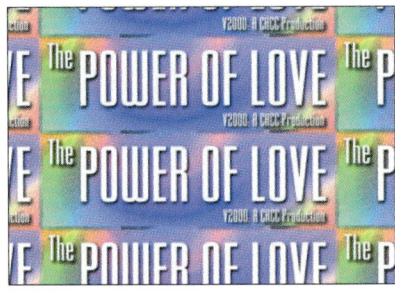

Figure 10.34
A large Merge Size setting produces a more extreme effect.

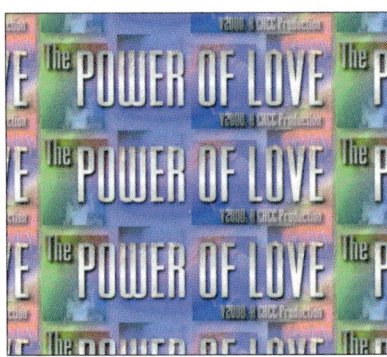

3. Once you've finalized your settings, click OK. This will return you to the PhotoImpact work area and your image will be waiting for you (see Figure 10.35). Save the image as a JPEG or GIF file (depending on the complexity of the colors) and reference it in your HTML program or with the PhotoImpact tools (we'll explain these later in this chapter).

Figure 10.35
Our final seamless tile.

TIP

If you're looking to use a flashy background but want to minimize its distracting nature, try changing the transparency.

Designing Entire Web Sites with PI 6.0

So far in this chapter we've covered a variety of the tools that you have at your disposal when creating Web graphics, backgrounds, rollover effects, image maps, image slicing, and optimization of every last pixel. The biggest change in the PhotoImpact line is that 6.0 now allows you to design entire Web sites, from start to finish, with HTML code and text support. This is a very ambitious move on Ulead's part, because it creates a new type of hybrid application that hasn't existed before—the graphic designer's HTML studio. It seems a logical extension: When I'm creating a site, the bulk of the initial work is in graphical concepts and design ideas, and that's all time spent in PhotoImpact.

I've developed a method of moving from PhotoImpact concept to actual HTML, but with PhotoImpact 6.0 many of the steps I used to take are no longer necessary. I can design the concepts, insert real HTML text, and export the stuff as a functional Web site. While PhotoImpact won't replace FrontPage 2000 as my overall site management tool, the features added into version 6.0 are a large step in the right direction.

The best way to show you how these new features work is to jump right into an example: I'm going to create a new graphical look for a personal Web site I have and use the new features in PhotoImpact 6.0 to do it. This example will be fairly lengthy and will incorporate many of the things we've covered in earlier chapters. Let's get started!

1.   File > New on the menu bar, select Standard for the image size, and choose Web page 600×440 (see Figure 10.36). I'm choosing this because I'm running in 800×600 resolution as I write there. Were I in my preferred resolution of 1280×1024, I would have chosen Web Page 750×550.

Figure 10.36
Starting a Web page with a standard file size.

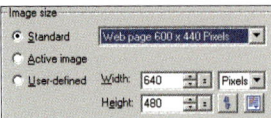

2.   Now that we have a blank canvas, it's time to get creative. The site I'm working on is a technology-oriented site that focuses on portable computing. I want a crisp, clean look, in muted tones of blues and grays. I also want a flat, 2D look to the site. I'm going to create a fairly standard left/top interface, and I'll use a few buttons along the way. The first step in creating the new design is to switch to the Path Drawing Tool and select Rounded Rectangle as my shape (see Figure 10.37).

Figure 10.37
Selecting Rounded Rectangle.

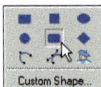

3.   I'm going to draw a shape near the top. This will be the location of the page header and logo. I want it to cover most of the top space but leave enough space free on the left for the other section (see Figure 10.38).

Figure 10.38
Creating our first shapes.

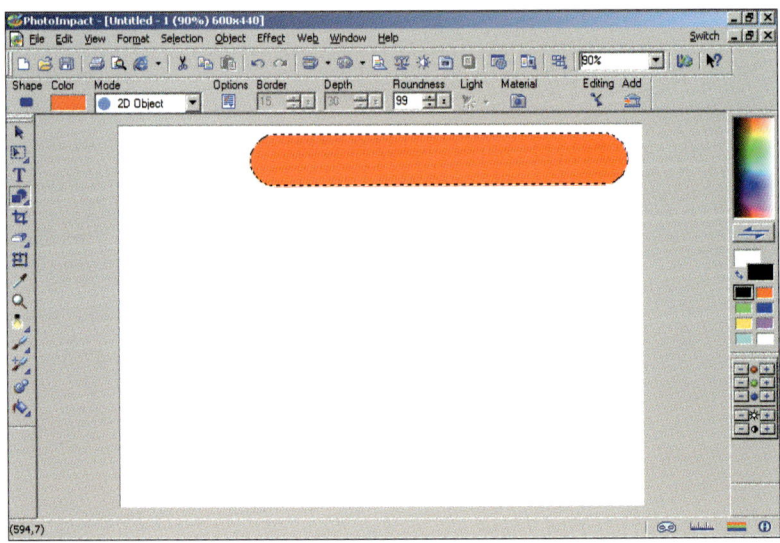

4. Both the color and the roundness of the edges are wrong. I'll change the color to my favorite shade of blue by clicking on the Color box and change the Roundness value to 30. This gives me the shape in Figure 10.39.

Figure 10.39
Our modified shape.

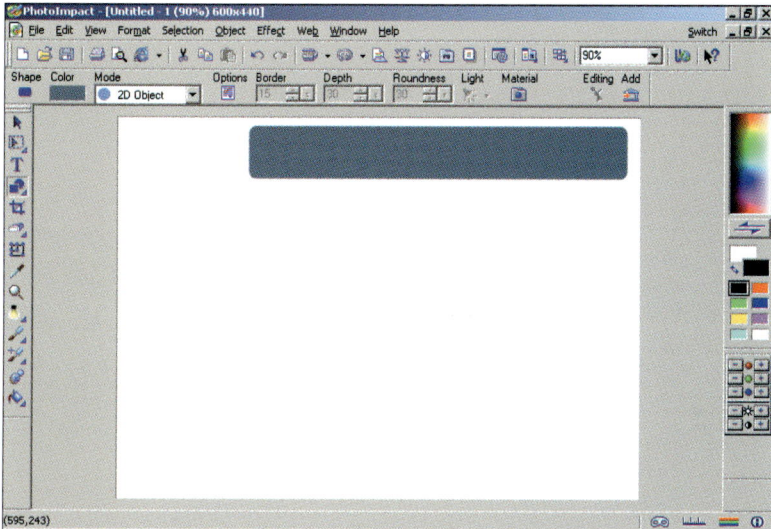

5. Next I want to create something to go in the top left. Because this is a site about mobile computing devices, some imagery might help. I'll go out and collect some images from the Web, copy them into a separate file, and resize them to fit in the corner as individual objects. Figure 10.40 shows the results of my efforts.

Figure 10.40
Adding some interest to our site.

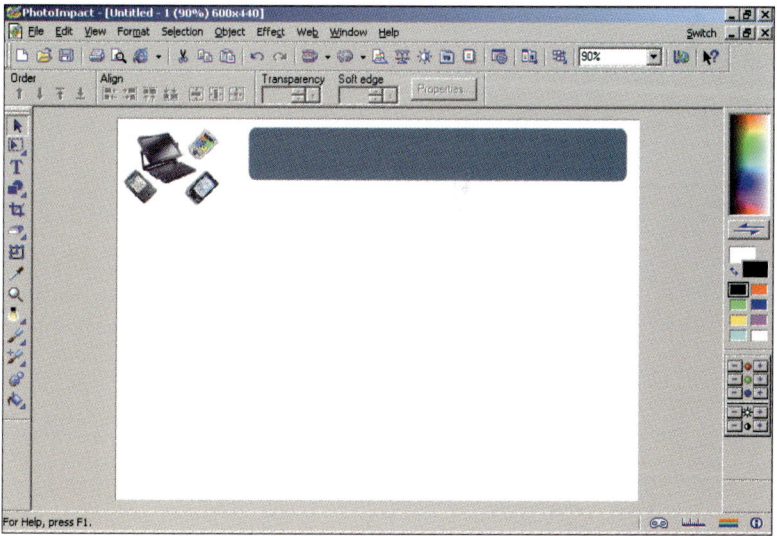

6. Next, I want to create a series of buttons below the device images. I'll use the Path Tool as before and create rounded rectangles with a roundness value of 30. Once I've created the first button, I'll hold down the CTRL key and click and drag on the image to create copies, while also holding down the Shift key to make sure they stay in vertical alignment with the original button. This sounds complicated, but it's really easy once you get the hang of it!

7. Next I'll select all the buttons by using the Pick Tool and holding down the Shift key to select each button. Then I'll right-click and Align > Space Evenly all the icons. The results are down in Figure 10.41.

Figure 10.41
Our buttons are in place.

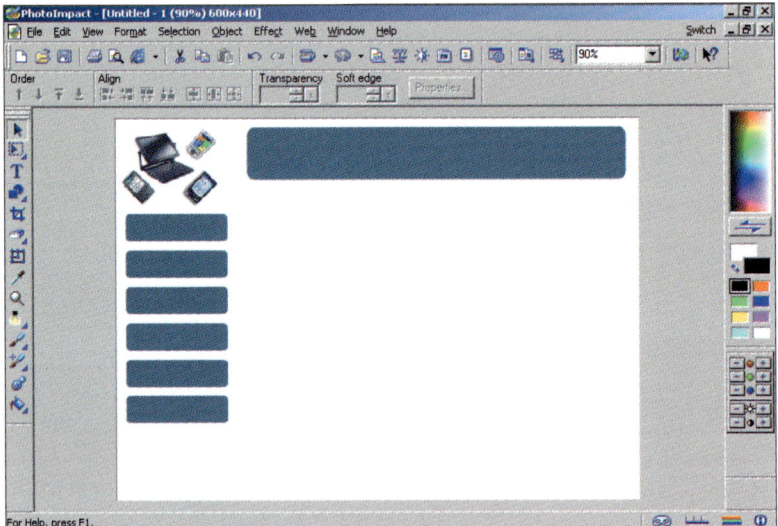

8. The large blue banner at the top is looking a little out of alignment with the other images, so I'll click on it. Using the arrow keys on my keyboard, I'll nudge the banner a few pixels down and to the left.

9. Now it's time to add some text to our buttons. I'll click on the Text Tool, then click on the first button for the location of the text. I'll enter the text (see Figure 10.42), guess at a font size of 15, and click OK. That font size was correct, so I'll click on the text once, hold down the CTRL key and the SHIFT key at the same time, and copy the text by dragging it, keeping it in perfect vertical alignment with the source text.

Figure 10.42
Entering text using the
Text Entry Box.

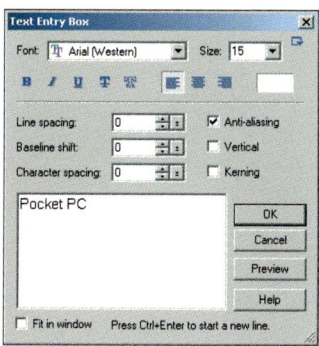

10. Once all the button text pieces are in place, I'll then change the text
    to the appropriate values (the different sections on my site).

11. I'll then add some appropriate text to the banner area at the top of my
    site. Using two fonts (Arial Black and Zombie), different font sizes for
    contrast, a drop shadow on two of the major objects, and a mild 3D
    Round effect on the two large text pieces, I end up with Figure 10.43.
    Looking at the whole page (see Figure 10.44), I can see it's starting to
    come together!

Figure 10.43
Our banner logo for
the site.

Figure 10.44
Things are starting to
come together!

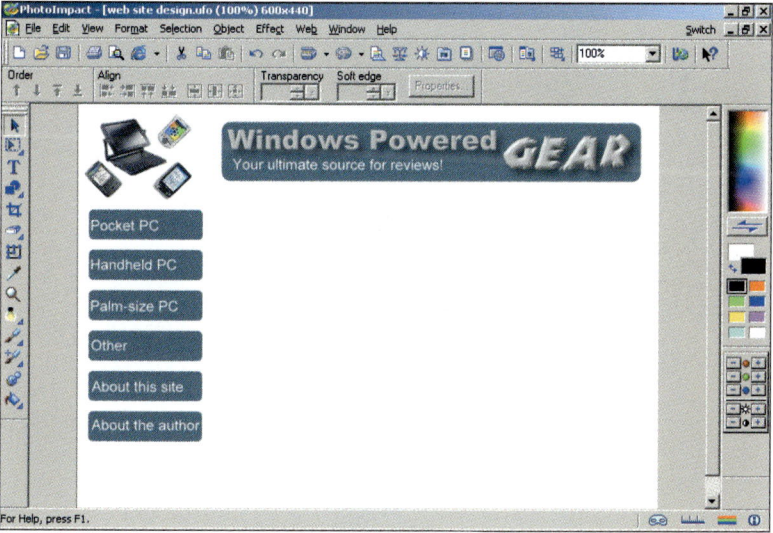

12. Next I need to fill in the middle space with something eye-catching. The EasyPalette Image Library has a hand figure I'll use, and when combined with some colored text, I get Figure 10.45.

Figure 10.45
Adding some central content.

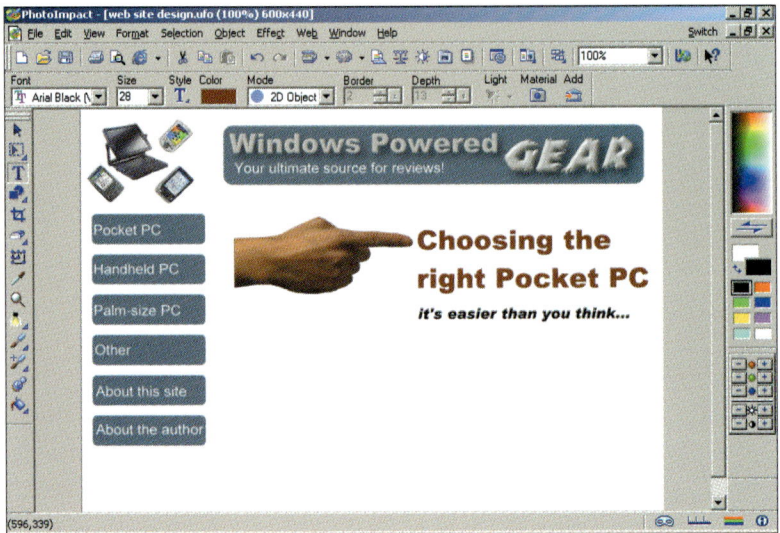

13. I've decided that I want to create rollover effects on the buttons. Because everything is object-oriented, this is easy to do at any step of the game. First, I'll select each of the buttons and text and make copies of them (see Figure 10.46).

Figure 10.46
Making copies of the buttons.

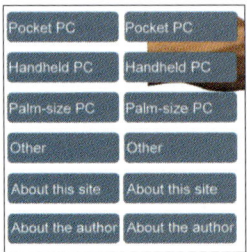

14. Now I need to change the color of the rollover buttons, both the background and the text. Yellow background and black text work well together. Using the Fill command (CTRL+F), I'll fill the blue buttons to yellow, and the white text to black (see Figure 10.47).

Figure 10.47
Changing button colors.

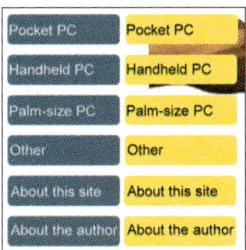

15. I'll then merge each button and text as a single object, then select the first set of blue and yellow buttons, and hit SHIFT+R into the Rollover tool. Once there, I'll enter the URL links, Alt text, and everything else I need. This procedure needs to be repeated for each button. When I'm done, my workspace looks just like in Figure 10.45 above.

16. Now I want to insert some HTML text content into the body of the image. Under the Web menu on the menu bar, I'll select HTML Text Object. This gives me a text box (shown in Figure 10.48) into which I can enter text. This tool allows you to create text that will remain as text when you export the project to HTML. This is a very critical feature because it allows you to actually create a full Web page with text, something you could not do in previous versions. You can specify the style (H1, H2, and so on), the font and weight, the size, create bulleted or numbered lists, indent the text, control the alignment, and manage the text color. Lastly, you can also create hyperlinks in your text by selecting the words you want to turn into the hyperlink, and then clicking the Hyperlink icon (to the left of Help). Once my text is entered, I click OK.

Figure 10.48
The HTML Text
Entry Box.

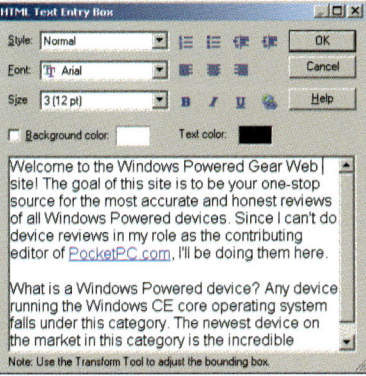

17. Once my text is completed, I can resize the box by adjusting the black box handles using the Transform Tool (see Figure 10.49).

Figure 10.49
Resizing boxes with handles.

18. My Web page looks like it's complete! Figure 10.50 shows the completed page, ready for export.

Figure 10.50
The final page, ready for export.

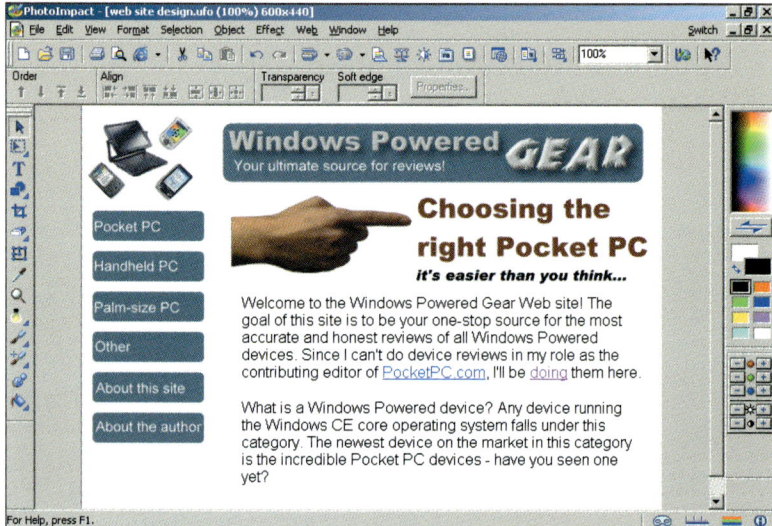

19. To export this page, I'll go to File > Save For Web > As HTML on the menu bar. Figure 10.51 shows the final project in HTML. The layout is duplicated exactly, which I have to admit excited me a lot the first time I saw it. I've been waiting for a true WYSIWYG graphic to HTML tool for a long time, and it looks like PhotoImpact is the first program to actually deliver on this promise.

Figure 10.51
All done—image to HTML, perfect layout match. Beautiful!

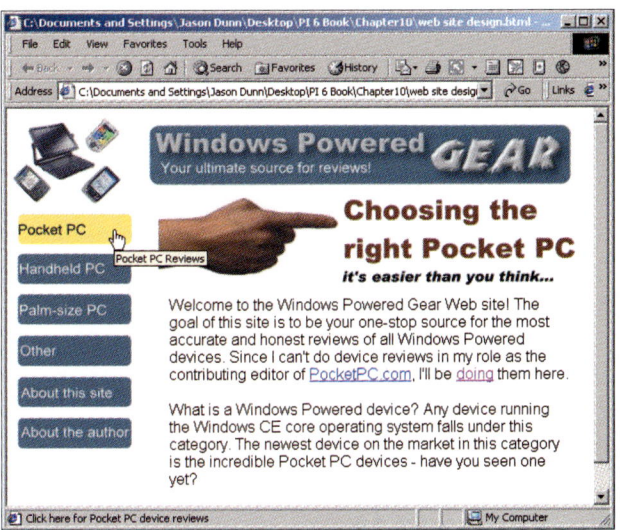

TIP

If you want to create an e-mail link in your HTML text object, put "mailto:" in front of your email address, without the quotes. In Step 16 above, I created my text object with an e-mail hyperlink. I did so by entering "mailto: jason@kensai.com" (without the quotes) into the Hyperlink field.

CAUTION

If you're exporting your project to HTML and you're getting error messages about the object not falling inside the boundaries of the document, try shifting the object away from the edge. If it's an HTML text object, shift it away from other graphical objects. If it's too close to the graphics, PhotoImpact will get confused and turn the HTML text into graphical text, defeating the whole purpose.

Other Ulead Web Design Tools

Ulead has made a name for itself in the world of Web design tools by creating applications that target a specific need that do it better than anything else on the market. In almost every area for which Ulead has developed an application, the product has won awards and industry praise. I'm one of those people who installs and uninstalls a few applications every day because I'm always looking for new programs to help make my tasks easier or help me to get creative and have some fun.

Although there are many excellent applications out there on the market, I usually end up coming back to the Ulead products because I truly believe they are among the best in their respective fields. Let's take a quick look at some of the Ulead products on the market.

Cool 3D

Trial Version: http://www.ulead.com/cool3d/

This 3D tool is used for creating 3D text, logos, and animation. It's fairly simple to use (although there's certainly room for improvement), but it has a lot of potential for creative use. Creating 3D text is easy in the program—all it takes is a few clicks and the application of some creative thought. It has many presets and textures, so you can customize the look of your graphic; and it also includes many objects and moving paths (for animation). It can import 2D graphics and through the use of a path editor, users can make 3D graphics out of their 2D logos and text. One of my favorite features is the support for animated GIFs and movie formats like AVI and QuickTime: You can create an animated sequence and then insert it into a movie project using Media Studio Pro. Very cool stuff! Figure 10.52 shows the user interface and a quick 3D graphic I created.

Figure 10.52
Cool 3D 3.0 in action.

SmartSaver Pro

Trial Version: http://www.ulead.com/ssp/

SmartSaver Pro can be thought of as a big brother to Image Optimizer. It's based on the same idea, but it offers a lot more in the way of options, has system-wide integration, and can be started up independently of PhotoImpact. It offers support for more complex rollovers than the PhotoImpact rollover tool can perform (including support for audio and remote rollovers); an integrated slicing tool; basic animation control; custom color palette design; and control over area quality in an image (meaning you can make one part of a JPEG image quality 80 while the rest is quality 50). My favorite features are the way it's integrated with the operating system and the coolness of its batch features. SmartSaver Pro will install itself as an option on a right-click menu, so when I need to resize a hundred digital images, I simply select them all, right-click, and activate the batch mode. I can resize images and save them in different formats, completely unattended, making this a fantastic timesaver for me. Figure 10.53 shows the SmartSaver Pro interface.

Figure 10.53
SmartSaver Pro 3.0.

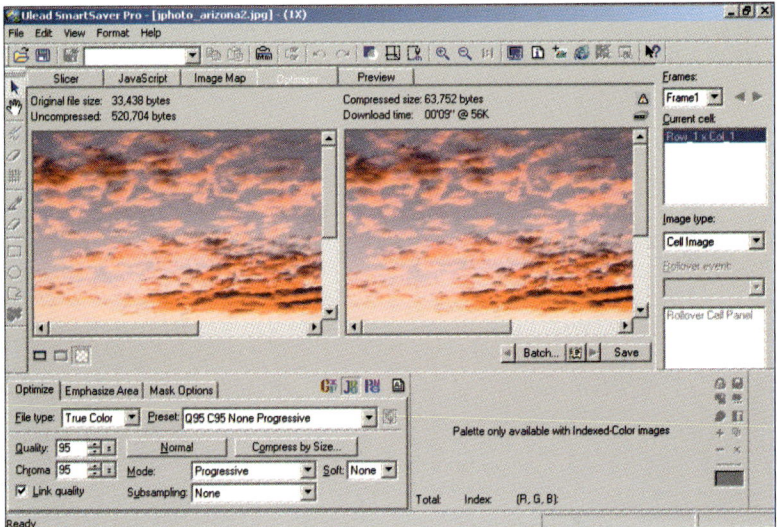

Photo Explorer

Freeware Download: http://www.ulead.com/pex/

Photo Explorer is an application that covers a lot of functions at once: It's an image browser, quickly creating thumbnails for whatever directory you point it at. It's also a slide show tool, allowing you to create Web-based slideshows of your images or to create self-extracting slide shows for distribution to friends and family. Photo Explorer also has built-in camera and scanner functions, allowing you to tie into both kinds of devices if they are connected. Wallpaper tools, auto-rename tools, thumbnail printing tools, and tight integration with Ulead's iMira service (covered in Chapter 13, "Gearing Up: Printing, Sharing, and More") make this free package a good tool for anyone to have. The freeware version has ads in it, but as a PhotoImpact owner, you should qualify for the ad-free version (check the Web site for more details). Figure 10.54 shows the interface of the program—I personally find it a bit cluttered, but it's totally customizable and you can't beat the price!

Figure 10.54
Photo Explorer 6.0.

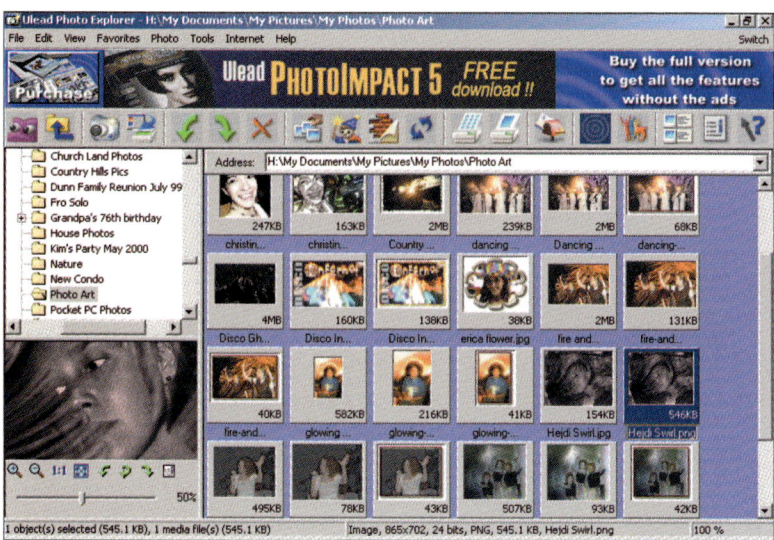

Other Ulead Applications

Ulead is involved in more than just the Web design realm. Its video-editing suite, MediaStudio Pro 6.0, has won many awards and is a viable contender to the competing Adobe Premier. Although I consider myself to be an amateur in the field of digital video, I've put together a few projects and found MediaStudio Pro to be an excellent tool for video work. Ulead also has a more entry-level video product called Video Studio. This is aimed at video beginners and offers simple methods for putting together videos.

A "little brother" to PhotoImpact is PhotoExpress. It's a more basic package that focuses on photo editing rather than Web graphics, but it also has an incredible number of templates and presets for cards, calendars, and so on. I find PhotoExpress to be quite fun to use, and it's perfect for beginners and experts who are looking to save some time by using a template. Ulead's Web site (**www.ulead.com**) has more information on all these products, and I'd encourage you to go check it out if any of them interest you. I've enjoyed using the company's applications for years now, and Ulead's quality releases continue to impress me.

11

Moving Pictures: GIF Animator 4.0

You already know that PhotoImpact itself is a juggernaut when it comes to making images for the Internet. That is its major strength. But what if, at some point, you'd like to make one of those neat animated banners you see online?

Making those animated banners is where GIF Animator 4.0 comes in. With PhotoImpact, this tool, and a little know-how, you can make GIF animations that equal or exceed those same ads and banners you find on the Internet.

Early in this chapter, I'll show you how to create a basic GIF animation. Later, I'll get more specific about GIF Animator's various wonderful features. You'll find out that it's very easy to make GIF animations with this tool in almost no time at all.

NOTE
GIF images never contain more than 256 colors in any given color palette.

GIF Animator and PhotoImpact: Peanut Butter and Jelly

Make no mistake, GIF Animator is a post-production tool. I wouldn't suggest using it all by itself. To make really nice GIF animations, GIF Animator needs PhotoImpact and PhotoImpact needs GIF Animator. Luckily for you, Ulead designed the two applications to work hand-in-hand when necessary.

There are many different ways that PhotoImpact can work with GIF Animator—I'm going to show you a way that I feel is one of the best to compose GIF animations.

It's important, first, to think of a GIF animation like a cartoon. It has a series of frames that continually overlap each other during the course of the animation to show the progress of the action—just like a cartoon. With that in mind, you compose your frames in PhotoImpact and then import them into GIF Animator to assemble the animation and to optimize the animation for download speed on the Web.

Making an Animated GIF Step by Step

In these next few pages, we're going to create a basic GIF animation, with illustrations for each step. We'll use the Animation Wizard tool to help us along. So let's get started!

Let's begin by taking a look at my example. Figure 11.1 shows the PhotoImpact workspace with a blank image open. I have my custom objects ready in the EasyPalette for use in the frames of the animation.

Figure 11.1
The PhotoImpact workspace with a blank image open and active.

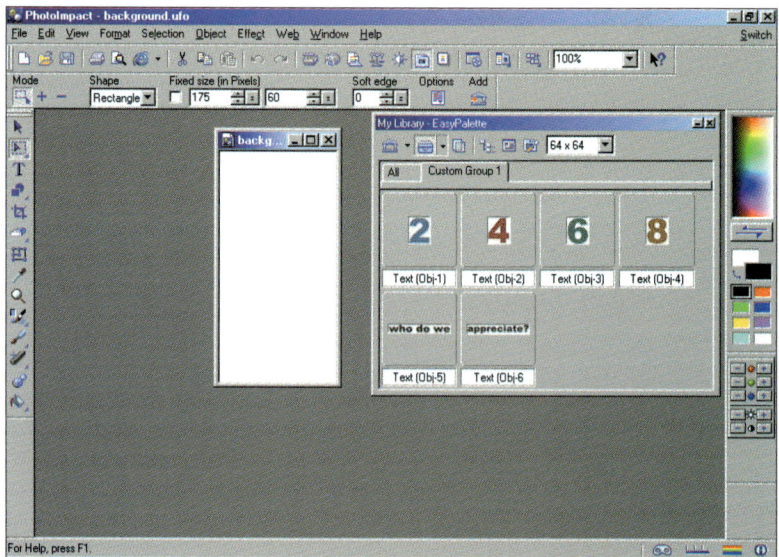

Using this one image, I begin to compose my frames.

TIP
Use "My Library" under the EasyPalette (CTRL+F1) to store objects for use in your animation.

I compose the first frame in my animation and then save it as "1.bmp".
By using CTRL+D on my keyboard, I can make an exact duplicate of this
frame. Figure 11.2 shows our first frame and a duplicate.

Figure 11.2
Frame one of my future
animation and its exact
duplicate.

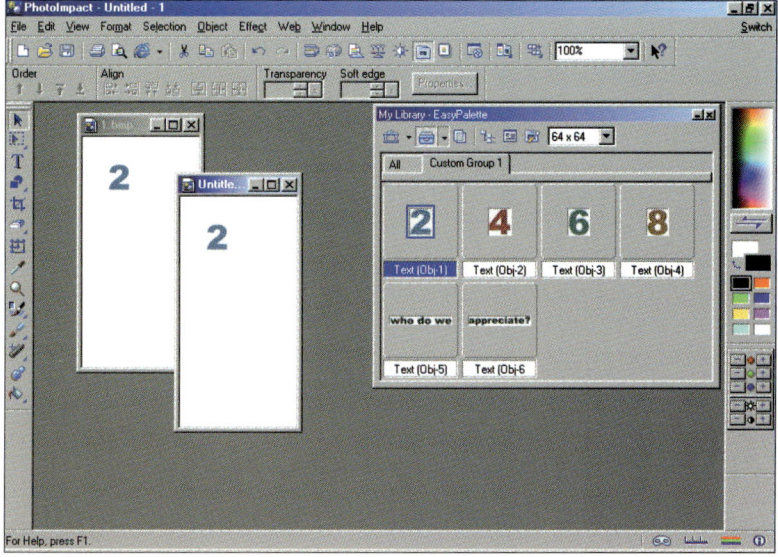

NOTE

Formats like BMP (Windows Bitmap) do not support the use of floating
objects or layers. PhotoImpact will warn you of that when you begin saving.
However, until you close the image, you can still work it and duplicates of it
as if you had the full capabilities of a typical PhotoImpact composition.

TIP

It's a good idea to save your frames in a custom folder on your Windows
Desktop for handy access and organization. I call mine, "GIF Animation
Frames." Title the frames in the animation with numbers (1, 2, 3…) or letters
(a, b, c…), because a numbering system makes it easier to distinguish between
frames in the animation.

As soon as I make a duplicate, I add to or modify the duplicate to represent the next frame for the animation by dragging an object from the EasyPalette onto the duplicate and then saving it, as shown in Figure 11.3.

Figure 11.3
The duplicate is now modified to reflect the next frame in the animation.

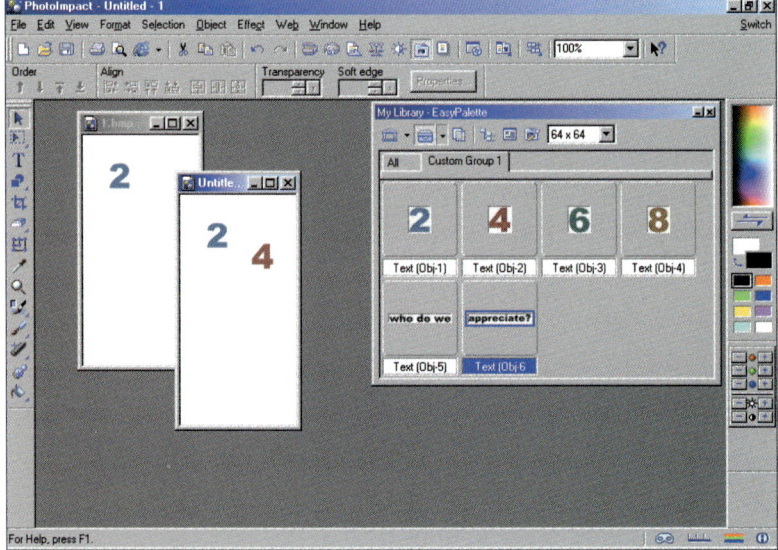

Using the same steps as before, I create successive frames for as many as I want in the animation. Figure 11.4 illustrates the entire set I'm going to use for this animation.

Figure 11.4
The complete set of frames.

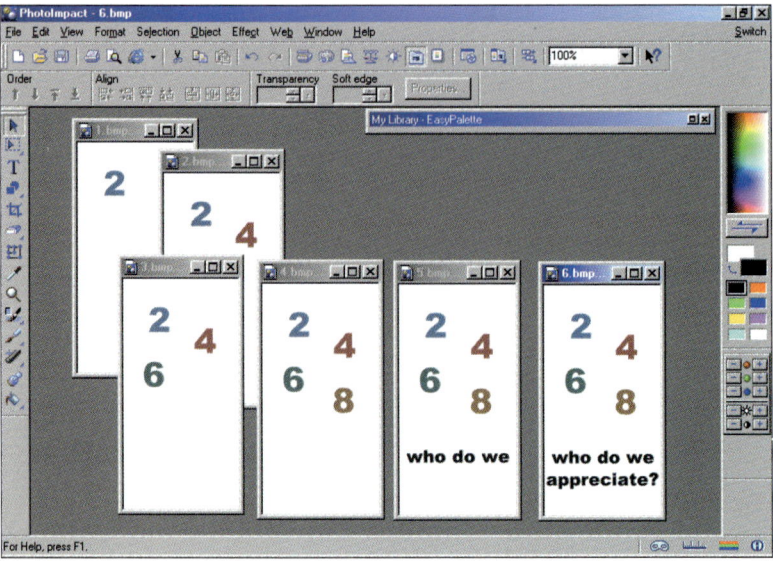

With that done, I can close the frames in PhotoImpact and open GIF Animator by clicking the Start button and choosing Programs > Ulead PhotoImpact 6 > Ulead GIF Animator 4.0.

When you first open GIF Animator, the Startup Wizard appears as shown in Figure 11.5. I click the Animation Wizard button.

Figure 11.5
The Startup Wizard.

Animation
Wizard

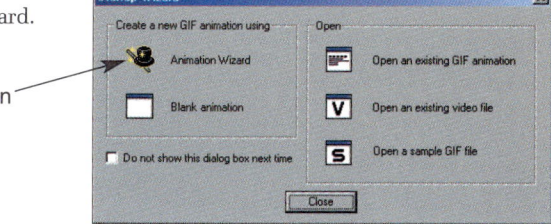

The Animation Wizard will next ask where the images are that you want to add to your animation (see Figure 11.6). Because I'm working with images, I click the Add Image button and browse to my GIF Animation Frames folder on the Windows Desktop. I click the Next button to continue.

Figure 11.6
The Animation Wizard—selecting the files. I can arrange the files in any order by clicking and dragging them accordingly in the list.

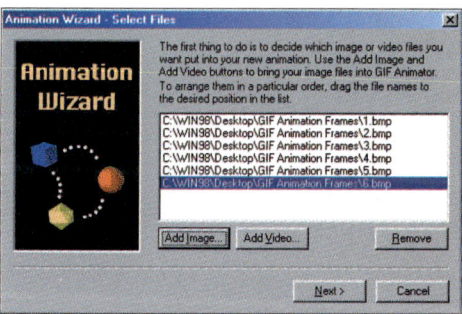

The Animation Wizard then asks which type of source files are being inserted: Type-oriented or Photo-oriented (see Figure 11.7). Because I have text-oriented frames here, I choose Type-oriented (Don't dither) and click the Next button.

CHAPTER 11

Figure 11.7
The Animaton Wizard—
source type.

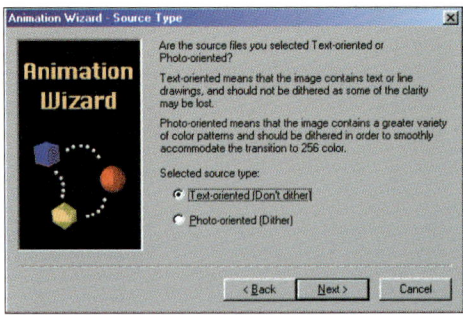

TIP

Always use Type-oriented if any of your source files contain text. The text
will look better. Use Photo-oriented if you have source files that contain
highly colored images, such as photographs, so that the dithering will
compensate for extreme color changes.

The Animation Wizard next asks what duration, in increments of
thousandths of a second, I want each frame in the animation to be
displayed (see Figure 11.8). Changing the value in Delay time also
changes the value of Specify by frame rate accordingly and vice versa.
I accept the defaults and click Next.

TIP

If you input 100 as a value in Delay time, it will equal one second of duration
for each frame. So, 100 equals 1 second, 200 equals 2 seconds, and so on.

Figure 11.8
The Animation
Wizard—frame
duration.

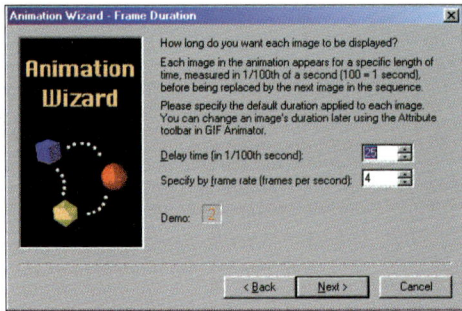

The Animation Wizard next tells me in Figure 11.9 that I'm finished with this part and I click the Finish button. I then wait for GIF Animator to insert my frames into the workspace (which doesn't take very long).

Figure 11.9
The Animation
Wizard—finished.

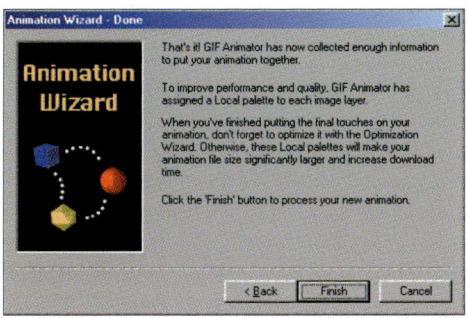

I'm almost done now. All I have left to do is optimize my animation for download speed on the Web. I press F11 to initiate the Optimization Wizard. The first thing this Wizard asks for, (see Figure 11.10) is whether I want to build a general, global color palette for all the images in my animation (thereby reducing file size) or whether I want to leave each frame's palette untouched. I use the recommended setting of using the Global Palette by clicking Yes and then clicking Next.

Figure 11.10
The Optimization
Wizard—the type of
palette.

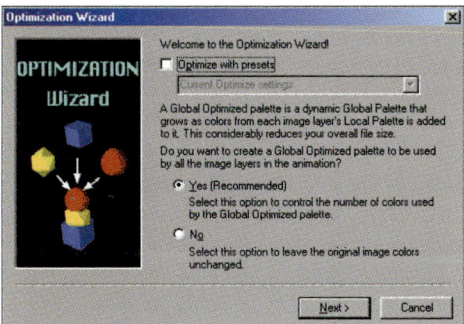

The Optimization Wizard then asks (see Figure 11.11) how many colors I want to include in the Global Palette, up to a possible 256, and whether I want to dither those colors. Because fewer colors means smaller file sizes, I choose 16 colors and no dithering, because I'm dealing with a text-oriented image.

Figure 11.11
The Optimization
Wizard—colors and
dithering.

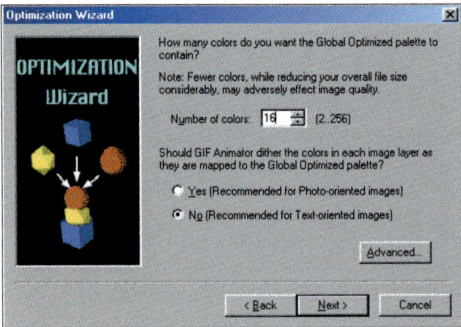

The Optimization Wizard next asks if I want to remove redundant pixels, all comment blocks, and all layer titles to reduce file size. I choose the recommend settings by clicking Yes for each option (see Figure 11.12) and click Next.

Figure 11.12
The Optimization
Wizard—redundant
pixels, comment blocks,
and layer titles.

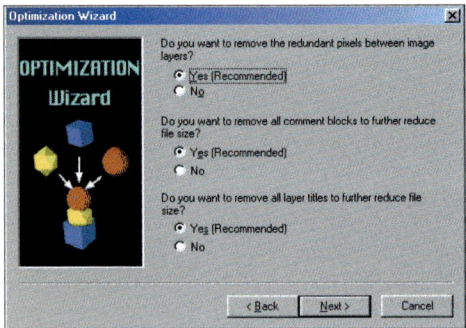

As a final step, the Optimization Wizard gives me a summary of the choices I made (see Figure 11.13). If I want to modify any of these choices, I may go back by clicking the Back button. I choose Finish and let GIF Animator do its thing.

Figure 11.13
The Optimization
Wizard—summary.

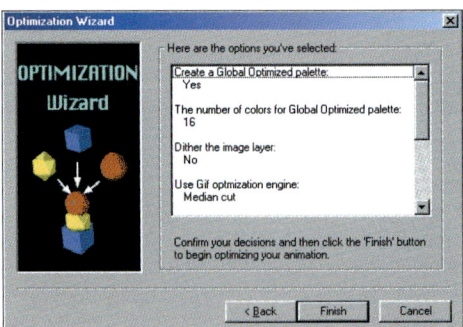

As soon as GIF Animator is done optimizing the image, it will present me with a window detailing the results of the process before and after the optimization, telling me how many bytes were saved and the download time based upon a typical 56K dial-up connection (see Figure 11.14).

Figure 11.14
The Optimization Wizard—optimization results.

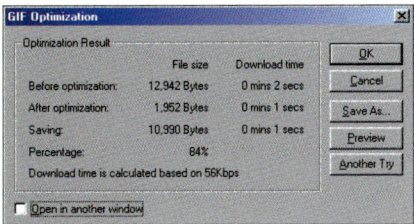

From here, I have several options open to me, including saving the optimized, animated GIF or taking another go at optimization if I don't like the results. I can even preview, frame by frame if I like, the optimized GIF before saving it. I clicked the Save As button and saved my final, optimized and animated GIF to a location on my disk.

> **TIP**
> You can, or course, name a final, animated GIF anything you like, such as, anigif_001.gif or my_animated_gif.gif. Just remember what you named it!

And that's it! I now have an animated GIF ready for the Internet! All I have to do is use my favorite HTML editor to insert and position the animated GIF on a Web page.

Now that you know how to make a GIF animation, let's next take a look at some more features and tips to help you create GIF animations with PhotoImpact and GIF Animator.

Customizing Your GIF Animations and How You Work

PhotoImpact and GIF Animator work together to provide the user with many options in customizing and individualizing your work. When it comes down to the line, that's what it's ultimately all about. You don't have to be stuck with any template or pigeonhole yourself with a wizard. This section will show what is available to you so that you can grow your talents and use them to create a GIF animation that's unique.

Animation Studio and Lighting Effects

With PhotoImpact's built-in animation effects, you have the choice of saving an effect on a composition as a still image or as an animation. In the case of the Animation Studio and Lighting effects, when you save the animation directly as an animated GIF, there is an additional option asking if you would like to open GIF Animator with this animation to further optimize it. When you check this option and save the animation, GIF Animator will automatically launch and insert the animation into its workspace. Figure 11.15 shows a typical example of saving an animation within PhotoImpact's Animation Studio and a subsequent chance of importing the animation into GIF Animator. This figure also shows the window you get when saving an animation using Animation Studio by clicking the Save button.

Figure 11.15
When saving an animation using Animation Studio, you have the option of opening the animation with GIF Animator right after saving.

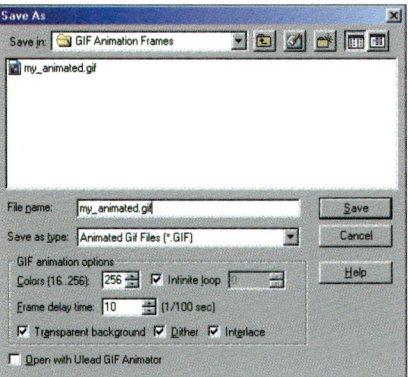

Artist Texture, Creative Warp, and Transform Effects

In the case of Artist Texture, Creative Warp, and Transform effects, you are asked if you want to save the animation as an animated GIF or as a sequence of images. When you save the animation as a GIF animation, GIF Animator automatically opens and inserts the animation for further editing. If you save the animation as a sequence of images, you are asked where to put the images and what title to give them. PhotoImpact will automatically append a number sequentially, beginning with 000, to each image. You can then launch GIF Animator on your own and insert these images yourself. Figure 11.16 shows a typical example of using the Creative Warp effect and the subsequent option of importing and opening the result within GIF Animator when you click the Save button.

Figure 11.16
With effects such as Creative Warp, you have the option of opening the animation directly within GIF Animator or saving it as a sequence of images that you can work with yourself.

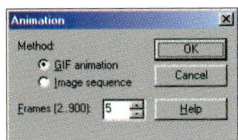

In short, saving an animation in PhotoImpact will simply provide you with the option of opening the animation within GIF Animator for further composition and optimization.

General Preferences

You can customize how you work with GIF Animator by specifying your preferences (see Figure 11.17). Click File > Preferences on the menu bar or use F6 on your keyboard to access these preferences.

Figure 11.17
By using F6, you can access and customize GIF Animator's many preferences.

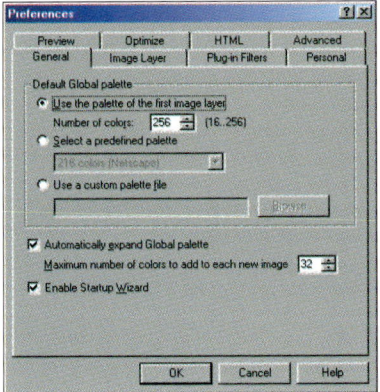

Want to add your own personal comment to your work of art? Click the Personal tab and enter a custom message, up to 512 characters. Figure 11.18 shows a comment that I use (and change regularly).

Figure 11.18
You can add your own personal comment block to your saved or optimized GIF animations.

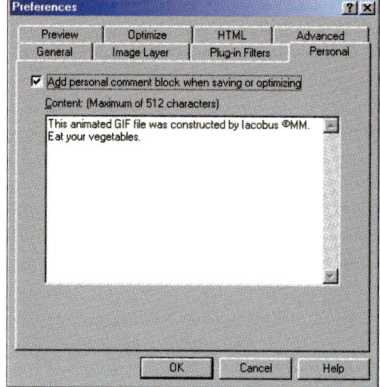

NOTE

This comment is visible only in animated GIF authoring software such as GIF Animator.

Getting to Know the Workspace

Figure 11.19 shows the GIF Animator workspace and its basic features.

Figure 11.19
The GIF Animator window.

Standard Toolbar

Attribute Toolbar

Layer Pane

Workspace

Palette Toolbar

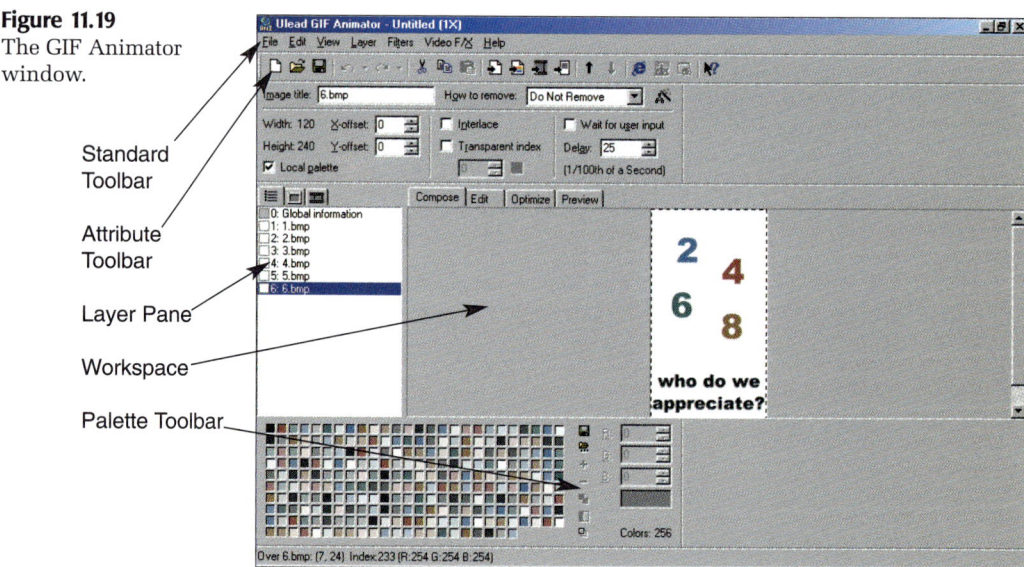

Adding Layers to Your Animation

The first thing to get acquainted with is how to add layers to the animation. There are several ways to do this.

One way is to use the Add Images button on the Standard Toolbar (see Figure 11.20) to browse your disks so you can insert images into your animation. You may add several images at once with this option. GIF Animator will sort the multiple images alphanumerically and put them into your animation. Add Video lets you browse for a video, such as videos in Quicktime or AVI format. You can even choose portions of the video for insertion.

Figure 11.20
The Add Images button, the Add Video button.

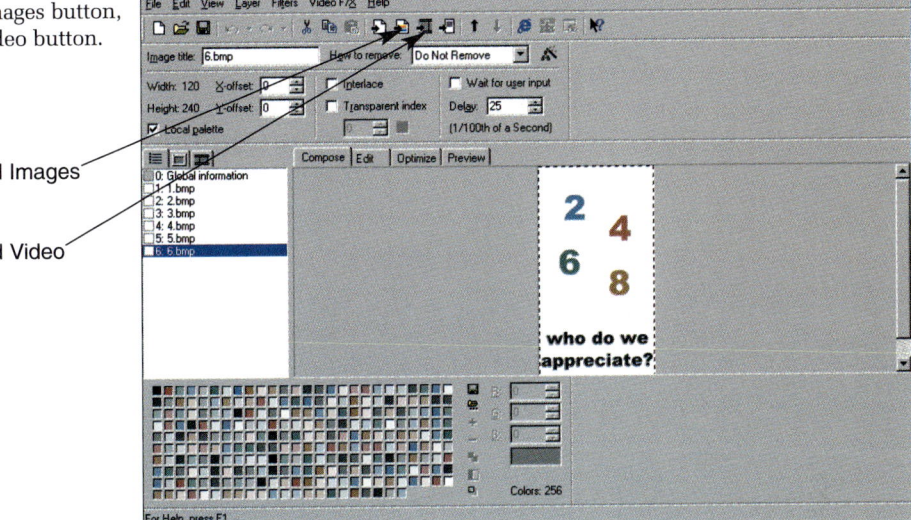

Add Images

Add Video

NOTE
Frames are also called layers or cels.

The Layer Pane

After becoming familiar with the two typical ways of inserting images into your custom GIF animation, get to know the Layer Pane. It will be your best friend. Once you get your frames inserted, the Layer Pane is where you'll organize the frames to your animation.

Moving Layers

The frames in the Layer pane can be moved up and down using the Move Layer Up and Move Layer Down buttons on the Standard Toolbar (see Figure 11.21). You can move single or multiple frames this way. Use the conventional Windows method of selecting files by holding down the CTRL key on your keyboard and clicking the frames you want to move up or down.

Figure 11.21
The Move Layer Up button and the Move Layer Down button.

The Move Layer Up button

The Move Layer Down button

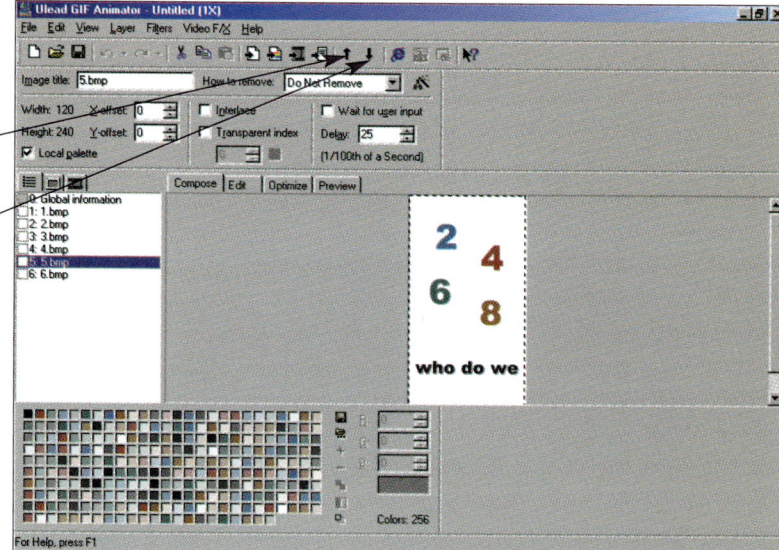

TIP

You can also use ALT+Up cursor key to move the layer or layers up and ALT+Down cursor key to move the layer or layers down.

You can reverse the order of the entire set of frames or a specified set of frames using Layer > Reverse Order command on the menu bar.

You can view multiple layers simultaneously by checking the box next to the layer's title in the Layer Pane. Figure 11.22 shows a typical example of this.

Figure 11.22
Viewing multiple layers
is as simple as checking
the box next to their
titles.

Checkbox to
Title of Layer

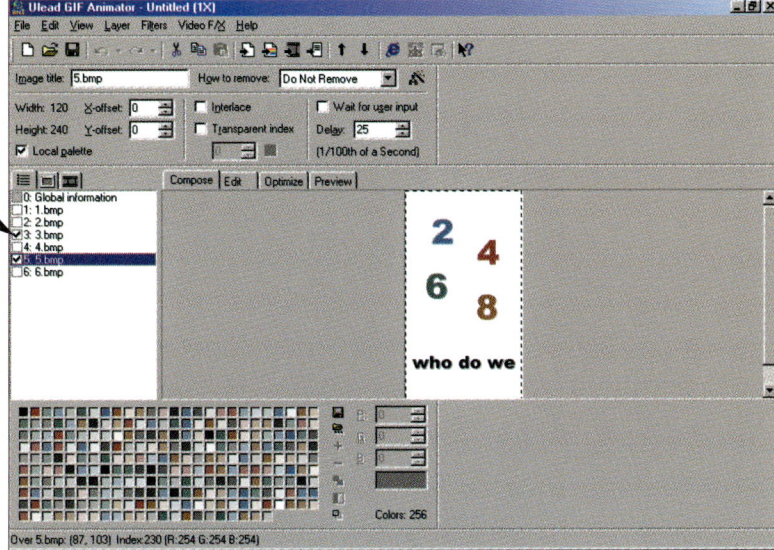

NOTE

This technique works best on layers that are transparent.

The Layer pane has three different views to choose from: List View, Thumbnail View, and Filmstrip View.

▶ **List View**—This is the default view and the one I recommend. It lists the frames in your animation by name.

▶ **Thumbnail View**—This view lists not only the name of the frame but also has a thumbnail of the frame. All thumbnails are of the same size and are centered.

▶ **Filmstrip View**—This function lists the name of the frame and shows the frame's position in relation to the other frames in the animation.

Now that you know how the Layer Pane helps you organize your frames, it's time to find out what you can do with the frames.

Deleting Layers

Deleting frames is a really straightforward task. Click on a frame or number of frames and press Delete on your keyboard.

Duplicating Layers

You may, if you'd like, make duplicate copies of a particular layer or layers. Use either the Edit > Duplicate command on the menu bar or press CTRL+D with the selected layer(s) active. This command is great if you'd like to create action out of a transparent layer. Figure 11.23 shows the Duplicate window.

Figure 11.23
The Duplicate window. You can enter values in pixels for shifting the layer(s) horizontally and/or vertically.

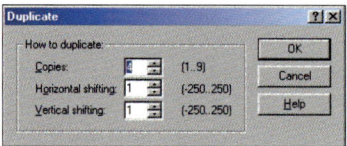

Merging Layers

You may also merge your layers together in different ways. There are two ways of merging: Either merge two or more images together or merge one or more images with a selected background. These options should be used with layers that have transparency applied to them.

Merge Images

The Merge Images function lets you merge two or more images together. With this command, you have an additional option of replacing the original image. Use Layer > Merge Images on the menu bar or CTRL+M on your keyboard. Figure 11.24 shows the Merge Images window.

Figure 11.24
The Merge Images window. Select the layers you'd like to merge together and click OK.

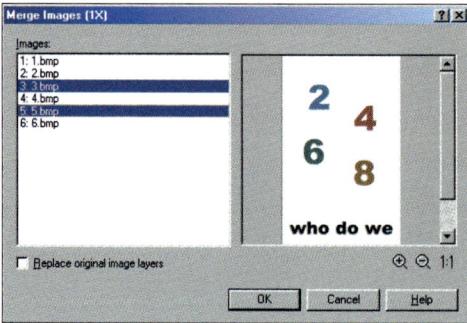

Background Merge

Background Merge, accessed by using Layer > Background Merge on the menu bar, lets you merge one or more images with a common background. Choose the background from the drop-down list and select the layers you'd like to merge the background with. This option works best when the images to be merged into the background are transparent. Figure 11.25 shows a typical example.

Figure 11.25
The Background Merge
window. Choose a
background.

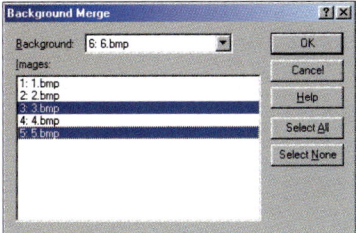

Now knowing how you can apply different ways to merge images
together, it's helpful to next know what properties your animation has as
a whole and what layers have for themselves independently.

Attributes of Layers

There are several useful attributes that affect the animation as a whole
and that affect layers independently.

Attributes Affecting the Whole Animation

The Global Information Layer's Attribute Toolbar (see Figure 11.26)
contains information pertaining to the entire animation:

Figure 11.26
The Global Information
Layer's Attribute
Toolbar.

Logical Screen

Global Palette

Looping

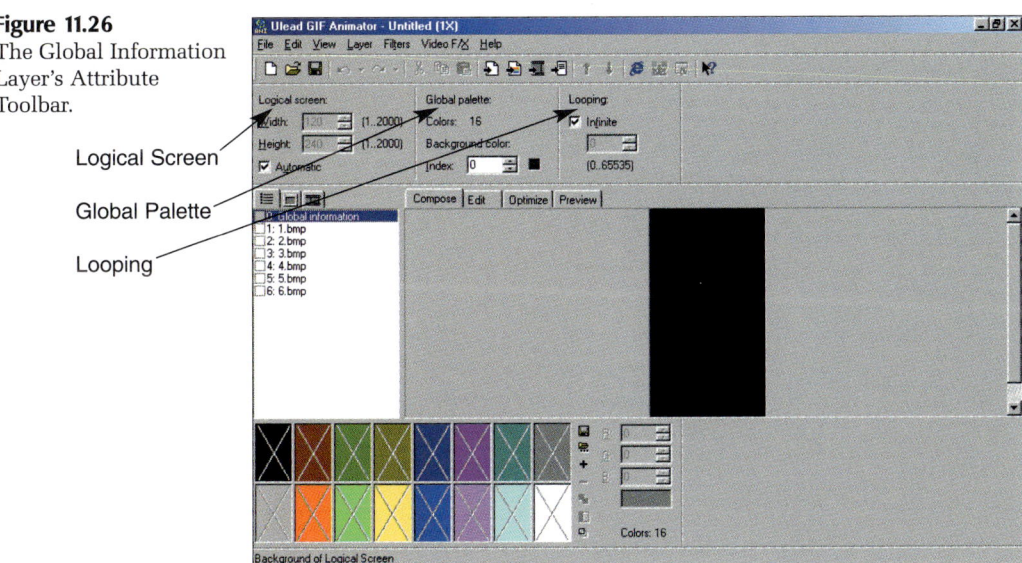

▶ **Logical Screen**—This pertains to the width and height, in pixels, of the entire animation's dimensions.

▶ **Global Palette**—This represents the color palette of the entire GIF animation. This palette does *not* apply to layers that have a Local Palette applied to them.

▶ **Looping**—This determines how many times the animation will play. Infinite is the default.

Independent Attributes

In addition to the above, layers can have attributes assigned to them independently. Figure 11.27 shows the various attributes:

Figure 11.27
The Attribute Toolbar for the independent layers.

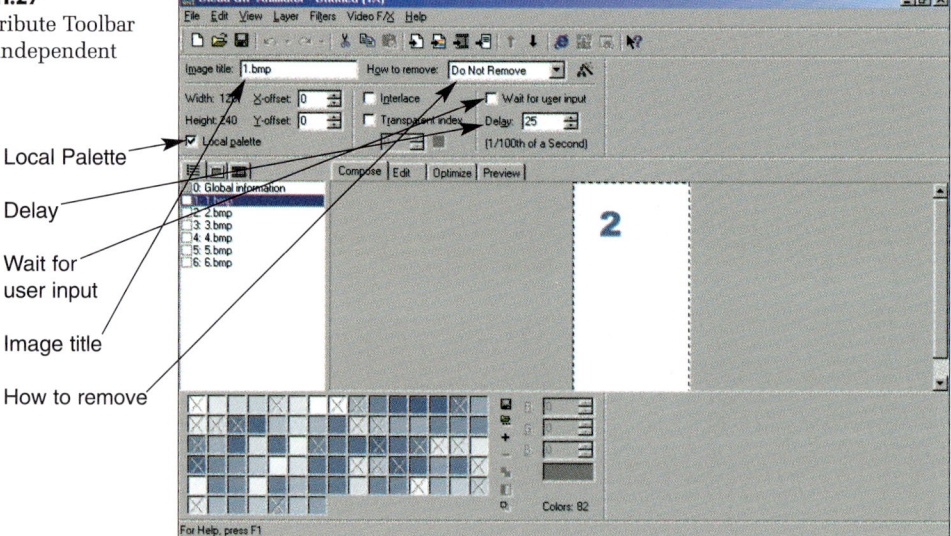

▶ **Local Palette**—This represents the color palette of individual layers. When checked, the particular layer has its own color palette and ignores the Global Information Layer's palette. This can result in a larger file size. The limit, as in the Global Information Layer's palette, is 256 colors.

So why use the Local Palette if it can result in a larger file size? You'd use this option if during the course of your animation a particular layer has a color palette that's drastically different from the rest of the animation.

▶ **Delay**—Delay can specify how much time (in hundredths of a second) passes on a specific frame before continuing on to the next frame in the animation. This is similar to the Animation Wizard, in that 100 equals 1 second, 200 equals 2 seconds, and so on.

▶ **Wait for user input**—This is not yet supported in Web browsers. It specifies that the user must click the mouse to freeze the animation and then click again to proceed with the animation.

▶ **Interlace**—This is another option not yet supported in Web browsers. It allows the particular layer to "focus" in as the layer loads in the animation.

▶ **Image title**—This function lets you name a particular layer if you so desire. The Layer Pane reflects the changes made here for the layer.

▶ **How to remove**—This function represents how the layer will remove itself and the animation will continue with the next frame.

There are four options under How to remove:

▶ **Web Browser Decides**—This option lets the browser decide the best way to remove the layer. You'll get different results with different browsers with this option. My suggestion is not to use it.

▶ **Do Not Remove**—This option is, in my opinion, the best choice for universal compatibility between the different Web browsers. This option makes the animation stack the layers on top of one another during the animation. The downside? If you have transparent layers, anything in the transparent areas will show through during the course of the animation. The best way to remedy this is to merge the transparent layers with a common background using the Background Merge command. Figure 11.28 shows an example of what happens when you use transparent layers with Do Not Remove.

Figure 11.28
A GIF animation using transparent layers and Do Not Remove. This is how a moving object will show up in a Web browser. Not a good idea.

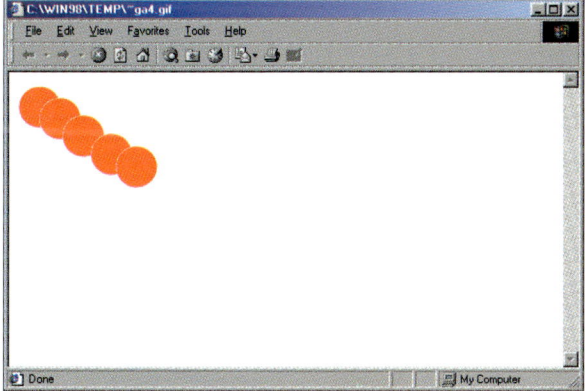

CHAPTER 11

▶ **To Background Color**—This removes and replaces the layer with the background color. You can use this option to achieve a smooth transition effect and your layers will overlap evenly.

▶ **To Previous State**—This is currently supported only by Microsoft Internet Explorer. It removes the layer and replaces it with the next frame in the sequence of the animation. This would be my preferred method because it's easier to make GIF animations this way, but since only Internet Explorer supports it, it can't be.

You now know the properties that affect the whole animation and its independent layers. There are different ways you can work with the layers in your animation, which I'll discuss next.

Using the Work Modes

GIF Animator has several modes that you can use to work with your animation.

▶ **Compose Mode**—What you see in Figure 11.29 is the default mode. You'll spend most of your time in this mode. It shows the present layer that is clicked on in the Layer Pane.

Figure 11.29
Compose Mode. This default mode lets you take a quick look a tone or more layers or of your animation.

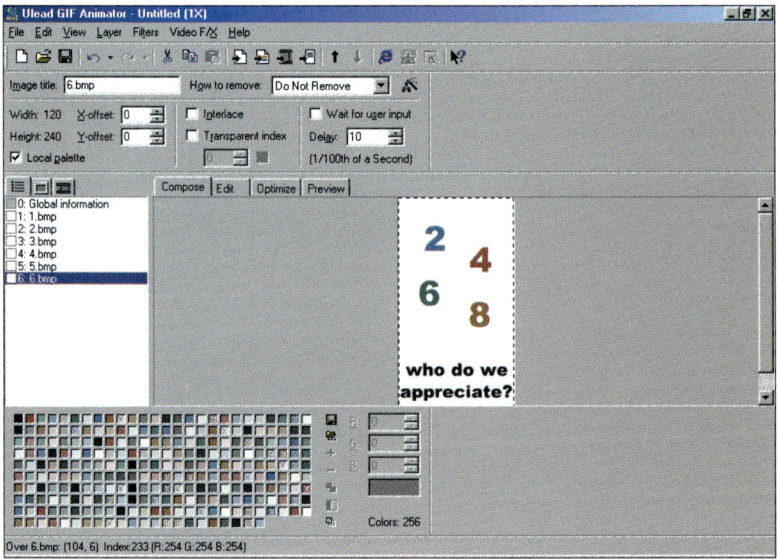

▶ **Edit Mode**—This mode, as seen in Figure 11.30, consists of several simple tools for you to use when cleaning up a layer. You can apply different edits, such as the Rectangle Tool, to make a selection on a frame and the Eraser Tool to erase parts of a frame with this mode.

Figure 11.30
Use Edit Mode to clean up the layers of your animation.

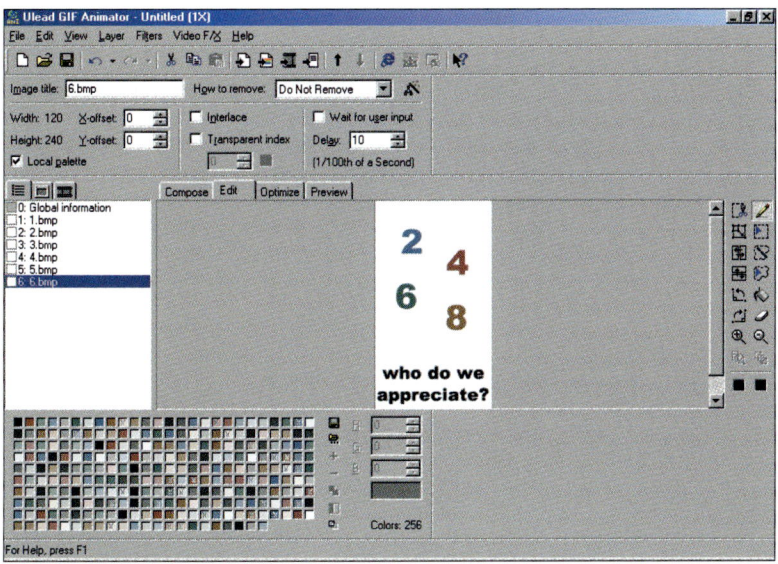

▶ **Optimize Mode**—In Figure 11.31, you can see that this works very much like the Optimization Wizard, with the exception of replacing the current animated GIF that's open in the GIF Animator workspace with the optimized version. Once you optimize the animated GIF, all you do is use File > Save on the menu bar to save over the existing animation or File > Save As to save the file separately. There's a button here for the Optimization Wizard if you'd like to experiment.

CHAPTER 11

Figure 11.31
Use Optimize Mode when you want to replace the current, open GIF animation with an optimized version.

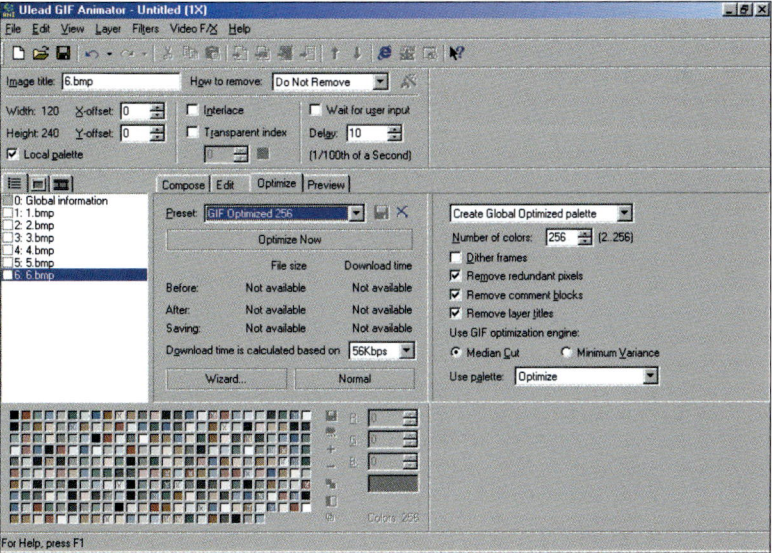

▶ **Preview Mode**—The image in Figure 11.32 simulates a Web browser. It lets you take a quick peek at how the animation looks as it stands in a Web browsing environment.

Figure 11.32
Use Preview Mode to see how your animation looks in a Web browser.

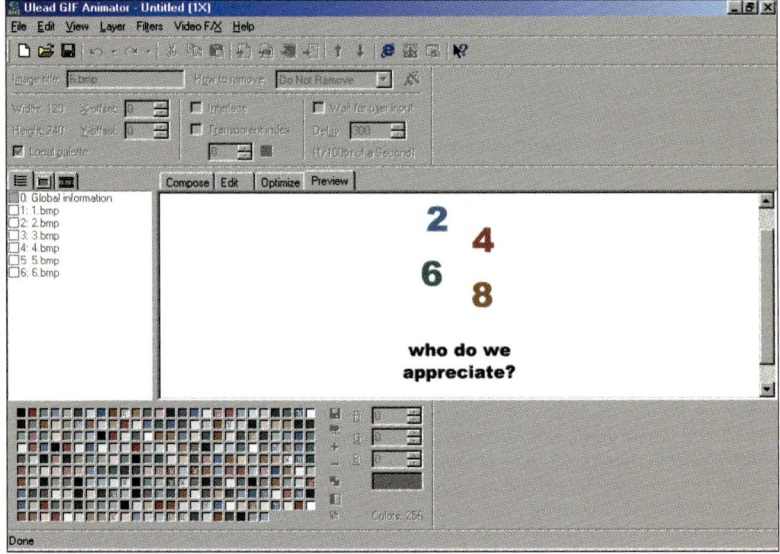

NOTE
You must have Internet Explorer 4.0 or higher installed or have Windows 98 as your operating system. If you don't have either environment, GIF Animator will use its own customized browser environment to view your animated GIF.

The different work modes will help you to compose, edit, optimize, and preview your animation. Get to know them well, and you'll thank yourself later.

Now let's take a quick look at the Global Palette and Local Palette.

Palette Toolbar

As I've said earlier, the animation can have a color palette for the entire set of frames, called the Global Palette; or it can have a color palette that applies only to a specific frame, called the Local Palette.

To find out the range of colors for either the Global Palette or the Local Palette, check out the Palette Toolbar.

With this toolbar (see Figure 11.19), you can add, delete, or replace a color within a given palette. You may also load or save a particular palette in this toolbar.

Next, let's take a look at the Video F/X that come with the program.

Video F/X

There are quite a few nice effects that come with GIF Animator. These effects are located under Video F/X on the menu bar. The effects have a video production quality to them and provide a nice alternative to creating your own ways of GIF animation in a snap.

Care should be taken when using these effects. By default, they use fifteen frames of animation. You can pare this down to fewer than ten. Because they act as a transition between two frames, it's recommended that you keep only two initial frames before applying these effects, one as the source and one as the destination. Figure 11.33 shows one of the many effects available to you.

Figure 11.33
One of GIF Animator's many built-in effects— Run and Stop-Push.

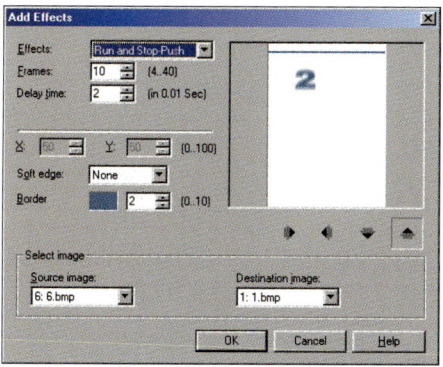

There are more effects to use with GIF Animator that are available to purchase—F/X for GIF Animator and GIF-X 2.0. For more information, consult the following Web sites:

http://www.webutilities.com/products/gifx/runme.htm
http://www.webutilities.com/products/fx/runme.htm

Beside the Video F/X, Ulead also included a number of simple yet effective transition and text effects, which I'll talk about next.

Simple Transition and Text Effects

All of these rather simple transition and text effects are located under the Layer menu on the menu bar.

▶ **Add Banner Text**—This function contains five different types of effects involving text in an animation: Simple, Neon, Gradient, Marquee, and Animation, all of them with a wealth of their own options. All of these effects apply thirty frames of animation (which might be a little too much depending upon the situation). As always, you can adjust the number of frames in the animation. Figure 11.34 shows one of the effects available under this option.

Figure 11.34
Add Simple Text, one of the many effects available under Add Banner Text.

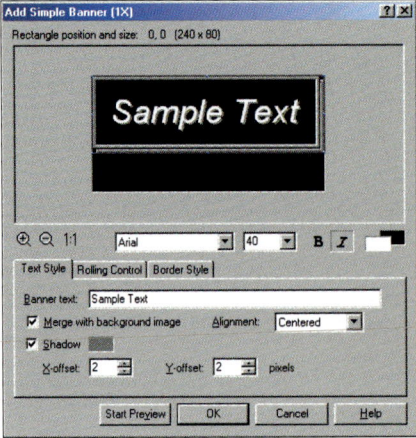

▶ **Add Simple Transition**—This function contains a number of very simple transition effects, like Wiping Down or Vertical Split. You can adjust the number of frames in the animation just like in Add Banner Text. Fifteen frames is the default. Figure 11.35 shows one of the effects available under the option.

Figure 11.35
Add Simple Transition contains a number of very simple but effective transitions.

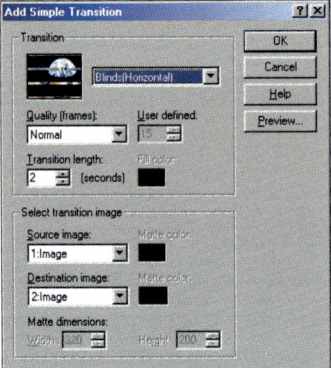

▶ **Add Color Animation**—This effect applies animation to a particular frame's chosen number of colors. Every color chosen adds a frame to the animation. Figure 11.36 shows a typical use of the effect.

Figure 11.36
The Add Color
Animation window.

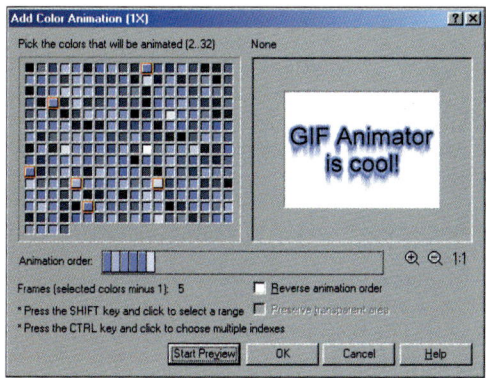

> ▶ **Add Cube Effect**—This device employs a simple "turning cube"
> animation between two frames, as if the frames were applied to a
> cube's faces. You can apply effects such as turning the cube from
> bottom to top and from left to right. Figure 11.37 shows a typical way
> to use the effect.

Figure 11.37
The Add Cube Effect
window.

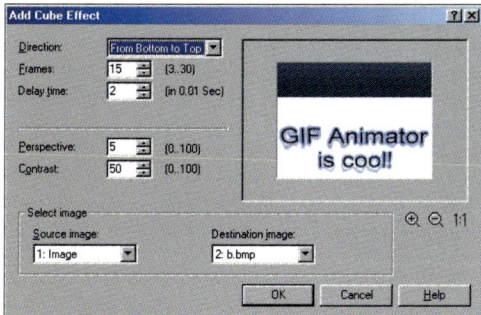

> ▶ **Add Scrolling**—As seen in Figure 11.38, this adds a simple scrolling
> effect to a chosen frame. You can choose to scroll the frame in and
> then out or just scroll in or scroll out.

Figure 11.38
The Add Scrolling
window.

In addition to now knowing that you can apply various simple effects to
your animation, you can also apply your own third-party Adobe
Photoshop-compatible plug-ins, which I'll talk about next.

CHAPTER 11

APS Plug-Ins

You can use your own commercial or freeware 32-bit Adobe Photoshop-compatible plug-ins to use with GIF Animator, including Flaming Pear Software's Designer Sextet or Kai's Power Tools (KPT). Press F6 to access GIF Animator's Preferences (as in Figure 11.39) and click the Plug-in Filters tab. Use the Browse button to choose the folder where your plug-ins will reside.

Figure 11.39
The Plug-in Filters tab under GIF Animator's Preferences.

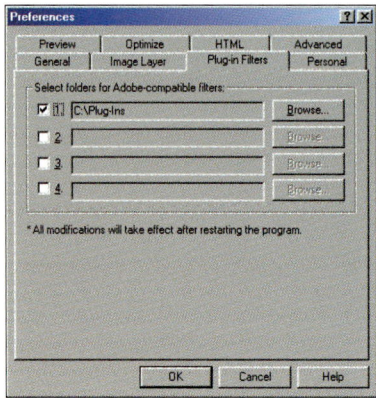

Once you specify the plug-ins you have installed, you'll have to close and relaunch GIF Animator for the program to activate them. From there, you just click the individual layer or layers and use the Filters menu bar command and choose your favorite plug-in to apply to one or more layers in your animation.

NOTE
Using plug-ins on a layer effectively replaces the layer. Use CTRL+Z to undo the plug-in effect on the layer if needed.

You now know a lot about GIF Animator's features. I'll next tell you some tips on how to use the features that GIF Animator provides combined with making animations appear uniformly in various Web browsers.

The Best Roads to GIF Animation Composition

Thus far, you've learned how powerful a tool GIF Animator can be for authoring GIF animation. It's now time to give you some very helpful tips on using GIF Animator and some standard procedures you should know about when composing GIF animations. Heed these tips well, and making animated GIFs will seem like second nature.

Anybody got any tips? I know I do.

These tips come recommended not only because they'll help make your GIF animations that much nicer, but also because you'll look like a pro (if you're not already one). They come straight from the heart, based upon my personal experiences.

The Best Removal Method

I mentioned earlier in the chapter about how GIF animations, depending upon the removal method used in the animation, can affect how the animation looks in the various Web browsers. If you want your animations to be as universally viewable as possible within most, if not all, Web browsers, there are some things you should know.

Unless you know what you're doing, using transparent layers to compose the frames in your animation can be an iffy proposition.

Your best bet is to make the whole animation's set of frames opaque and at the same size when possible. Also, set their removal method under the How to remove option to Do Not Remove on the Attribute Toolbar and then let GIF Animator's Optimization Wizard do the optimizing for you. As I've said earlier, the Optimization Wizard will get rid of any redundant pixels during the course of the animation, thereby reducing the overall file size.

Use PhotoImpact to Make Your Frames

That being said, it's a good idea to compose most, if not all, the frames in your animation within PhotoImpact. By using duplicate copies of an active composition in combination with the EasyPalette, you can ensure the continuity of your animation as well as provide yourself with full-size frames for optimization later within GIF Animator's Optimization Wizard.

File Size and Presentation

For compact GIF animations, I would suggest a final optimized file size no bigger than 30K. It's sometimes OK to go above this number, especially if there aren't many graphics on the page. Remember that the goal is not to make the absolute smallest GIF animation but to make the most presentable. A slightly larger-than-normal GIF animation that looks good is better than a very small GIF animation that looks terrible.

Keep It Simple and Keep It Quick

The most attractive GIF animations involve simplicity, such as a blinking text message or an animating arrow pointing to an element you want people to notice. Most people aren't going to sit there while it takes a minute for your animation to play through, so keep it to five to eight seconds total.

Don't Limit Yourself

Don't forget there are a few uses for GIF animations other than just banners. Use the format to animate an element on a Web site, such as an animated e-mail image. Such elements will also spruce up an otherwise static page. Or use it to make a simple animation for a JavaScript rollover image. Simply call the animated GIF just as you would a regular GIF in your JavaScript code for the rollover. Remember to keep the rollover animated GIF relatively small.

Put Yourself in Their Shoes

Keep in mind your own Web surfing habits and ask friends and family about their surfing habits. For example, you may ask how long you or your friends are willing stick to around for a GIF animation to complete its duration. I bet it isn't very long. You may also ask about what gets their attention.

Time is on Your Side

One of the most frequent uses in your custom GIF animation will be the Delay option on the Attribute Toolbar. If you'd like to make a smooth, quick action during an animation, select the frames in the animation and enter a value of 10. If you want the person to be able to read and absorb something like a text message, enter a value of 300, which will make the assigned frame stick around for three seconds.

The Optimized Palette and the Browse-Safe Palette

In earlier chapters, we covered optimized and browser-safe palettes. The same applies in deciding which palette to use within GIF Animator for a GIF animation. If you absolutely want to include everyone, use the browser-safe palette. That setting ensures that the animation will look the same across the board no matter what color depth or operating system a person is using, but it also has the potential to reduce the quality of your images. Because nearly all Internet users are browsing in color depths of 16 bits or higher, I recommend using the optimized palette in all cases.

Keep the Number of Colors Low

You really shouldn't have to use the entire range of 256 available colors when optimizing. More colors in the palette equals bigger overall file size. Try to use 64 colors or fewer within the optimized animated GIF's color palette. Thirty-two or even 16 colors can work even better and the results are not that much worse at all. Figure 11.40 shows the Optimization Wizard's step asking how many colors to use: in this case, the Global Palette with 64 colors.

Figure 11.40
Specifying 64 colors or fewer in the Optimization Wizard will help to reduce the file size of your animation.

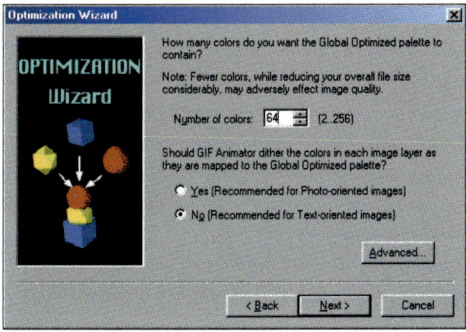

Use the Global Palette When Possible

Try to use the Global Palette for all the frames in the entire animation. Use a Local Palette on a particular frame only when that particular frame's color palette is drastically different from the rest of the animation.

Compose It Raw

When compiling and adding/importing the frames to your custom animation, keep in mind GIF Animator works with many different graphics file formats, such as BMP or TGA, which are essentially lossless formats (the quality of the image doesn't degrade). You'll want to keep the frames in your image as true as to the original as possible before optimizing, so save the frames in a format like BMP in PhotoImpact before importing them into GIF Animator.

Online Help is Your Friend

Almost all of the time, a quick question can be answered by conferring with GIF Animator's online help. Use Help > Help on GIF Animator's menu bar.

Experiment, Experiment, Experiment!

This is the mantra I live by: Experiment. Don't expect to make your animation in just one shot. GIF animation takes a lot of practice and some patience.

So there you have it. Armed with this information, you now should be able to compose your very own captivating GIF animations using PhotoImpact and GIF Animator. All it takes is a little effort and a lot of imagination.

12

PhotoImpact Album 6.0: A Digital Photographer's Dream

Just like printed photos, digital images have to be stored somewhere, and once they start to accumulate, keeping track of them can be difficult. PhotoImpact Album is designed to give you a central storage place for all your digital images that allows you to classify them, browse through them, search for particular images, and use them once you've found them.

Storing Images in Albums

PhotoImpact Album shows a thumbnail representation of each image stored in an album file. Without moving the original file, Album collects information about it and stores that information so that you can search for and open the original image within an album file. Images can be stored in more than one album, and you can have as many albums as you want. For example, you might have an album for each of a group of photographers, one for each type of photo (such as landscapes and portraits), or one for each type of subject matter.

> **NOTE**
> You can use Album to store any kind of file, not just image files. Because this book is about creating images with PhotoImpact, this chapter focuses on using Album with images. You can, however, experiment with storing video, audio, or text files in Album as well.

Viewing and Searching for Images

You can use as many albums as you want at the same time. All the albums PhotoImpact Album knows about are stored in the Album Panel at the left side of your screen, with closed albums displaying a cover that shows a representative image and open ones appearing to have their covers folded back (see Figure 12.1). You can determine which thumbnail represents the album in the Album Panel—its cover—by clicking the Play button at the top of the panel to rotate through the images in the album. Then click the Stop button when you see the one you want to use.

Figure 12.1
Your albums are stored in the Album Panel for easy access. The album shown here is in Attribute Mode.

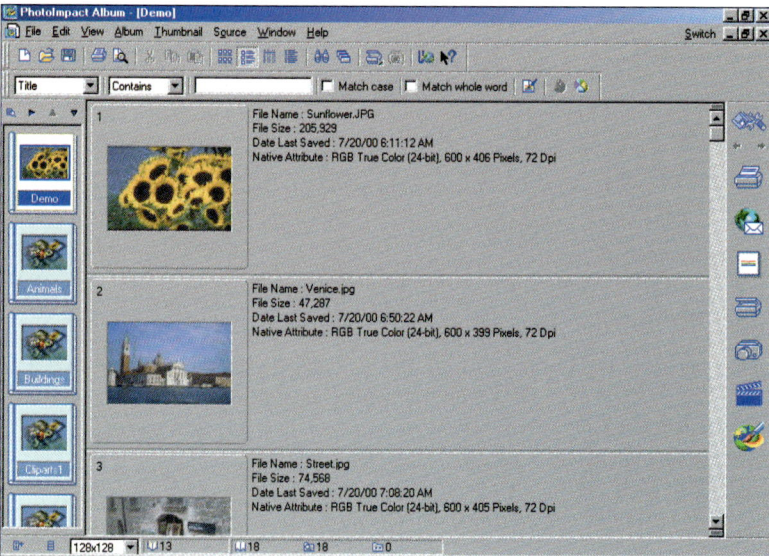

Viewing Albums

To open an album, click its thumbnail in the Album Panel. The album opens in the viewing mode that was last used with it; to change viewing modes, click one of the four Mode buttons on the Standard Toolbar:

▶ **Thumbnail Mode**—All images (or other kinds of files) are displayed in gray rectangles that look like slide holders, with the filename underneath each thumbnail.

▶ **Attribute Mode**—Thumbnails are displayed in a vertical list, each one accompanied by the attributes of its original file.

▶ **File Name Mode**—No thumbnails are visible, just filenames and attributes; click a header to sort the list by the values in that column.

▶ **Data Entry Mode**—Fields defined for this album are displayed next to the thumbnail; you can click in a field to add or change data (see "Entering Data in Fields," ahead).

You can view an album in more than one mode by splitting its window: Drag the splitter at the bottom of the right-hand scroll bar upward (see Figure 12.2). The Mode buttons on the Standard Toolbar control the top pane. To change the viewing mode of the bottom pane, right-click and choose an option from the Mode submenu in the contextual menu.

Figure 12.2
To view an album in two different modes at once, you can split the window. The upper pane here shows Attribute mode, while the lower pane shows Thumbnail mode.

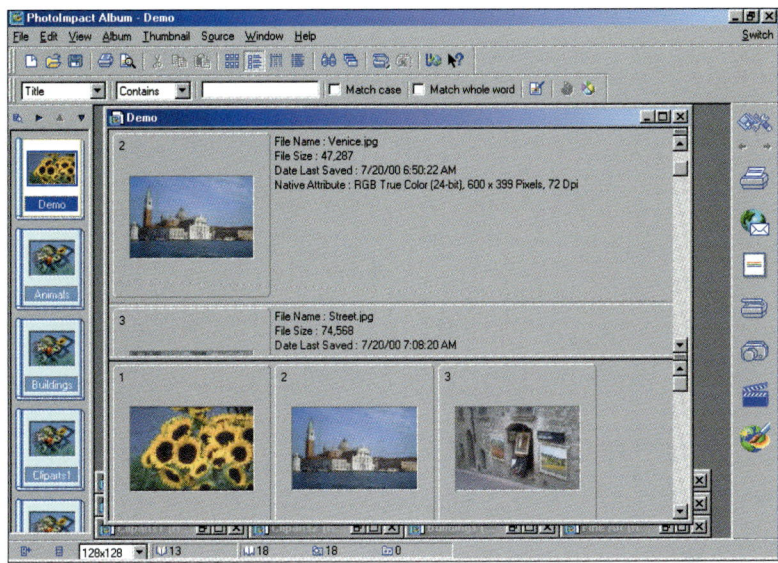

If the standard viewing modes don't include the information you want to see, you can edit their layouts to add the information you're looking for. Choose View > Mode > Layout on the menu bar and click on the tab for the mode you want to change. Then click to select the fields whose information should be included in that mode. You can also change the appearance of the image thumbnail frames by choosing an option from the Thumbnail format radio buttons on the right.

The simplest way to view particular images in an album is to scroll through the album to find them. In Thumbnail, Attribute, or Filename Mode, you can use the scroll bar at the right-hand side of the album window to move through the album. If you're in Data Entry Mode, four buttons at the top right corner of the window allow you to move to the beginning of the album (Top), one record back (Backward), one record ahead (Forward), or to the end of the album (Bottom). Or, if you want to review the contents of an album without having to scroll through it yourself, choose View > Auto Scroll on the menu bar.

You can also find thumbnails with specific characteristics by changing the album's sort order. Choose Thumbnail > Sort on the menu bar to open the Sort dialog box; click on a field name in the Basic tab, choose Ascending or Descending, and click OK.

TIP
If the order of the thumbnails in the album doesn't suit you, you can rearrange them by dragging the thumbnails within the album window.

CHAPTER 12

Searching Albums

Album offers two ways to search an album: using the Search Toolbar or using the Search dialog box. The former method is the quick-and-dirty version—you can keep the Search Toolbar visible all the time for quick searches, but it doesn't have all the options available in the Search dialog box. It searches only the album you're currently working in, while the Search dialog box allows you to search all open albums.

To view the Search Toolbar, choose View > Toolbars & Panels > Search Toolbar on the menu bar. The first drop-down menu contains fields you can search—some are data entry fields and others are information that's automatically saved about every image, such as file size. The other interface elements on the toolbar change depending on your choice from the menu. For example, if you choose a text field, the second drop-down menu has the choices Contains and Empty, with Contains followed by a text entry field so that you can enter the text you're searching for. Press Enter to begin the search.

For slightly more complex searches in which you can use logical operators such as AND, OR, and NOT, click the Edit Criteria button on the Search Toolbar. This brings up the Edit Search Criteria dialog box (see Figure 12.3), in which you can enter multiple search terms separated by operators. For example, you can search for "tree NOT autumn" to find only green, summery trees. If you want to use multiple words as single terms, surround them with the selected delimiter (by default, double quotation marks). Enter your search terms and choose operators from the menu as they're needed, then click OK to return to the Search toolbar, and press ENTER to begin the search.

Figure 12.3
This search will find thumbnails that contain sad clowns and those that contain clowns who are not specifically indicated as happy.

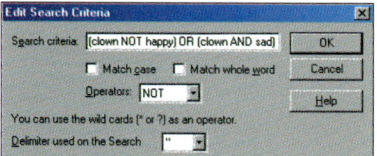

Once you've completed a search, only those thumbnails are shown in the album. If you want to clear the search results and go back to viewing all the thumbnails, click the View All button at the end of the Search Toolbar.

For the most complex searches, Album provides the Search dialog box, with many more options. To get there, choose Thumbnail > Search on the menu bar or click the Search button on the Standard Toolbar (see Figure 12.4). Here you can set up as many search criteria as you're likely to need by entering the information at the top of the dialog box in the same way as you do in the Search Toolbar. As you set up each criterion, click on And or Or to determine whether the criterion is added to the list as an alternative (Or) or a requirement (And), then click Add. That criterion is added to the list in the middle of the dialog, and you're free to begin the search or add more search criteria. To change a criterion, click on it in the list, make changes at the top of the dialog box, then click Change.

Figure 12.4
You can create complex searches using the Search dialog box, and you can save the criteria for future use.

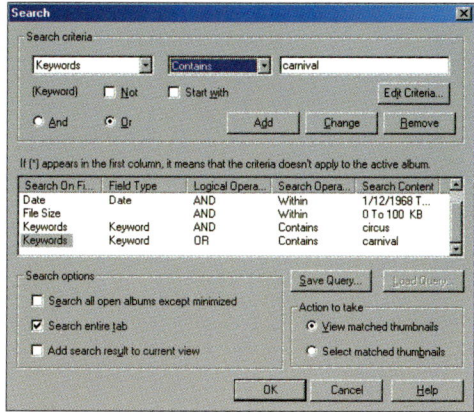

Several options allow you to determine what thumbnails you'll come up with:

▶ **Search all open albums except minimized**—This is self-explanatory.

▶ **Search entire tab**—This searches only the current visible tab.

▶ **Add search result to current view**—This option doesn't dismiss the current search results; instead, it adds the new search results to them.

You can also choose whether to select the located thumbnails (the selection won't show up in Data Entry Mode) or just view them. Once your search options are chosen, you can either save the search (click Save Query) for future use or go ahead and begin the search by clicking OK. If Album doesn't find any thumbnails that match your search criteria, it lets you know with an error message. Otherwise, the found set is either displayed (with the other thumbnails hidden) or selected (with the other thumbnails still visible but unselected).

TIP

If you want to move certain thumbnails in an album to another album or use them to create a new album, use the Search dialog box with the Select matched thumbnails option turned on. Once the search is complete, the thumbnails are selected and ready to drag to another album. Or you can choose Edit > Make Album on the menu bar.

CHAPTER 12

NOTE

The results you get from your search will only be as good as your keywords. If you're serious about having a searchable database of images, get into the habit of entering keywords for every new image—your future searches will be much more accurate.

Marking Thumbnails

Once you've located a thumbnail you've been looking for, it's a good idea to mark it so that you can go on sorting through your other images and still find this one when you need it again. Marking works is similar to keywords, but marks are visible on the designated thumbnails, so you can use them even in Thumbnail Mode. You can assign your own values to marks, but they appear on thumbnails as letters of the alphabet (which means you can use twenty-six different marks within each album).

To mark thumbnails:

1. Choose View > Toolbars & Panels > Mark Panel on the menu bar.

2. Double-click a letter in the Mark Panel and enter your own description of what the mark will signify, then click OK (see Figure 12.5).

Figure 12.5
Each letter can be keyed to a text description of what you want the mark to indicate.

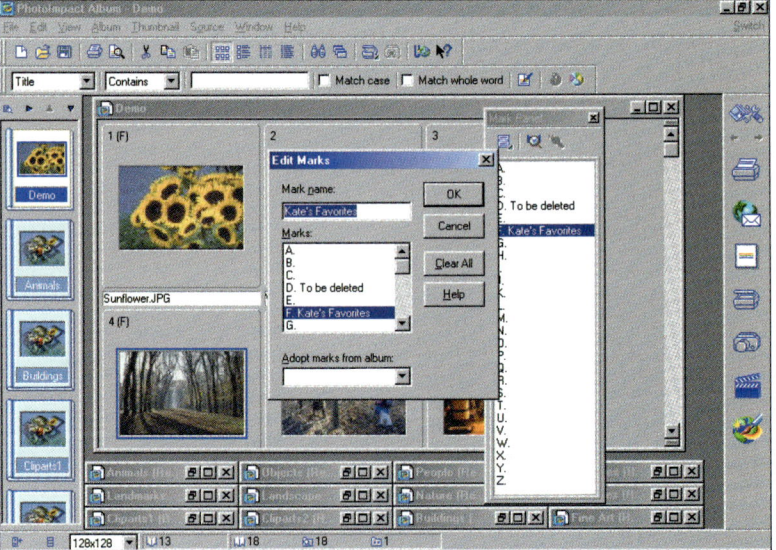

3. Click in the Mark Panel to select the mark you want to assign, then click the Assign Marks button.

4. With the Mark cursor (a magic wand with an "M" at the end), click on each thumbnail you want to mark (see Figure 12.6).

Figure 12.6
You can mark an image with more than one code at a time.

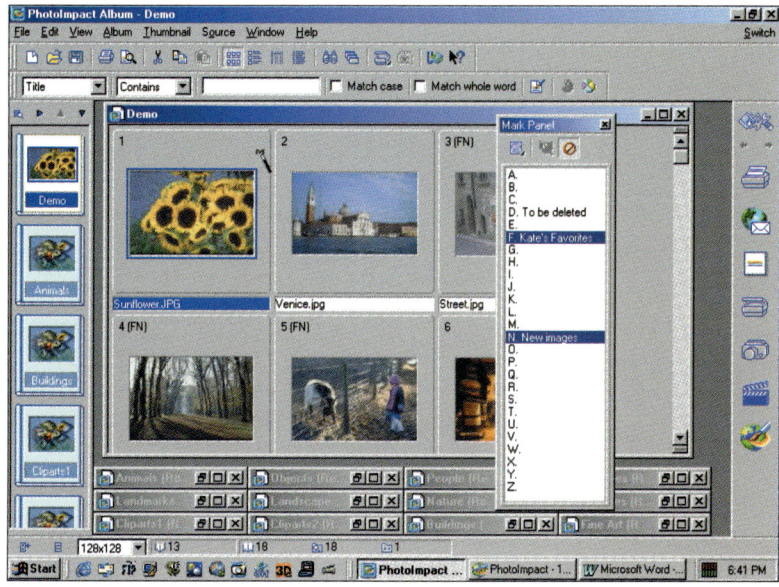

5.   When you're done marking, click on the Assign Marks button again.

TIP
You can assign more than one mark at a time by SHIFT+clicking in the Mark Panel to select a range of marks or CTRL+clicking to select noncontiguous marks.

Once files are marked, you can see the mark letter next to the thumbnail number. You can't sort by marks, but you can search for marked thumbnails.

Adding Images

As you create images, you'll want to add them to your albums right away so you won't lose track of them. Album allows you to insert images that you already have, as well as acquire images directly from a scanner or digital camera and put those right into albums at the same time as the original files are created.

Adding Existing Images

There are five methods for adding existing images to an album, four that are based on locating the original file and one that's a helpful shortcut if the images are already in another album. Here are your options:

▶   With the album open, choose Thumbnail > Insert on the menu bar and then choose an option: Insert files from a folder allows you to choose specific files, while Collect files from a folder (and subfolders)

CHAPTER 12

adds all the files in the selected folder. Click OK, then locate the files you're looking for. Click to select the ones you want to add to the album, then click Insert (or Collect if you chose Collect files from a folder).

▶ With the album open, choose Thumbnail > Visual Insert on the menu bar (see Figure 12.7). Visual Insert allows you to look at thumbnail images, while Insert just shows you a standard file tree. Locate the files you're looking for, click to select one, then click Open—you can add only one file at a time.

Figure 12.7
If you remember images better than filenames, Visual Insert is the thumbnail insertion method for you.

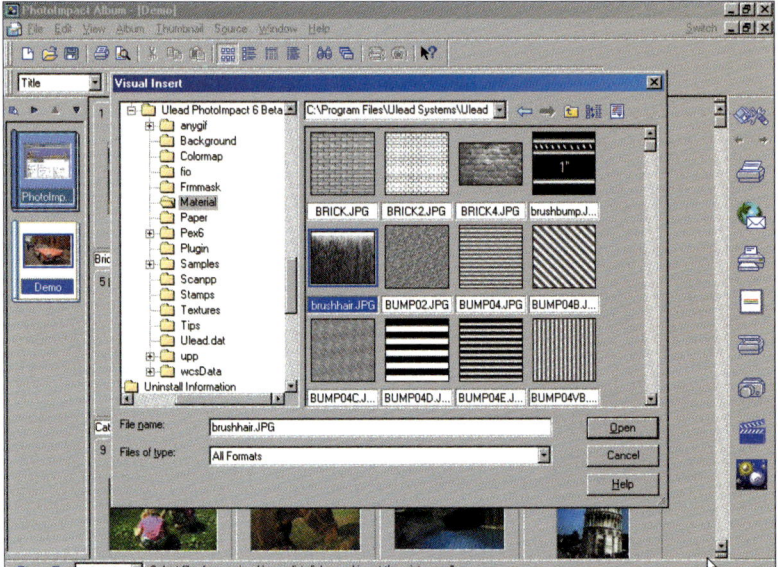

▶ Open the album, then locate the image files in Windows Explorer and drag them into the album window.

▶ When you're saving an image from PhotoImpact, click the Album button in PhotoImpact's Save As dialog box. In the Insert Thumbnails Into Album dialog box, choose an album from the list or click New Album to create a new album in which to catalog the file.

▶ If the images are already cataloged in another album, open both albums, SHIFT+click to select the thumbnails you want to move, then just drag them into the window of the destination album. If you want the thumbnails to be copied from the current album to the new one, hold down CTRL as you drag; then the thumbnails will exist in both albums.

Remember, because the thumbnail in an album is only a reference to its image file, you can catalog an image in as many different albums as you want.

Acquiring Images from Scanners and Digital Cameras

If you're generating a lot of images from a scanner or a digital camera, it's even more important to keep track of them as you create them. Album allows you to add images to an album immediately when you scan them or acquire them from a digital camera. To do that, choose File > Scanner or File > Digital Camera on the menu bar or click the Acquire from a scanner or the Acquire from a digital camera button on the Standard Toolbar.

> **TIP**
>
> Before you can acquire images from a scanner or digital camera, you'll need to set up PhotoImpact to use that device. For scanners, choose File > Scanner > Select Source on the menu bar; for digital cameras, choose File > Digital Camera > Select Source.

Retrieving Images

Once you've cataloged all your images in albums, what can you do with the albums? The obvious answer to that is that you can locate and use the images that you've cataloged. There are a number of ways you can open the original images via their thumbnails.

Probably the easiest method is to drag and drop the thumbnail either into another program's workspace or onto a program icon on Album's Tool Panel, either of which opens the original image in that program.

If the Tool Panel isn't visible, choose View > Toolbars & Panels > Tool Panel on the menu bar (see Figure 12.8). This panel starts out "preloaded" with the PhotoImpact programs, but you can add other program icons to it by clicking the Tool Panel Menu button at the top of the panel and choosing New. In the New Group dialog box, create a program group for your own programs by entering a name and clicking New, then click Browse to locate the program you want to add to it. Click New again to add the program to the panel, then click Close. To switch between the default Tool Panel and the one you've created, click the Tool Panel Menu button and choose a panel from the list—the preloaded panel is called "internal."

CHAPTER 12

Figure 12.8
The built-in ToolPanel group contains icons for Album commands such as Email and Print.

To delete icons or groups from the Tool Panel, chose Delete from the Tool Panel Menu and choose what you want to delete in the Delete dialog box.

TIP

You can add program icons to the Tool Panel quickly by dragging them from Windows Explorer onto the Tool Panel.

If you prefer to drag and drop thumbnails directly into another program's workspace, what happens to them there depends on whether there's a file open in the second program. If you drag the thumbnail into an open file, it will be either embedded or linked, as follows:

▶ If you don't hold down any modifier keys as you drag, the image is linked to its originating program.

▶ If you hold down CTRL as you drag, the image is embedded in the document.

▶ If you hold down CTRL+ SHIFT as you drag, the image is linked to Album.

Linked objects are updated each time their original file is modified, while embedded ones stay the way they were when they were embedded in the container document.

TIP

Switch to Compact Mode to hide most of Album's windows and toolbars, so that you can see other programs behind it. This makes it a lot easier to drag images into other programs. Choose View > Compact Mode on the menu bar.

Creating a New Album

Album comes with one album file, called Demo, but you'll want to create your own albums customized to reflect the way you want to organize your files. There are several ways of doing this, including creating a new album as you save a file from PhotoImpact (click Album in the Save dialog box, then click New). The other methods are as follows:

▶ To create a new, empty album, click the New button on the Standard Toolbar.

▶ To create a new, empty album, choose File > New on the menu bar in Album.

▶ To create a new album from thumbnails in an existing album, select the thumbnails and choose Edit > Make Album on the menu bar.

Once you've done any of these, you need to set up the new album in the New dialog box. First, choose a template from the Album template list. As you click on each template name, its description is shown in the Album description field and its fields are listed so that you can see what kind of information it can hold. If you don't find a template that's exactly what you want, choose the closest one and click Customize to change its fields for your uses (see "Creating and Modifying Fields" for more information on setting up data entry fields in an album). Finally, enter a name in the Title field and click OK.

Adding Image Data to an Album

All data about an image is stored in fields. If you've worked with databases before, you're probably used to this concept. If it's new to you, think of each field as a slot designed to hold a particular piece of information. Although you can customize the fields in each album file, it's a pretty good bet that you won't have an image album without at least one field that contains each image's filename. And you'll probably want more fields to keep track of other information about each file.

Creating and Modifying Fields

When you're creating an album, you start with a list of templates, each containing predefined fields of various types. For example, the Scrapbook template includes six fields: Members in Photo, Event, Place, Date, Keywords, and Description. From this starting point, you can modify each template to change existing fields or add new ones. Each field has a type that ensures only the right kind of data ends up there, as follows:

▶ **Number**—Any number from 0 to something over 4 billion

▶ **Date**—Dates between 1/1/100 and 12/31/4099

▶ **Text**—Text as long as 255 characters

▶ **File Name**—File names as long as 259 characters

▶ **Keyword**—As many as 32 keywords from a list that you set up

▶ **List**—One term from a predefined list that you set up

▶ **Memo**—Text as long as 65,535 characters

If you try to enter text in a date field, for instance, Album tells you it's "unable to change the current field."

To define fields in an existing album:

1. Choose Album > Properties on the menu bar to display the Album Properties dialog box.

2. Click on the Fields tab to see the list of fields that already exist (see Figure 12.9).

Figure 12.9
Each field has a name and a type.

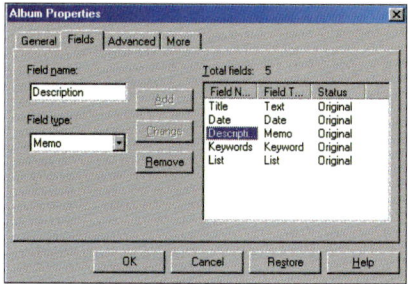

3. To add a new field, type its name in the Field name field and choose a type from the Field type menu, then click Add.

4. To edit an existing field, click on it in the list of fields, then change its name or field type and click Change.

5. To remove a field, click on its name and then click Remove.

6. To restore the field list to its original condition, click Restore.

7. To add, delete, or edit keywords or list values for a field, click on the field, and then click the Edit Keyword or Edit List button (see Figure 12.10).

Figure 12.10
The Edit Keywords dialog box shows all the keywords that have been added to an album.

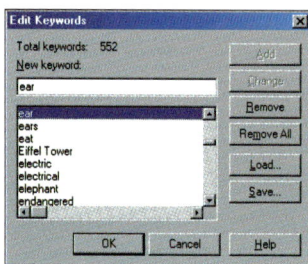

—To add a term, enter it in the New keyword or New value field and click Add.

—To delete a term, click on it in the list and click Delete.

—To edit a keyword, click on it in the list, make changes in the New keyword or New value field, and click Change.

8. Click OK when you're done editing the terms.

9. When you're done editing the fields, click OK.

Entering Data in Fields

To get started, click the View in Data Entry Mode button in the Standard Toolbar. This displays the data fields next to each image thumbnail, and you can just click in a field and start entering data.

TIP

Click in any field and check the status bar at the bottom of the Album window for a clue as to what data the field's looking for.

Entering Keywords

To enter a keyword, double-click in the keyword field to open the Keyword dialog box (see Figure 12.11). Although predefining the keywords forces you to be consistent in entering them, you can create new keywords as you go; either choose one from the list labeled Current keywords available or type a new one in the New keyword field and click Add.

Figure 12.11
If you didn't enter the keyword you need when you set up the fields, you can enter it on the fly in the Keywords dialog box.

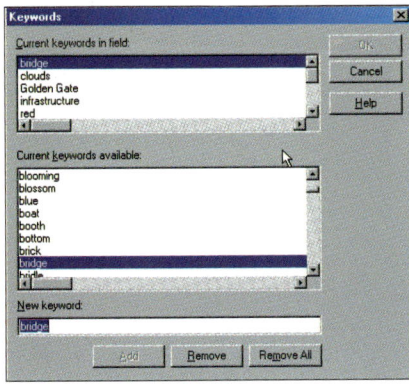

CHAPTER 12

If you want to use keywords you've created in one album for another album, go to the Fields tab of the Album Properties dialog (choose Album > Properties on the menu bar), click on a keyword field, and click Edit Keyword. In the Edit Keyword dialog box, click Save to export the keyword list as a text file. To import into another album, return to the Edit Keyword dialog box and click Load. You can load any text file (filename extension .txt), so you can create lists of keywords in any program that will save as text-only.

Entering List Values

List fields require you to set up the list values ahead of time, like keywords, but they're intended to operate more like multiple-choice questions. For example, in an image database, you might have a field called Image orientation in which the list values are portrait (for images that are taller than they are wide) and landscape (for images that are wider than they are tall). A list field for a thumbnail can have only one value, so the values have to be exclusive, rather than overlapping—in other words, each image must fall into one and only one category in a list.

To enter a list value, double-click in the list field and choose an option in the List dialog box (see Figure 12.12).

Figure 12.12
The List dialog box works the same way as the Keywords dialog box.

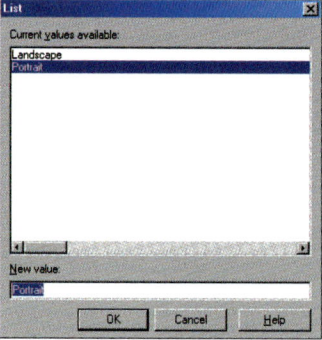

TIP
If you're using an album that contains a field with list values, you can use the values as the basis for tabs. Choose View > Show Tabs on the menu bar—each tab will be labeled with one of the list values.

If tabs are showing, you can change the value of one or more thumbnails by selecting the thumbnails to change (SHIFT+click to select more than one) and dragging them onto another tab. This moves their thumbnails to the other tab and changes the value entered in their list fields.

Exporting Data from an Album

In addition to allowing easy access to the original images an album catalogs, Album allows you to create catalogs in other formats, such as a slide show of images that you can post on the Web for others to view, or, similarly, a photo album of images that you can post on the Web. You can also export the text data that you've entered about each thumbnail.

Creating a Web Slide Show

A Web Slide Show consists of an HTML file and copies of all the included images in GIF format, which can be displayed on the Web. All the images you want to use in the slide show have to be in the same album, so if you have images scattered among several albums, you'll need to copy them to a new album for the purposes of creating the slide show. Here's how to create the slide show:

1. Select the images you want to include.

2. Choose Thumbnail > Export > Web Slide Show on the menu bar to display the Export Web Slide Show dialog box.

3. In the Output tab, click on Save as Web pages and choose an Output folder in which the files will be saved (see Figure 12.13).

Figure 12.13
The Output tab of the
Export Web Slide Show
dialog box.

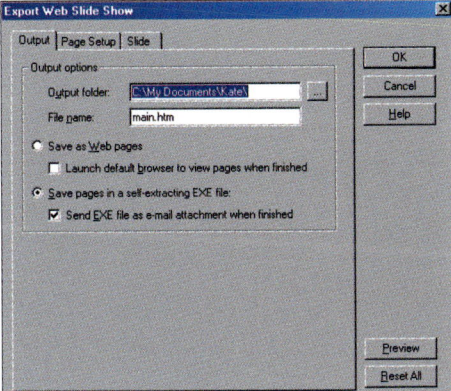

4. In the Page Setup tab, click on all the elements you want to include, such as a *Page title*, a *Heading*, and *Page numbers* (see Figure 12.14). For those elements that have customizable content (including Heading), enter your own information.

Figure 12.14
The Page Setup tab of the Export Web Slide Show dialog box.

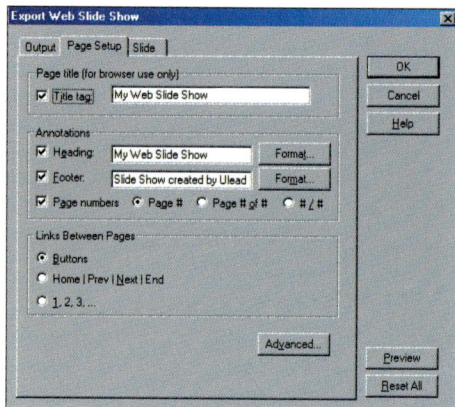

5. In the Slide tab, set a maximum size for the images, choose a compression level, and click on or off Automatically advance to next page (see Figure 12.15). If you leave this option on, enter a number of seconds between images.

Figure 12.15
The Slide tab of the Export Web Slide Show dialog box.

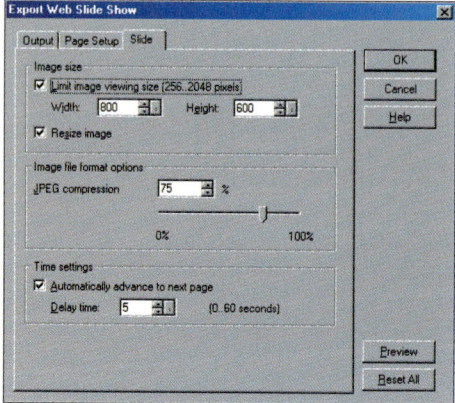

6. Click OK to create the album. If you selected *Launch default browser to view pages when finished* under the Output tab, you'll see the album immediately; if not, you'll need to locate the album HTML file and double-click on it to view the album (see Figure 12.16).

Figure 12.16
The final slide show has navigation buttons, a title, and page numbers.

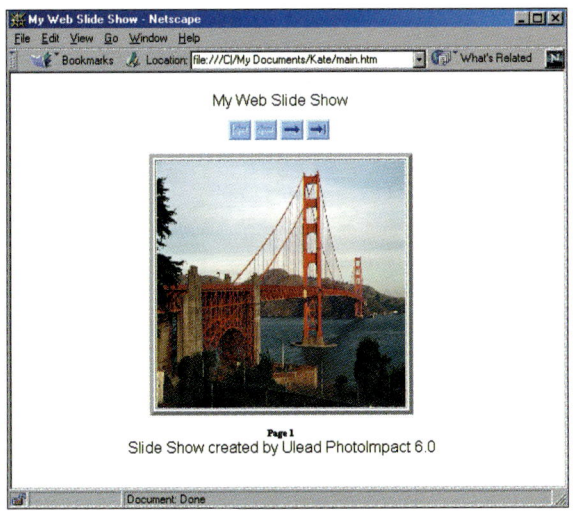

> **TIP**
>
> If you want to package up the Web album and e-mail it to another person, check Save pages in a self-extracting EXE file in the Output tab of the Export Web Slide Show dialog box; then you have only to attach the file to an e-mail message.

Creating a Web Album

If you want to show off a large selection of images, and give your audience a choice of which images to view at full size, a Web Album is a better choice than a Web Slide Show. It starts out by displaying small thumbnail images. Clicking on one of these displays the full-size image. You can also display thumbnail data along with each image. To create a Web Album, follow these steps:

1. Select the images you want to include.

2. Choose Thumbnail > Export > Web Album on the menu bar to display the Export Web Album dialog box (see Figure 12.17).

CHAPTER 12

Figure 12.17
The Export Web Album dialog box looks very much like the Export Web Slide Show dialog box.

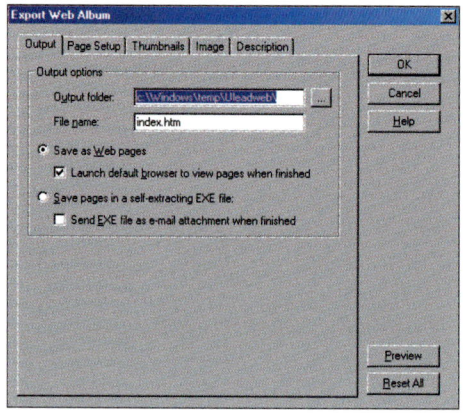

3. In the Output tab, click on Save as Web pages and choose an Output folder in which the files will be saved.

4. In the Page Setup tab, click on all the elements you want to include, such as a Page title, a Heading, and Page numbers. For those elements that have customizable content (including Heading), enter your own information.

5. In the Thumbnails tab, enter numbers of rows and columns to determine the album's layout, along with the size of the thumbnails in pixels (see Figure 12.18). Click Show thumbnail in frame at the top of the dialog box if you want the thumbnails to be visible at the same time as a full-size image.

Figure 12.18
The Thumbnails tab is unique to the Export Web Album dialog box.

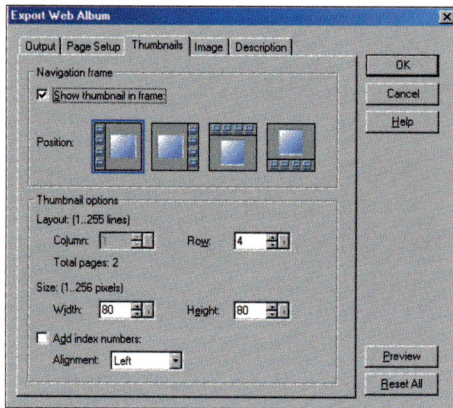

6. In the Image tab, set a maximum size for the images and choose a JPEG compression level.

7. In the Description tab, click to select the information that will be displayed with each image, then choose an option at the bottom of the dialog box for where the data should be placed (see Figure 12.19).

Figure 12.19
The Description tab allows you to determine what text information is included in a Web album.

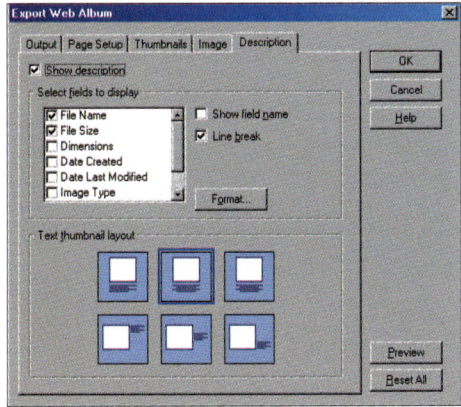

8. Click OK to create the album. If you selected Launch default browser to view pages when finished, you'll see the album immediately; if not, you'll need to locate the album HTML file and double-click on it to view the album (see Figure 12.20).

Figure 12.20
The appearance of the final album can be customized in several ways. Here a frame shows thumbnails while a larger frame contains a full-size image.

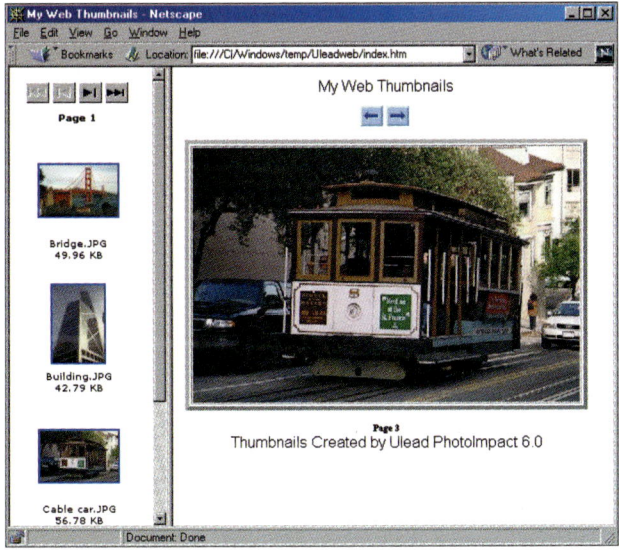

TIP
To customize the appearance of any of the text that's used in an album, click the Format button that appears within the Select fields to display option under the Description tab in the Export Web Album dialog box.

Exporting Text Data

Once you've entered all that useful information into an album, you'll be pleased to hear that you can get it out again for use in other programs. For instance, you might want to export caption information for use in a newsletter that's going to contain some of the images in your album. To export text from Album:

1. Select the thumbnails whose data you want to export. If you want to include all the thumbnails, make sure either all or none are selected.

2. Choose Thumbnail > Export > To File on the menu bar.

3. In the File tab, enter a name for the export file and then choose a format based on what formats are supported by the program with which you'll be using the data (see Figure 12.21).

Figure 12.21
The File tab looks much like a standard Save dialog box.

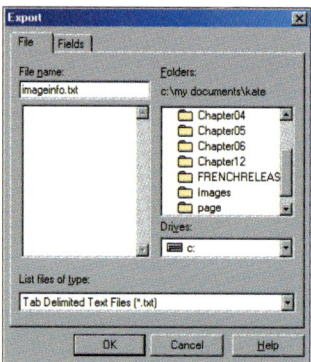

4. Switch to the Fields tab and click in the checkboxes next to the names of the fields you want to include in the export file (see Figure 12.22).

Figure 12.22
In the Fields tab, you specify what data should be included in the text file.

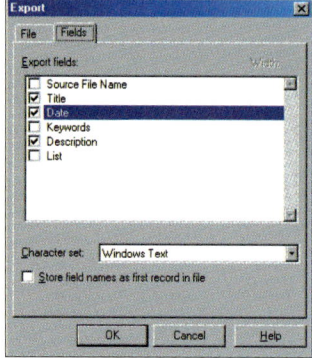

5. Choose Windows Text or DOS Text from the *Character set* menu.

6. Click Store field names as first record in file if you want the names of the fields included.

7. Click OK to save the file.

Maintaining Albums

Once you've created an album, you need to keep it up to date and make sure that its structure continues to work for your needs. You can accomplish these functions using Album's Properties and its backup and updating functions.

Editing Album Properties

An album's Properties contain several options (along with the data entry fields) that you can set to make your album more responsive or save memory, whichever suits your situation. To display the Properties dialog box, choose Album > Properties on the menu bar or right-click an album cover and choose Properties from the contextual menu (see Figure 12.23). Here are the tabs you'll see:

Figure 12.23
The Properties dialog box is, in a sense, the heart of an album.

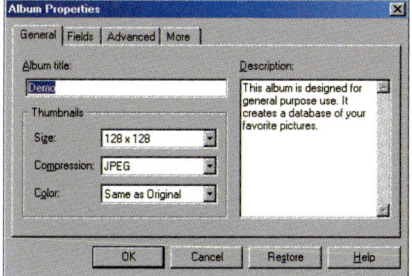

▶ **General**—Here you can change the album's title and description, along with the size, compression mode, and color mode of its thumbnails. You'll generally use JPEG compression for thumbnails, even though it may degrade the image quality slightly. Thumbnails are only for reference, and their compression doesn't affect the original files.

▶ **Fields**—This tab is where you set up fields for data entry; the tab shows each Field name, its **Field Type,** and the number of Total fields. See "Creating and Modifying Fields" for more information on setting up data fields.

▶ **Advanced**—The first option in this tab is Folder monitoring, which automatically adds images to the album when they're placed in the specified folder. You can choose from several formats so that only images of specific types are included in the album. Be sure to click on Enable folder monitoring—just choosing a folder doesn't start the process up. The other option in this tab is to create a Password so that the album can't be opened by unauthorized people.

▶ **More**—The information in this tab is purely statistical data about the album itself.

CHAPTER 12

Backing Up and Restoring Albums

Album allows you to back up an album and all the associated image files in a neat package that contains copies of all the files. You can save backups to your hard drive, removable media, or floppy disks. To create a backup follow these steps:

1. Open the album you want to back up.

2. Choose Album > Backup on the menu bar.

3. Choose a folder in which to save the backup files.

4. Click Backup selected files only to include only the selected thumbnails.

5. Click Compress files to use compression to minimize the size of the backup files.

6. If you're saving to removable media (such as floppy or Zip disks) and the space required for the backup files is more than will fit on one disk, enter the size of the removable media at the bottom of the dialog box.

7. Click OK to begin the backup process.

Once an album is backed up, you can delete the original files. To use them again, you need to restore the backup, as follows:

1. Choose Album > Restore on the menu bar.

2. Locate the folder containing the album backup files.

3. Enter a location for the restored files in the Restore to field.

4. Click OK.

Keeping Thumbnails Up to Date

Because albums don't store the original files, but rather information about them, it's possible for them to become out of date as changes are made to the original files. This section covers ways to make sure that you're always looking at the correct thumbnails for the images in your albums.

Refreshing Thumbnails

If you're sharing an album over a network (choose Album > Sharing on the menu bar), sometimes the album falls behind on reflecting changes made to the original image files. Choose Album > Refresh on the menu bar to update the thumbnails in your copy of the album.

For both shared and standalone albums, you'll sometimes need to update just one or a few of the thumbnails. For instance, if you just modified their source files, you know those are the only ones that need updating. To do this, select the thumbnails you want to update and choose Thumbnail > Update—From Source File on the menu bar.

Checking Image Links

When changes are made to the original files cataloged in your albums, the thumbnails need to be updated. You can check to see if any of the original files have moved or changed by choosing Album > Check on the menu bar to open the Check Album dialog box. Two tabs in the dialog box are labeled Missing Files and Modified Files. To relocate the missing files, click on each and then click Relink. For the modified files, all you have to do is select them in the list and click Update; Album makes a new thumbnail image and updates the data for each file listed.

If you want to relink just a few specific files, SHIFT+click to select them and choose Thumbnail > Relink on the menu bar. Locate the image folder for each file in the Relink dialog box and click OK.

Setting Up Album Preferences

You can adjust Album's preferences to save space on your hard drive, speed up Album's operation, and customize the way Album works to your liking. To open the Preferences dialog box, press F6 or choose Edit > Preferences. The following sections cover the options you'll find there.

PhotoImpact Album

The preferences dialog is divided into two sections; this section covers behavior specific to Album, while the other affects system settings that have to do with how Album operates. There are three subsections within the PhotoImpact Album's Preferences (see Figure 12.24).

Figure 12.24
In the Preferences dialog box, you can control both Album's behavior and your computer's behavior regarding Album.

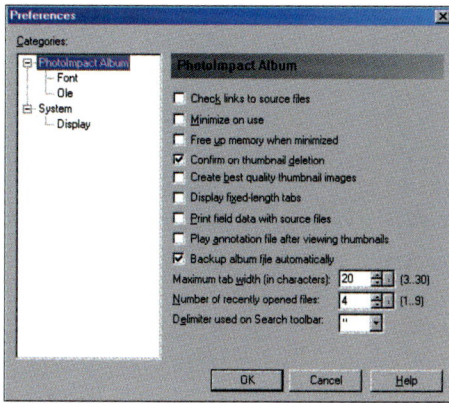

CHAPTER 12

PhotoImpact Album

Most of these settings affect the speed and efficiency of Album's operations. Here's a rundown on what you'll find in the main section of the PhotoImpact Album's Preferences:

▶ **Check links to source files**—Check this box to have Album constantly monitor links between its thumbnails and the original files and notify you of any problems it runs into. This will slow the program down some.

▶ **Minimize on use**—This setting minimizes Album as soon as you drag a thumbnail into another program, keeping it out of the way while you're not using it.

▶ **Free up memory when minimized**—Checking this box saves memory by allocating Album's memory to other programs when Album is minimized.

▶ **Confirm on thumbnail deletion**—With this setting, deleting a thumbnail produces a confirmation dialog box before the thumbnail is actually removed.

▶ **Create best quality thumbnail images**—This setting improves the quality of thumbnail images but increases the time needed to create them and display them.

▶ **Display fixed-length tabs**—If some of your tab names are so long that those tabs are crowding the other tabs out of the window, check this setting to keep the tabs all the same width.

▶ **Print field data with source files**—When you're printing source files from Album (choose Source > Print on the menu bar), this setting includes the image data you've entered with the printout.

▶ **Play annotation file after viewing thumbnails**—This setting automatically plays attached audio annotations when you view thumbnails (to add recorded annotations, choose Thumbnail > Annotations > Add on the menu bar).

▶ **Backup album automatically**—If your computer crashes frequently (or you're just the careful type), click here to automatically create backup copies of your album as you work with it.

▶ **Maximum tab width (in characters)**—Here you can choose a maximum number of characters to be displayed in a tab name. This is another answer to the problem of overlong tab names.

▶ **Number of recently opened files**—This setting determines the number of recently opened files listed in File > Recent Files on the menu bar for quick access.

▶ **Delimiter used in Search toolbar**—You can determine the default delimiter for multi-word search terms here.

Font

This section of the Preferences dialog box contains the following menus:

▶ Font

▶ Font style

▶ Size

Album uses these font settings both in its on-screen display and when it prints text. You can choose from all the fonts installed on your computer and a variety of preset sizes between 8 and 18.

OLE

These settings determine the treatment of thumbnails that are dragged into other programs. The Object thumbnail link is broken checkbox makes Album the source application for thumbnail images, while the Object representation format area controls how drag-and-drop images are displayed in other programs:

▶ **Source object**—This option displays the original image in all its glory.

▶ **Thumbnail only**—Save time by using this option to show only the low-resolution thumbnail image.

▶ **Low resolution place holder**—Speed things up a bit more by using an even lower-resolution placeholder image.

▶ **Album program icon**—If you're really in a hurry and you don't need to see the image at all on-screen (it will still print at full resolution), choose this option to display an icon based on the Album program icon.

Finally, the checkbox labeled Convert images as display mode will convert images that are copied into other programs using the Clipboard to the current display mode of your system (making them smaller files). This option is only available if your monitor is set to 256 colors.

System

Here you'll find settings that control how Album interacts with Windows and with the other programs you use. The options here are the same as those in PhotoImpact's System preferences.

System

Here you can control the memory and hard drive usage of Album. If you want to use more hard-drive space as virtual memory—which will give you more memory but slow down your computer—set additional folders under Define additional folders for virtual memory. To specify an upper limit for how much space should be used for virtual memory, enter a number of megabytes under Limit hard disk usage to ____ MB. And if you don't have a lot of memory (RAM) in your computer, you can specify that Album shouldn't use any more of it than you want it to by entering a number under Limit RAM usage to ____ MB.

Display

These settings improve the way that Album uses your monitor to display images, as follows:

▶ **HiColor dithering**—If you're using High Color display, True Color images will display better if this setting is turned on.

▶ **View images with a common palette**—If your monitor is set to display 256 colors, this setting will speed up your work by displaying all indexed color images using the system palette, so there's no need to redraw the screen when moving from image to image.

▶ **Ignore background quality**—This setting skips repainting background images when you change views, speeding up operations.

▶ **Monitor gamma**—Adjust this setting until the two gray rectangles are the same color. This will calibrate your monitor for the best display quality.

13

Gearing Up: Printing, Sharing, and More

This is the catch-all chapter that deals with an assortment of topics that didn't quite fit anywhere else in the book. These are, however, very important topics. Learning about Quick Commands is critical if you have a lot of images to work with and want to save yourself hours of time, so we'll go over the basics of how and when to use them. Knowing how to print your images, both locally and via Web-based photo printing services, also will be covered in this chapter. In addition, we'll cover the basics of sharing your images with other people. The Internet obliterates barriers of time and space, so if you have family and friends you want to share images with, read on!

Quick Commands

A batch file is a type of computer file that is a series of commands contained inside a single file. Early batch files from the DOS days helped boot your computer—each line would contain commands meant to initialize your CD-ROM, sound card and so on. Macro commands are another form of this concept. A macro will, when called with a certain keystroke or trigger, perform a function or series of functions. For instance, as I write this book in Word 2000, I have a simple macro set up to replace the word "easy" with "EasyPalette" to save me some time. One of my favorite programs is called Activewords (**www.activewords.com**). It allows me to trigger text replacement on a system-wide basis, in any program I'm in. I use it to insert e-mail signatures into newsgroup postings or quickly paste in a series of URLs when someone asks a question I've seen before. Traditional batch files aren't used very often any more, but the concept is alive and well in PhotoImpact's Quick Commands: You can record a series of PhotoImpact actions and play them back later on a singular or mass scale. This is an incredibly powerful tool when you get the hang of it.

Imagine this typical scenario, in which I find myself quite often: I've just returned from an event where I've shot a hundred to a hundred and fifty digital images, usually in JPEG resolutions of 1536×1024. Each image is between 300 and 400 KB, giving me a good 40 megs' worth of images. I'll keep them in this max resolution for archival purposes, but I normally post them to a Web site so people can see them—and I can't do that with such huge images! So I need to resize each image, sharpen the image after the resize, and resave it at a specified JPEG quality level, and then close it—150 times! The thought of doing this manually makes me shudder, so it's a lucky thing Quick Commands exist! What would normally take me hours can be done in minutes, and even seconds, with a powerful computer (this is where a fast CPU comes into play).

Quick Commands vs. Batch Convert

Now that you know what Quick Commands are, you may wonder what the Batch Convert function (found under the File menu on the menu bar) does. At first glance, it seems these are the same, but you can think of Batch Convert as a very specific form of Quick Command. While Quick Commands can be created to handle a wide variety of commands, the Batch Convert tool is used for one purpose only: converting several files in one format into several files in another format. Figure 13.1 shows the interface—very simple, few options. There aren't any resize options or any way to apply filters or any other commands. It's brute force file format changing, but it works well. If you have a folder full of BMP screenshots and want to turn them into GIF files for Web use, this is the tool to use. If you need to resize images or apply filters, stick to Quick Commands.

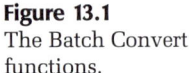

Figure 13.1
The Batch Convert functions.

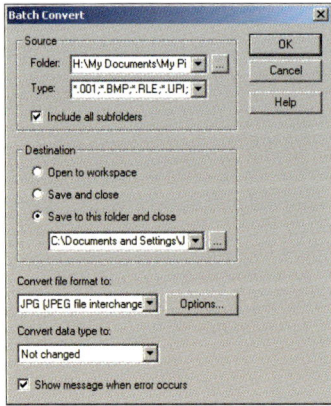

Using Quick Commands

Quick Commands, which contains what are called Tasks, are accessed via the Quick Command Panel (see Figure 13.2), either by View > Toolbars & Panels > Quick Command Panel on the menu bar or by pressing CTRL+F2 on your keyboard. Once the panel is loaded, you'll see a drop-down menu with the tasks. PhotoImpact has ten task presets, which serve more as an example of how to build your own rather than being of any serious use by themselves (although the Soft Focus Task, shown in Figure 13.3, works very nicely). You can also learn some interesting tricks by looking at the settings they use. For example, in the Monochrome Task under the Quick Command Panel, rather than using the Monochrome function under Effect > Special on the menu bar, it uses a Saturation value of -100. This was a new trick to me!

Figure 13.2
The Quick Command Panel.

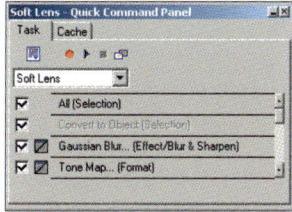

Figure 13.3
The Soft Focus Task under the Quick Command Panel is wonderful for portraits.

Using a Quick Command Task is simple: Select the appropriate task from the drop down menu, then click the Play button.

PhotoImpact will then run through the steps of the Quick Command Task, and the amount of time to do this depends entirely on how large and how many images you have and the speed of your computer. If you're quick with the mouse, you can click the Stop button in the middle of the action. If you want to activate a single step at a time, you can click on the step. This will open the setting screen so you can view the settings and OK each individual step.

Once you've created your own Quick Command Task, you'll see them in the drop-down list with the other tasks. Unfortunately, there's no way to reorder the task listing. Any tasks you create will be at the bottom of the list.

> **TIP**
>
> If you want to see how a Quick Command works in a step-by-step fashion, you can play it and then use CTRL+Z (Undo) and CTRL+Y (Redo) to walk backwards and forwards through each step.

Creating Your Own Quick Command Tasks

The real power of tasks is using them to automate your own work. Creating tasks can be complicated, but when you grasp the nuances of how to create them, you'll wonder how you ever lived without them. I'm going to show you how I created one of my typical tasks. I'll focus on the settings here rather than screenshots of the tools, because they've all been shown in previous chapters.

1. If it's not already open, open the Quick Command panel (CTRL+F2 on your keyboard).

2. Click on the Task menu commands button and, from the menu, select New.

3. A small window will pop up and request a task name and comment (see Figure 13.4). It's a good idea to give it a descriptive name and comment. As your task list grows, distinguishing between them will be important. A good comment is also helpful when sharing tasks with others. When I've entered the info, I'll click Record to start things off.

Figure 13.4
Enter the task name and comment.

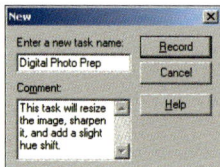

4. The default high-resolution images I work with are 1536×1024, so the first step is resizing. CTRL+G brings up the Dimensions window, and I'm going to use a value under Unit of 30 percent in Width and Bicubic under Resample method. This makes my image 460×307—perfect for a Web site. Clicking OK finishes this step.

5. Next I want to tweak the brightness. CTRL+B on the keyboard brings up the Brightness & Contrast window, and I'll use the upper-right preset, which has +12 brightness and +12 contrast values. Clicking OK finishes this step.

6. CTRL+E brings up the Hue & Saturation window, allowing me to adjust the hue of the image. My digital camera has a tendency to make flesh tones a little too red under certain lighting conditions, so after checking the Preview box, I'll set a Hue value of 6 and a Saturation value of 10. Clicking OK finishes this step.

7. Under Effect > Blur & Sharpen on the menu bar, I'll select the Sharpen function. A Sharpen value of 1 is enough to offset the slight blur that resizing the image has produced. Clicking OK finishes this step.

8. We're done! Figure 13.5 shows the final task list. You can see each individual step listed, and by right-clicking on an individual step, it can be deleted using Delete or altered using Properties.

Figure 13.5
Our final task.

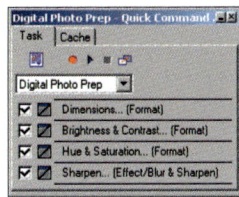

Batch Task

The Quick Command task I created above will take a large digital image and prep it for display on the Web. But opening up 150 images and clicking Play isn't much of a time-saver, so thankfully we have the Batch Task function to make this a completely painless process. What the Batch Task function does is to apply a task to a folder, or to a series of folders, and give you options to bypass dialog boxes that would slow the process down. Let's apply my Digital Photo Prep task to a folder full of images.

NOTE

PhotoImpact remembers the last JPEG setting that was used, so if you're going to use the Batch Task function to save in the JPEG format, first make sure it's set properly. To check this, look under the File menu on the menu bar and select Save As. Click Options and set your preferred quality and mode. Click OK, then Cancel from the Save As window. The JPEG settings you just changed are global, and any save to the JPEG format will use those settings.

CAUTION

There's no way to undo the changes made to your files. When you're first learning to use the Batch Task tool, it's a good idea to make a copy of your image folder and experiment first rather than risk wrecking your original images.

1. On the Quick Command Panel, click the Task menu commands button and select Batch Task.

2. The settings window for the Batch Task function will appear (see Figure 13.6), allowing to you select your Task from the drop down menu.

Figure 13.6
Preparing the batch task process.

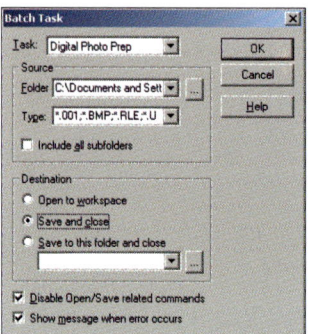

3. Next, select the Source folder (the location of the images you want to apply the Task to) and the image type. In most cases, you can leave it on All Formats, but if you have a folder with a mixture of file types, you can select the one file type you want and leave the others unaffected. Check off Include all subfolders if you want it to burrow through all the folders, changing images as it goes (but use this feature with caution).

4. Under the Destination area, in most cases you want to use Save and close. This will open your image, apply the task, save it, and close the file. If you want to do it this way, make sure to check off the Disable Open/Save related commands box.

5. Click OK and go for a break. This process will use up nearly 100 percent of your CPU, so unless you're running a dual-CPU machine, your computer will be fairly unresponsive during this process. The faster your CPU, the faster this task will complete.

6. When the task is complete, click OK on the dialog box, and a Task Report window will appear, showing you that the task was applied to each file successfully. See Figure 13.7.

Figure 13.7
The Task Report
window.

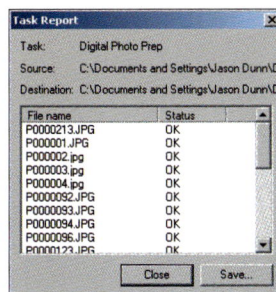

NOTE

Although SmartSaver Pro has powerful batch tools built in for resizing and saving, it can't be used to apply filters. Although creating Quick Command tasks takes longer, the final results are much more flexible than SmartSaver Pro, since that tool is mostly for optimization rather than producing effects on images.

NOTE

Quick Commands can't cope with object insertion. As a digital photographer, I usually place a visible watermark on each of my images so my work is protected from digital theft. When I'm converting dozens of images, being able to insert an object at a specified size and at exact X,Y coordinates would be extremely useful. Unfortunately, PhotoImpact 6.0 Quick Commands can't track object insertion or object placement. (Maybe in 7.0?)

Printing from PhotoImpact

Creating digital masterpieces is great, but if you're the only one to see them, what's the point? Every artist needs an audience, and printing your images is a good way to share them. PhotoImpact offers the standard tools for printing—nothing fancy, but they work. If you're looking for enhanced printing options, check out Photo Explorer (discussed in Chapter 10, "The PhotoImpact Web Design Studio") or try a Web search. One of my personal favorites in the realm of photo printing software is the Iomega Photo Printer (**www.iomega.com/software/completed/win95.html**). Although I think that company's hardware products are unreliable (I had three defective ZIP drives in two years) this software is wonderful—and free. It allows you to print a variety of photo sizes through a simple drag-and-drop interface, but it isn't Windows 2000 compatible and doesn't support PNG or TIFF files. There are dozens of applications out there for printing photos, so if one doesn't suit your needs, keep looking.

Limitations of Bitmap Printing

As I described in Chapter 1, bitmap images are not ideal for printing at sizes larger than their original size, and the quality is highly dependent on the original dpi of the image. As you make a bitmap image larger, the pixels are expanded, resulting in a jagged, digitized look that no one finds appealing. Bitmap images usually have anti-aliased edges, resulting in a smooth on-screen appearance, but when printed, these edges can cause problems: Text will have "fuzzy" edges, and depending on size and dpi, it will look jagged. Figures 13.8 and 13.9 illustrate this. The first figure was created in PhotoImpact at 72 dpi, and the second figure is a vector-based font character.

Because of the limitations around bitmap images, PhotoImpact really shouldn't be used for complex print work. If you're going to design a brochure or a book cover, a tool like Microsoft Publisher or CorelDraw should be used instead. That being said, if you have a powerful computer and can work with high-resolution images, crank the dpi of your files up to 300 and your print pieces will look very close to the printed products from a vector-based program. While I wouldn't suggest to a beginner that PhotoImpact is the optimal tool for print design work, in the hands of a skilled graphic designer, it can be used in very impressive ways.

Figure 13.8
A bitmap letter "A."

Figure 13.9
A vector letter "A."

Printing in PhotoImpact is accomplished by looking under the File menu on the menu bar and selecting Print, pressing CTRL+P on your keyboard, or clicking the Print icon on the Standard Toolbar. When you do any of these, the Print window will appear (see Figure 13.10), giving you some basic information and a few options:

Figure 13.10
The Print window.

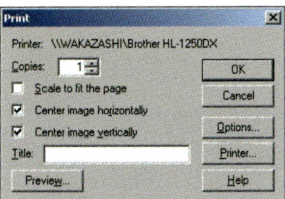

▶ **Printer**—This shows you the default printer your file will be printed to. If this isn't correct, click the Printer button and select a new printer.

▶ **Copies**—This shows the number of times your image will be printed.

▶ **Scale to fit the page**—This will force your image to fix the page. If the image is too large, it will be scaled down. If the image is too small, it will be scaled up, but the quality will drop the more it needs to be scaled up.

▶ **Center image horizontally**—This forces the image to be centered horizontally in the print area.

▶ **Center image vertically**—Forces the image to be centered vertically on the print area.

▶ **Title**—This is plain text that is inserted on the printout to the above left of the printed image.

▶ **Preview**—This activates the Print Preview function (detailed ahead).

Clicking OK on this window will begin the printing of your images. Many color printers have specific settings for quality and paper type that need to be adjusted prior to printing. Clicking in the Printer button will bring up the Windows Print Setup screen, and from there you can go into the properties for you printer. The Options button is for advanced functions like tweaking the color calibration and halftone adjustment. These settings override your printer drivers, so in most cases I'd suggest you stay away from them.

Print Preview

The Print Preview function is a function I use every time I print: It's handy to see exactly how the image will look on the page. Is it big enough? Have I cropped it properly? Looking at the preview will answer all these questions right away.

To access the Print Preview function, you can either hit the Preview button from the Print window (see Figure 13.10 above) or press CTRL+ALT+P on your keyboard to jump right to it. The options in the Print Preview window (Figure 13.11) are straightforward: You can set the number of copies (from 1 to 99), the image margins (different from your printer margins), add a text title, center and scale the image as discussed above, zoom in/out, and preview it with a ruler.

CHAPTER 13

Figure 13.11
The Print Preview
dialog window.

Once you're sure the image is set up properly, hit the Print icon and you're done.

Online Digital Print Services

Something wonderful has happened in the world of photography over the past year: It's now possible to order high-quality and affordable prints over the Web, using your browser as the interface for getting it all done. As I mentioned before, I spent a fair bit of money on a color printer, but after discovering the world of digital print services, I haven't used my printer in months! I've tried several different services like this, and I'll say this much about all of them: Regardless of how good your printer is, nothing can match seeing your high-res image on the thick, high-gloss photo paper. These companies invest a great deal of money in cutting-edge printing technology, and through the wonders of the Internet, you can get prints for as little as 49 cents each.

Using a digital print service is a snap. The general concept works like this:

1. You create an account with the service; in most cases, this will be free.

2. You upload your digital images via your Web browser or the free software the service provides for you.

3. Using your browser, you can apply special effects to the images and order multiple prints and sizes, frames, photo T-shirts, and other photo-related gifts.

4. With a credit card, you place your order and usually within a few days your prints will be delivered to you via mail or courier.

Kodak PhotoNet Online

www.photonet.com

This was the first service I tried, and I thought that because it was Kodak, it would be top-notch in every way. Was I ever wrong! The Web site doesn't allow for the easy drag-and-drop uploads that the other sites do, the print quality was noticeably worse than Ofoto and Shutterfly (my prints looked muddy and dark), and, worst of all, in order to upload your prints you need to buy a virtual "roll of film." After shelling out six bucks, you can upload thirty-six images, but the "roll" lasts only 30 days! Considering that I routinely shoot a hundred or more images at every event, I'd be spending $20 each month just to host my images. On the plus side, they have interesting photo gifts like mouse pads, coffee mugs, jigsaw puzzles, and T-shirts. Neat gifts aside, I can't recommend this service. Kodak makes fantastic digital cameras, but it just doesn't "get it" when it comes to online digital print services.

Shutterfly

www.shutterfly.com

Shutterfly wins major points in the creative realm! After you upload your photos, you can choose from dozens of creative borders—everything from romantic hearts to unusual textures. You can also change the hue of your image, crop it, adjust the saturation, and add a soft focus effect to your image—all in your browser! The print quality from Shutterfly is decent, although not quite as good as Ofoto. Image storage isn't a problem. You can upload as many images as you want, for as long as you want. They've also recently begun shipping outside the United States, making them an option for customers around the world.

Ofoto

www.ofoto.com

Ofoto is my number-one choice for digital prints. The quality is much higher than the Kodak service, has a little better color saturation than Shutterfly, and prices are great. When I first signed up, I was given fifty free 4×6 prints, and at the time of this writing that promotion is still going on. You can upload your images via the browser or use their free OfotoNow software package to crop and correct images, then upload in bulk. Ofoto has an incredible selection of great frames. I found their customer service to be fantastic as well. Although they've made minor errors on two of my four orders since I've been a member, I've received e-mail responses back the same day and the errors are always promptly fixed. Perfection is hard to find in any company, so great customer service is a must! Lastly, they don't charge for storing photos. I have more prints of, and the images can stay up there for as long as I want. Hard drive space being as cheap as it is, offering this to consumers only makes sense (Kodak, are you listening?). Ofoto will also process your 35mm film for free and load the scanned images into your account. Lastly, Ofoto ships to the United States, Canada, and overseas. One thing I wish they'd add is support for PNG files. When I'm editing a digital photo, I don't want to resave it as a JPEG and have another generation of quality loss, so I always output as a PNG file.

iMira

www.imira.com

Although I haven't seen the print quality from this service, I thought it was worth mentioning in this lineup because iMira is Ulead's creation. They've integrated an iMira "drop spot" into Photo Explorer, making it simple to upload your photos. iMira offers a lot of free services, including guest book, electronic greeting cards, and photo galleries you can share with others. They offer (for a fee) digital prints of your images, in sizes from 4×6 up to 11×14. I found their site a little confusing to use: After I uploaded a photo into my gallery, I couldn't see a simple way to request prints of the image. The only way to get a print was to upload the image again through a different section of the Web site.

TIP

If you want to see how much better these digital print services are than your own printer, get a print sample of the same image from both. Using the best paper possible and the highest quality setting on your printer, print out a sample image (the more colorful and complex the better). Then upload the same image to the sites and request print samples from each one. This will give you a good benchmark for comparison.

NOTE

If you have a digital camera, you know that the quality for most cameras is measured in terms of megapixels: one million pixels (1000×1000 pixel resolution). The higher the resolution, the higher the quality of your prints and the more choices you have in print size. For instance, a 640×480 resolution image will look good as a 4×6 print, but anything larger will result in pixellation of the image. One-and-a-half or higher megapixels is required for quality 8×10 prints. So when you're taking your digital pictures, always use the highest quality setting possible if you plan on printing them out later.

Sharing Your Images with Others

The explosion in popularity of e-mail and the Web has enabled people to easily send images and URLs to Web pages. Digital images tend to look best when kept digital: Even the best printers have difficulty exactly recreating the screen image on paper. Besides, the Web offers many more creative avenues for posting and manipulating those images. PhotoImpact gives you a few different ways to share your creativity—digitally.

E-mailing Images

Under the File > Export menu, you'll find options for exporting your image. One of them is Send—selecting this option will trigger a dialog box (see Figure 13.12) with options for sending your image via e-mail. There are two options to chose from: Web Page or Image File.

Figure 13.12
The Send function.

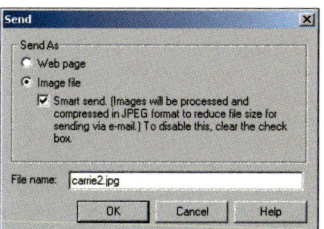

The default selection is Image file. When you select this, it will compress the image in JPEG format. Image file will give you a quality setting of around 75 and open up a new e-mail message. You can change the file name if you want by typing in a new one, but remember to leave the .jpg extension on the end of the file or it will come through as an unknown file type at the other end.

Selecting Web page saves the image, creates HTML code, and bundles them together in a single compressed .exe file that is attached to a new e-mail message (see Figure 13.13). When the user receives the e-mail and double-clicks on the attachment, it will decompress itself and open in the default browser. The recipient doesn't need to have any special software, just a Web browser.

Figure 13.13
The Send function.

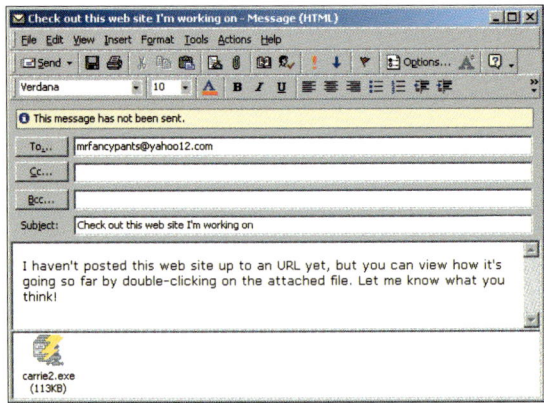

This method is great for sending actual Web pages to another person. It will maintain rollovers, image maps, and every other HTML setting you've created.

iMira.com Web Album

Also under the File > Export menu, you'll find the Post to iMira function. When you select this, the iMira Drop Spot will appear (see Figure 13.14). If you haven't already done so, click on Create New Account on the Web. This will bring you to the iMira Web site, where you can create a new account. As an iMira member, you'll get 20 megs of storage. This should accommodate at least a hundred photos.

Figure 13.14
The iMira Drop Spot.

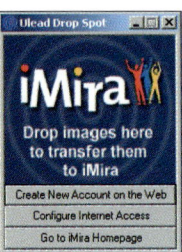

iMira offers some interesting services, including Web albums. In order to upload images to iMira, you need to drag and drop your files onto the Drop Spot. The problem is that if you're working in PhotoImpact, you can't drop your image onto the Drop Spot. You first need to save your image to a file, then drop that *file* onto the Drop Spot. In essence, all the menu item does is open up the Drop Spot.

Clicking on Configure Internet Access brings up a series of tabbed windows where you set your Internet connection type, username and password for iMira (if you already have an account), and size settings. Until you've created your account, you can ignore these settings.

Once you post your images to the iMira Web site, they are added to an album (see Figure 13.15). This album can be shared with others. When people visit, the site will track the number of visitors your site gets; it even offers a guestbook where people can leave comments.

Figure 13.15
My iMira Image Gallery.

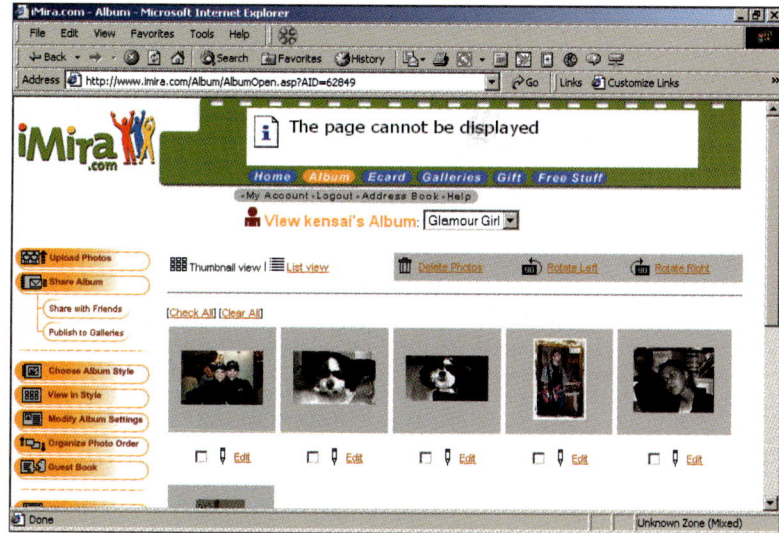

CHAPTER 13

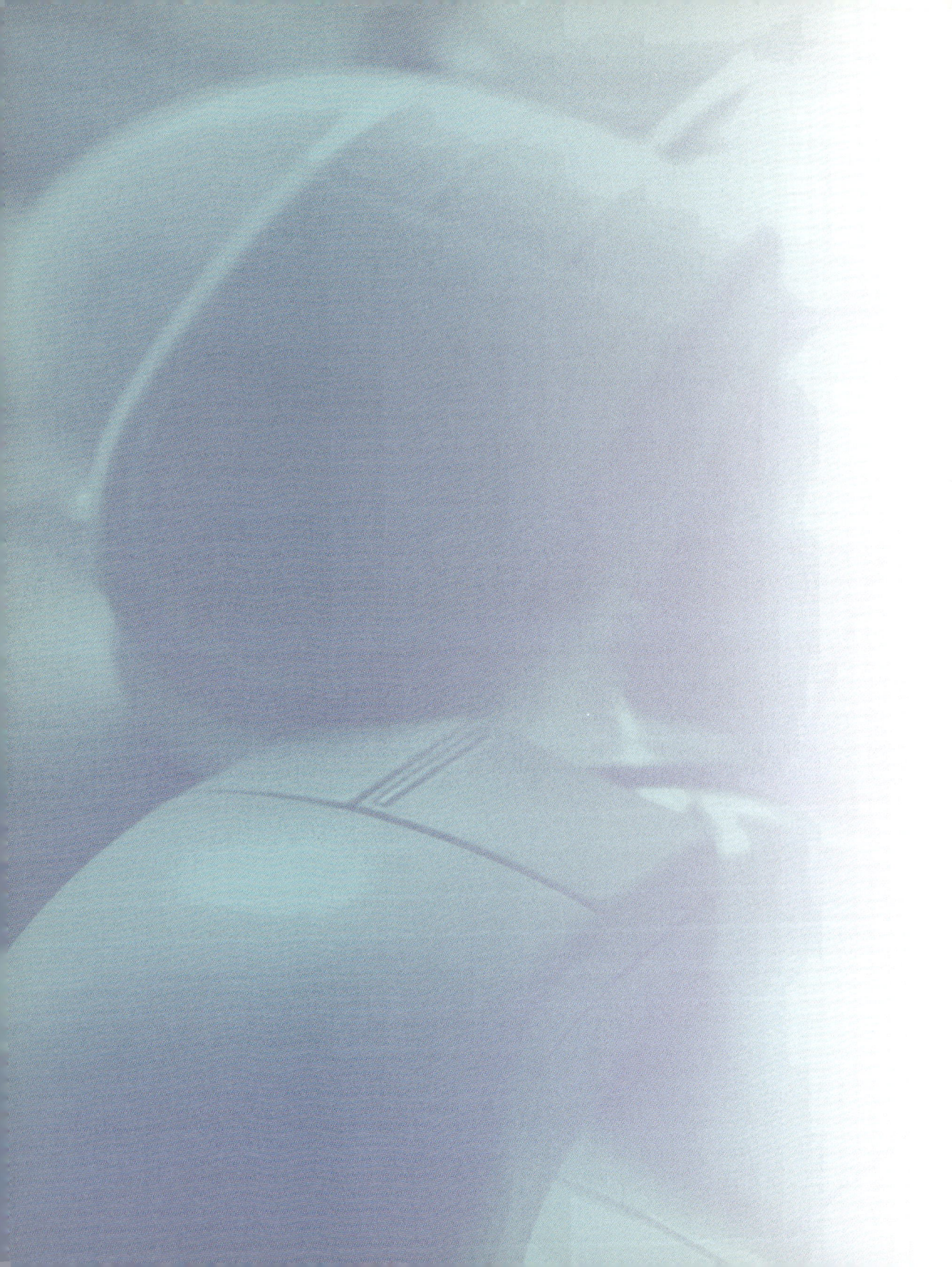

Index

INDEX

INDEX

MUSKA&LIPMAN

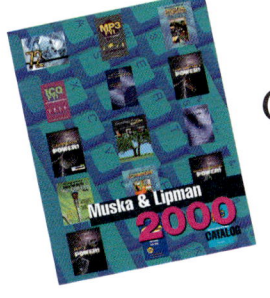

Order our free catalog by visiting
http://www.muskalipman.com

Order Form

Postal Orders:
Muska & Lipman Publishing
P.O. Box 8225
Cincinnati, Ohio 45208

Online Orders or more information:
http://www.muskalipman.com
Fax Orders:
(513) 924-9333

Title/ISBN	Price/Cost

Genealogy Basics Online
1-929685-00-9
Quantity _____
× $24.95
Total Cost _____

Digital Camera Solutions
0-9662889-6-3
Quantity _____
× $29.95
Total Cost _____

Title/ISBN	Price/Cost

**PhotoImpact 6
Resource Kit
CD-ROM** Quantity _____
× $19.95
Total Cost _____

Scanner Solutions
0-9662889-7-1
Quantity _____
× $29.95
Total Cost _____

Ship to:

Company _____

Name _____

Address _____

City _____ State _____ Zip _____ Country _____

E-mail _____

Educational facilities, companies, and organizations interested in multiple copies of these books should contact the publisher for quantity discount information. Training manuals, CD-ROMs, electronic versions, and portions of these books are also available individually or can be tailored for specific needs.

Subtotal _____

Sales Tax _____
(please add 6% for books shipped to Ohio addresses)

Shipping _____
($5.00 for US and Canada $10.00 other countries)

TOTAL PAYMENT ENCLOSED _____

Thank you for your order.

PhotoImpact Extras

EasyPalette Effects Reference

Parched

Light

Stars

Flashlight

This free download shows built-in EasyPalette effects as applied to images, objects, and text. See what each effect creates before using it with Web graphics and your personal photo collection. Save time and produce better images with this reference.

Free Download

Visit www.muskalipman.com/photoimpactsolutions

PhotoImpact 6 Resource Kit

RESOURCE KIT

PHOTOIMPACT
6
by Jason Dunn

by Jason Dunn

The PhotoImpact Resource Kit CD-ROM is a collection of tools and material for PhotoImpact users. The CD-ROM provides picture tubes, masks, photo objects, 3rd-party plug-ins, photos, animated GIFs, and utilities. Compiled by a PhotoImpact expert, this kit is a valuable enhancement for using PhotoImpact 6.

Only $19.95

Order at www.muskalipman.com/photoimpactkit